Collins
SCOTLAND

Contents

Road maps 2-21
Urban area maps 22-23
    Edinburgh, Glasgow
Index to place names 24-28
Street maps 29-69
    Aberdeen 30-35
    Edinburgh 36-51
    Glasgow 52-66
    Dundee 67
    Inverness 68
    Perth 69
Ferry information 70
Airport information 71
Distance chart 72
Administrative areas map 73

Key to road map pages

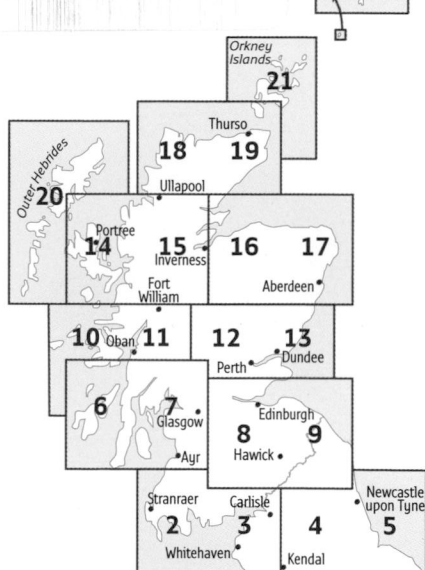

Published by Collins
An imprint of HarperCollins Publishers
Westerhill Road, Bishopbriggs, Glasgow G64 2QT

www.harpercollins.co.uk

Copyright © HarperCollins Publishers Ltd 2018
Collins® is a registered trademark of HarperCollins Publishers Limited
Mapping generated from Collins Bartholomew digital databases

Mapping on pages 29-59 uses map data licensed from Ordnance Survey
© Crown copyright and database rights (2018) Ordnance Survey (100018598)

Contains Ordnance Survey data © Crown copyright and database right (2018)

Printed in China by RR Donnelley APS Co Ltd
ISBN 978 0 00 827639 3   10 9 8 7 6 5 4 3 2 1
e-mail: roadcheck@harpercollins.co.uk

 facebook.com/collinsref    @collins_ref

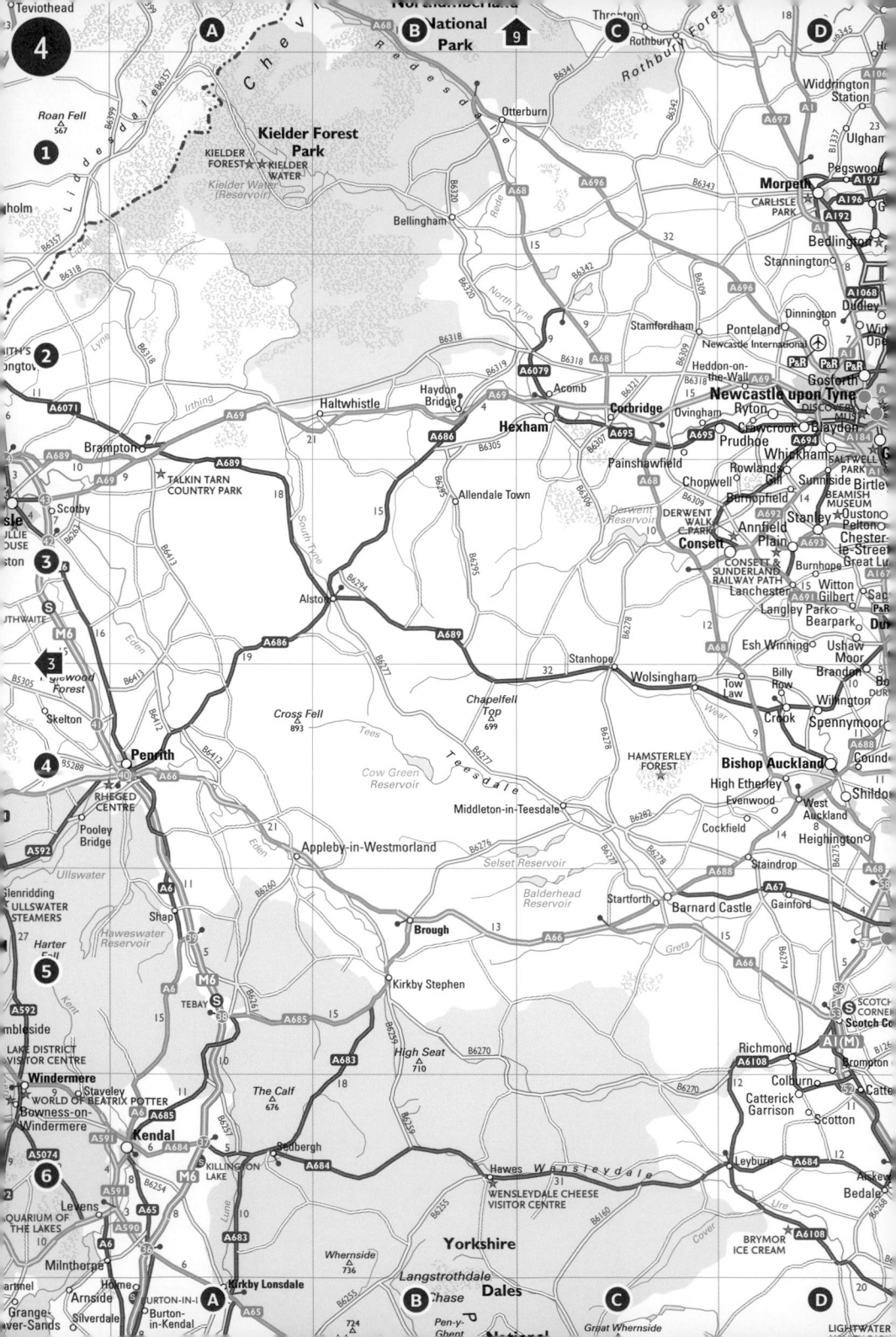

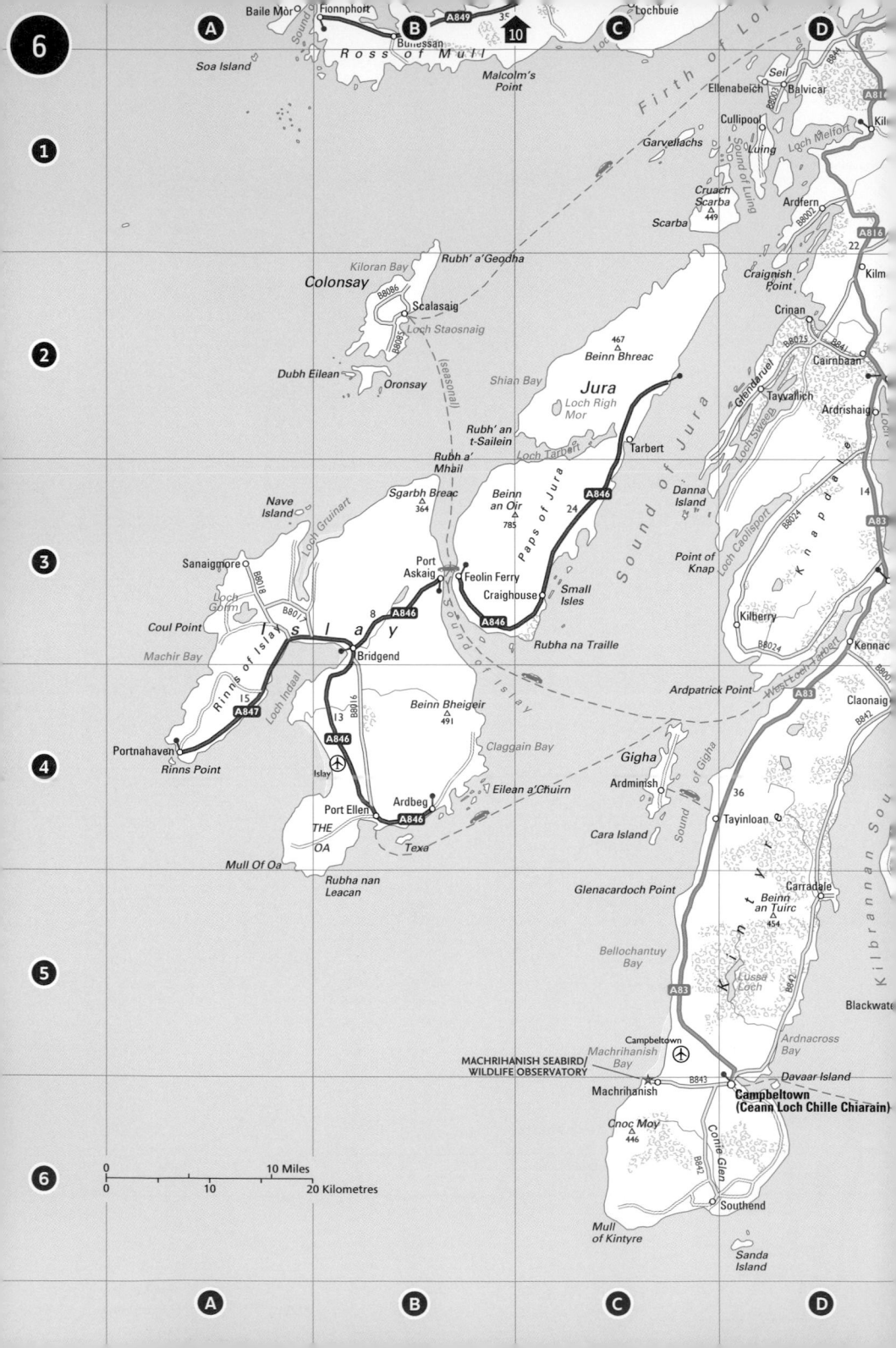

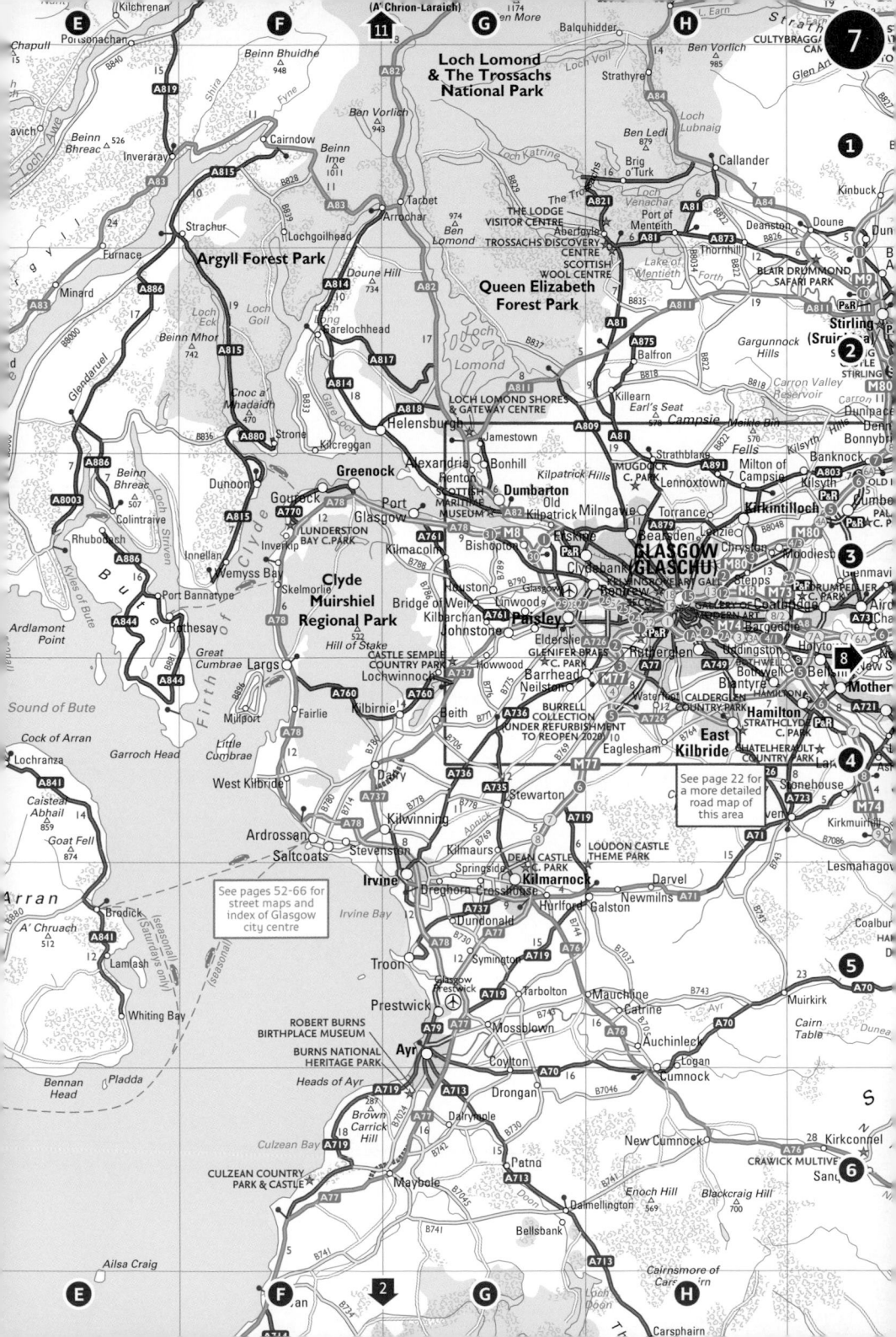

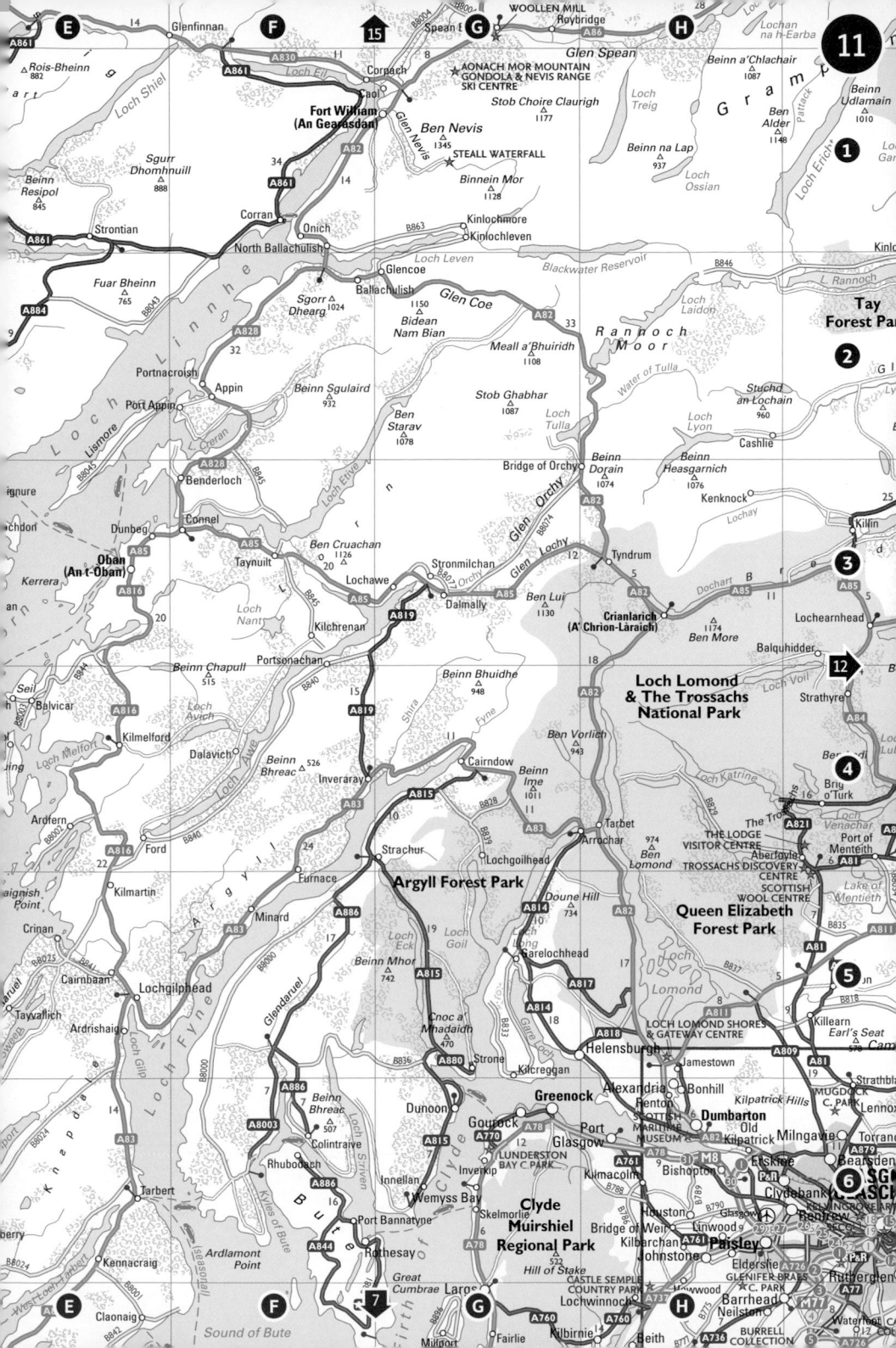

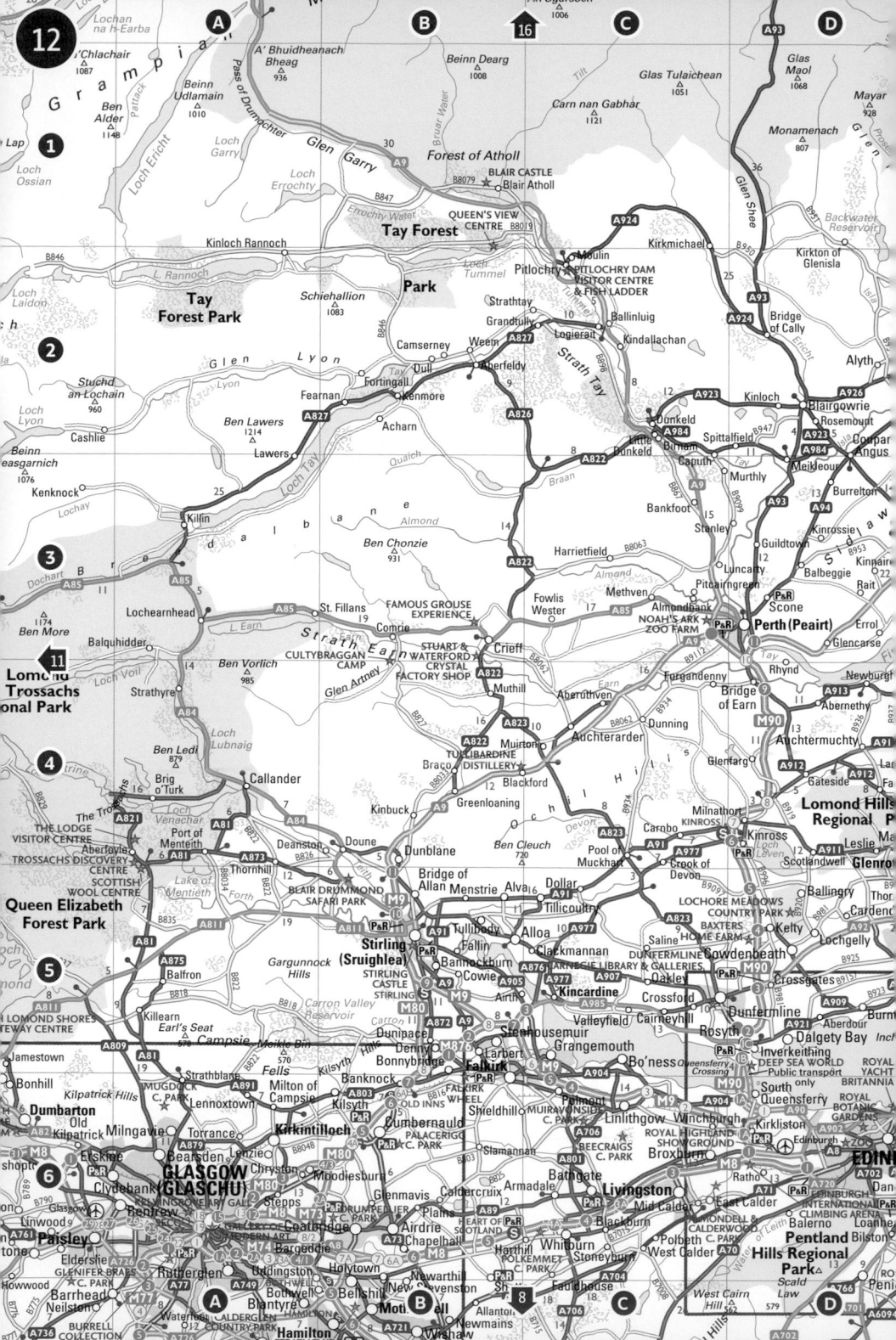

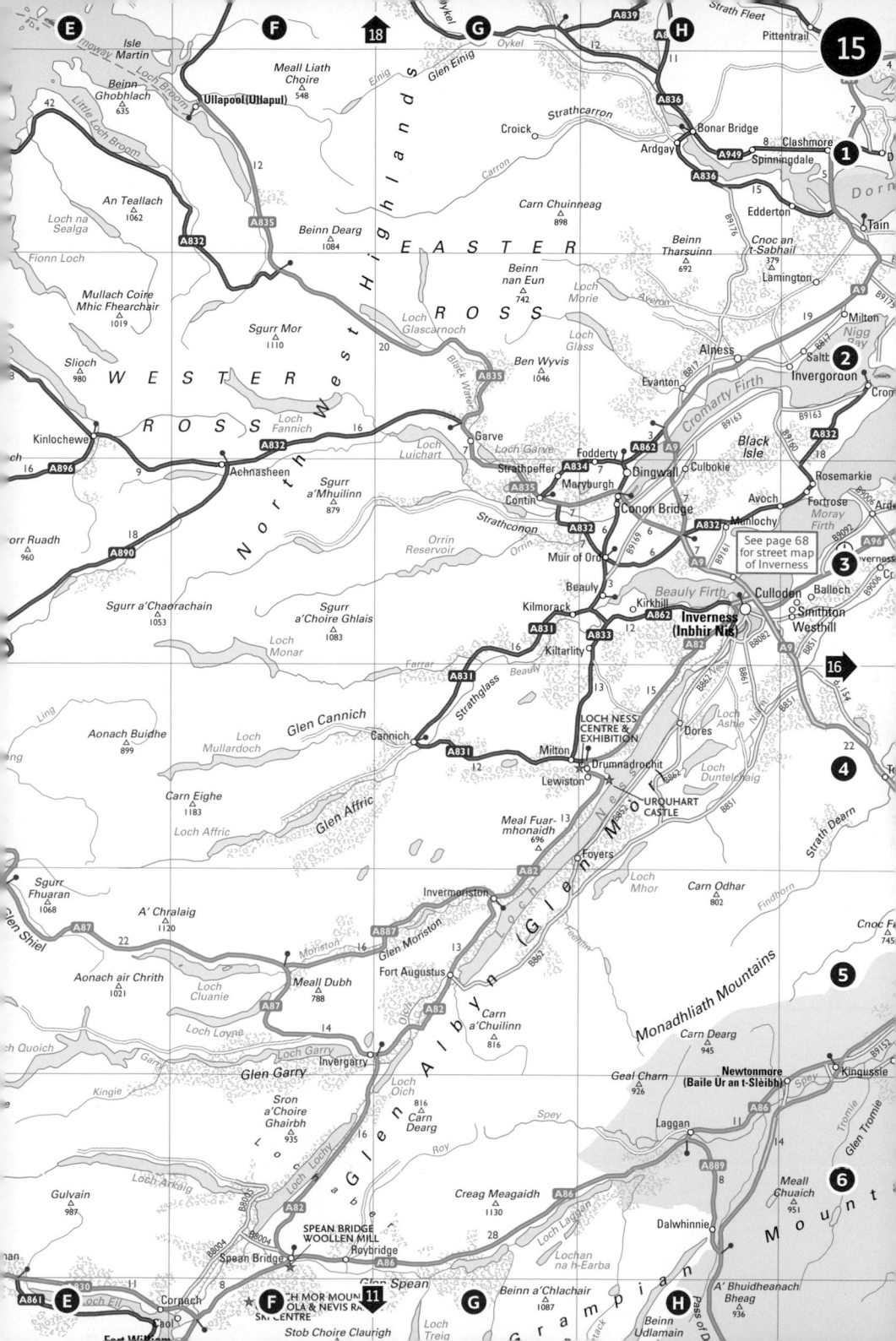

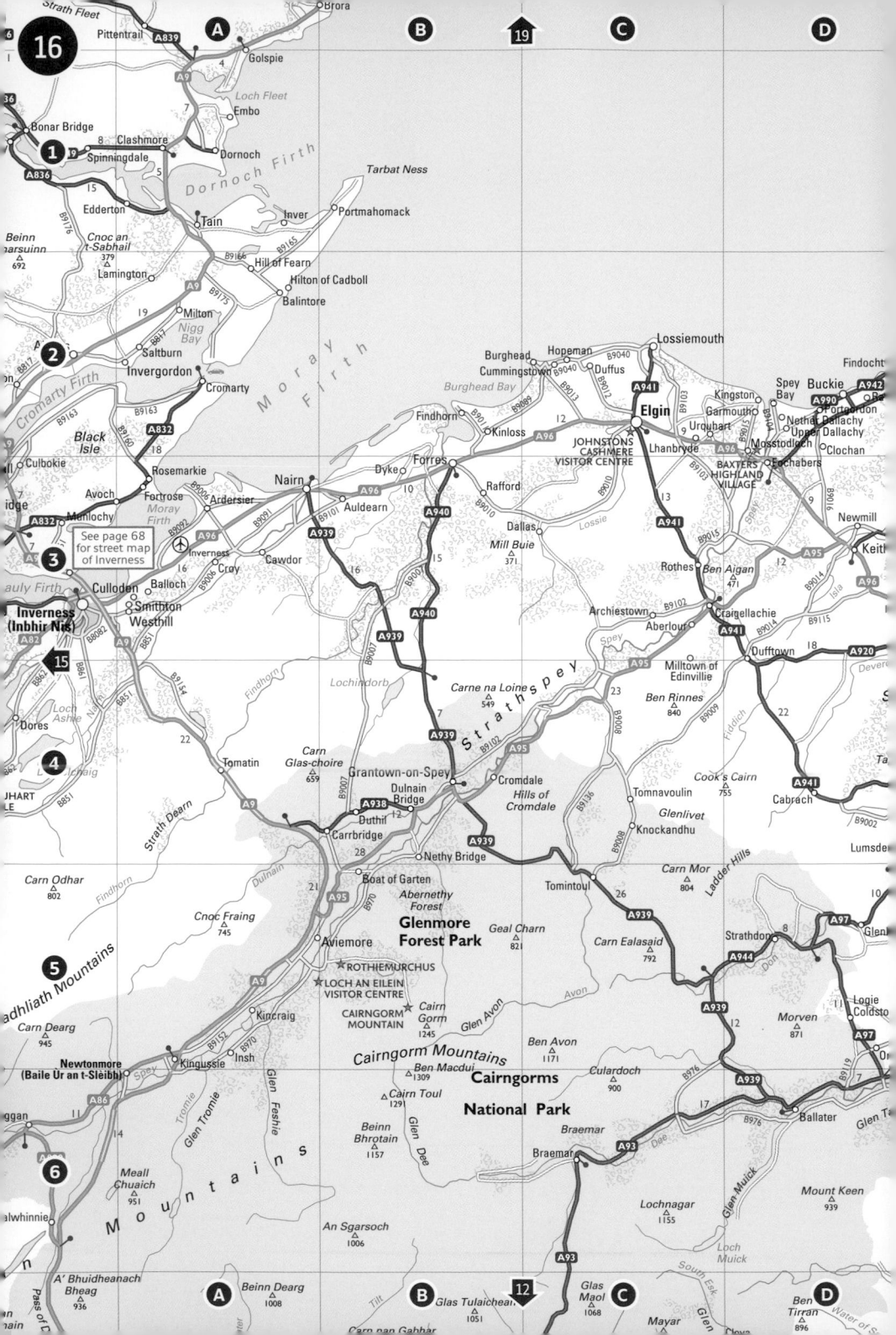

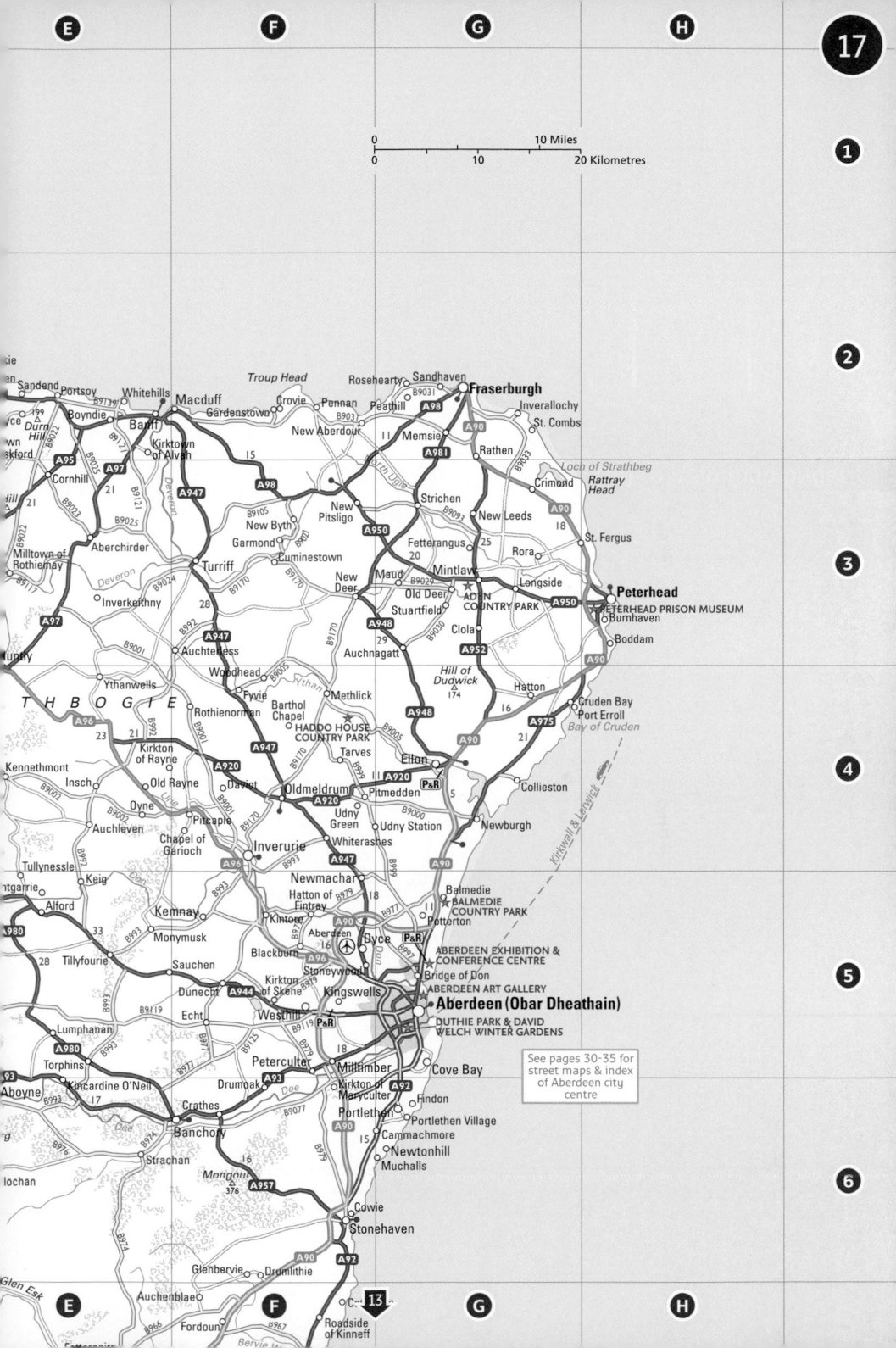

1

2

3

4

5

6

0   10 Miles
0   10   20 Kilometres

Sandend Portsoy
Whitehills Macduff Troup Head Rosehearty Sandhaven **Fraserburgh**
Boyndie Durn Hill B9139 Banff Gardenstown Crovie Pennan Peathill B9031 Inverallochy St. Combs
199 B9121 Kirktown New Aberdour 11 Memsie A90 A98
A95 A97 of Alvah A98 15 A981 Rathen Loch of Strathbeg
Cornhill Deveron Strichen New Leeds Crimond Rattray Head
21 B9025 A947 New B9093 25 18 St. Fergus
B9022 B9024 Pitsligo A950 Fetterangus Rora
Milltown of Aberchirder New Byth Garmond 20 Mintlaw A950 **Peterhead**
Rothiemay B9117 Cuminestown Maud Old Deer Longside PETERHEAD PRISON MUSEUM
B9170 New ADEN B9029 Burnhaven
A97 Turriff Deveron 28 Deer Stuartfield COUNTRY PARK Boddam
Inverkeithny B9024 A948 Clola A90
Auchterless B992 Auchnagatt 29 A952
THBOGIE Ythanwells Woodhead B9005 Hill of Hatton
Fyvie Methlick Dudwick 16 Cruden Bay
Kennethmont Rothienorman Barthol 174 Port Erroll
A96 23 Kirkton Chapel HADDO HOUSE A948 A975 Bay of Cruden
21 of Rayne A920 COUNTRY PARK Tarves 21
Insch Daviot B500 Ellon A90
Old Rayne Oldmeldrum Pitmedden A920 P&R 5 Collieston
Oyne A920 Udny Newburgh
Auchleven Pitcaple Green Udny Station
Tullynessle Chapel of Whiterashes
Keig Garioch **Inverurie** B999
ntgarrie Newmachar Balmedie
Alford Kemnay Hatton of 18 BALMEDIE
A980 Fintray COUNTRY PARK
33 Monymusk B979 Kintore Potterton
28 Tillyfourie Sauchen A96 Dyce P&R ABERDEEN EXHIBITION &
Lumphanan Blackburn Kirkton of Stoneywood CONFERENCE CENTRE
Torphins A980 Echt Skene Bridge of Don ABERDEEN ART GALLERY
Aboyne Kincardine O'Neil 17 Dunecht A944 Kingswells **Aberdeen (Obar Dheathain)**
B993 Westhill P&R DUTHIE PARK & DAVID
Crathes Peterculter WELCH WINTER GARDENS
Drumoak A93 Milltimber Cove Bay
Banchory Kirkton of A92 Findon See pages 30-35 for
Strachan Maryculter Portlethen street maps & index
16 A957 Portlethen Village of Aberdeen city
Glen Esk Mongour Cammachmore centre
376 Newtonhill
Muchalls
Cowie
Stonehaven
Glenbervie Drumlithie A90 A92
Auchenblae 13
Fordoun Roadside Bervie
of Kinneff

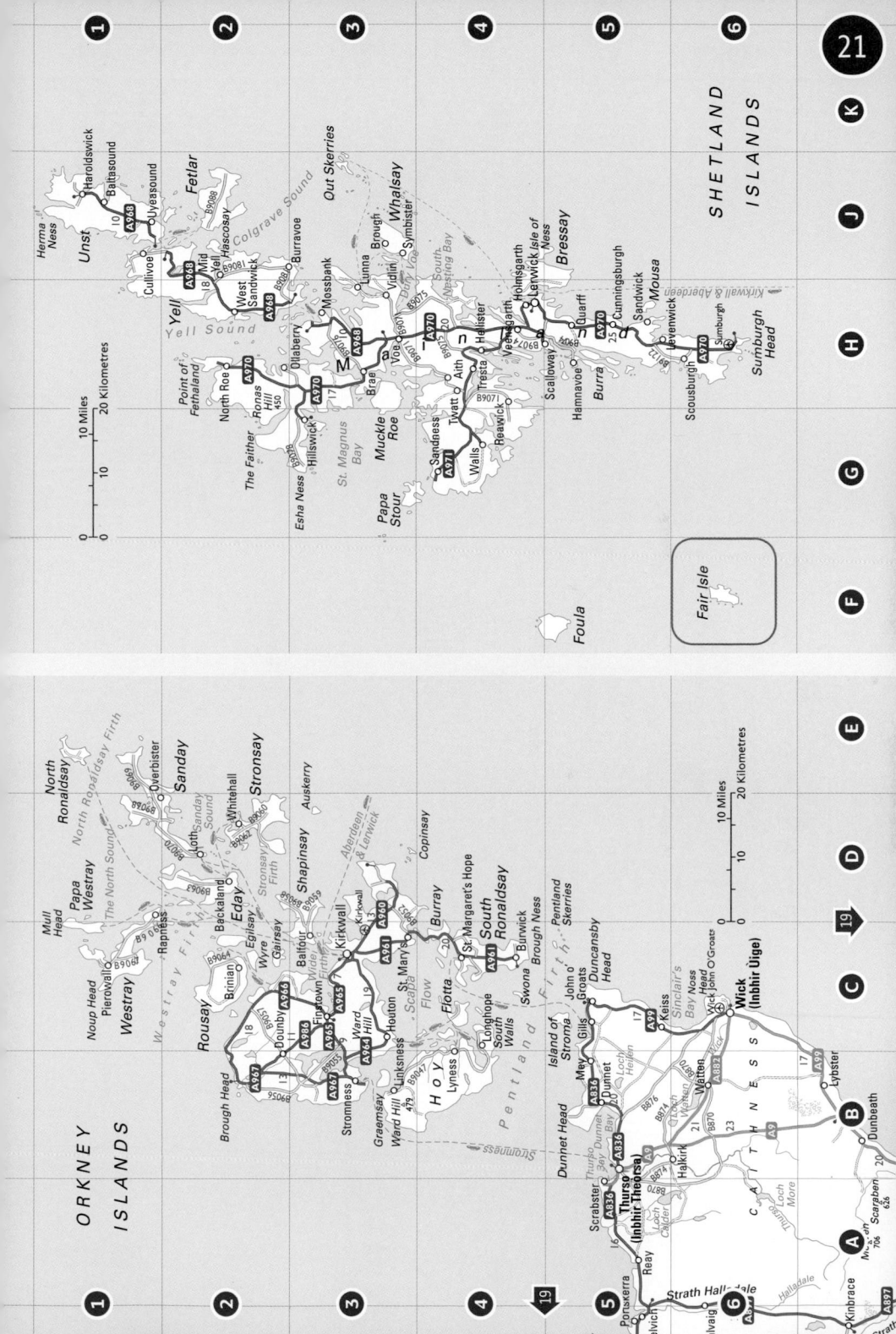

ORKNEY ISLANDS

SHETLAND ISLANDS

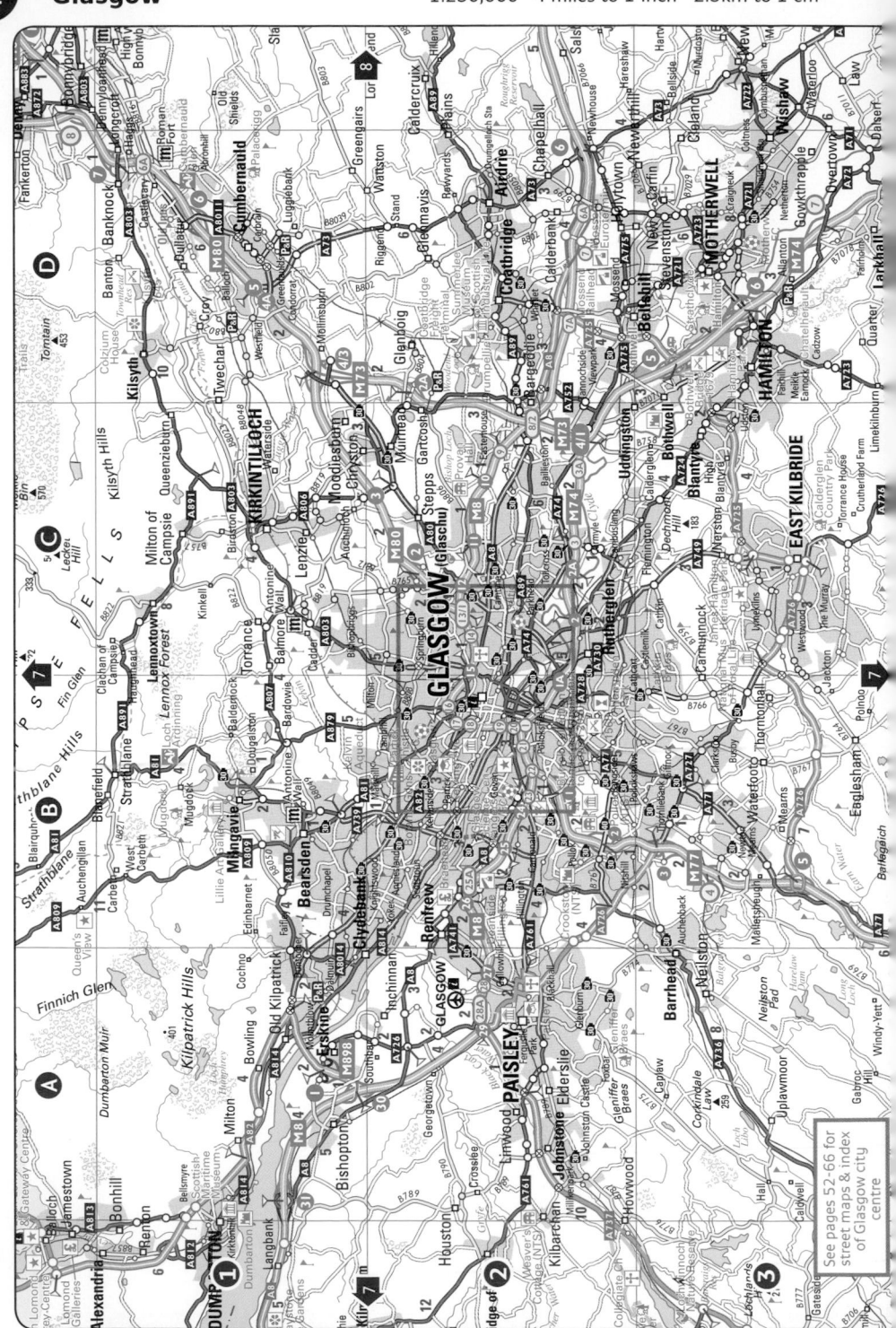

See pages 52-66 for street maps & index of Glasgow city centre

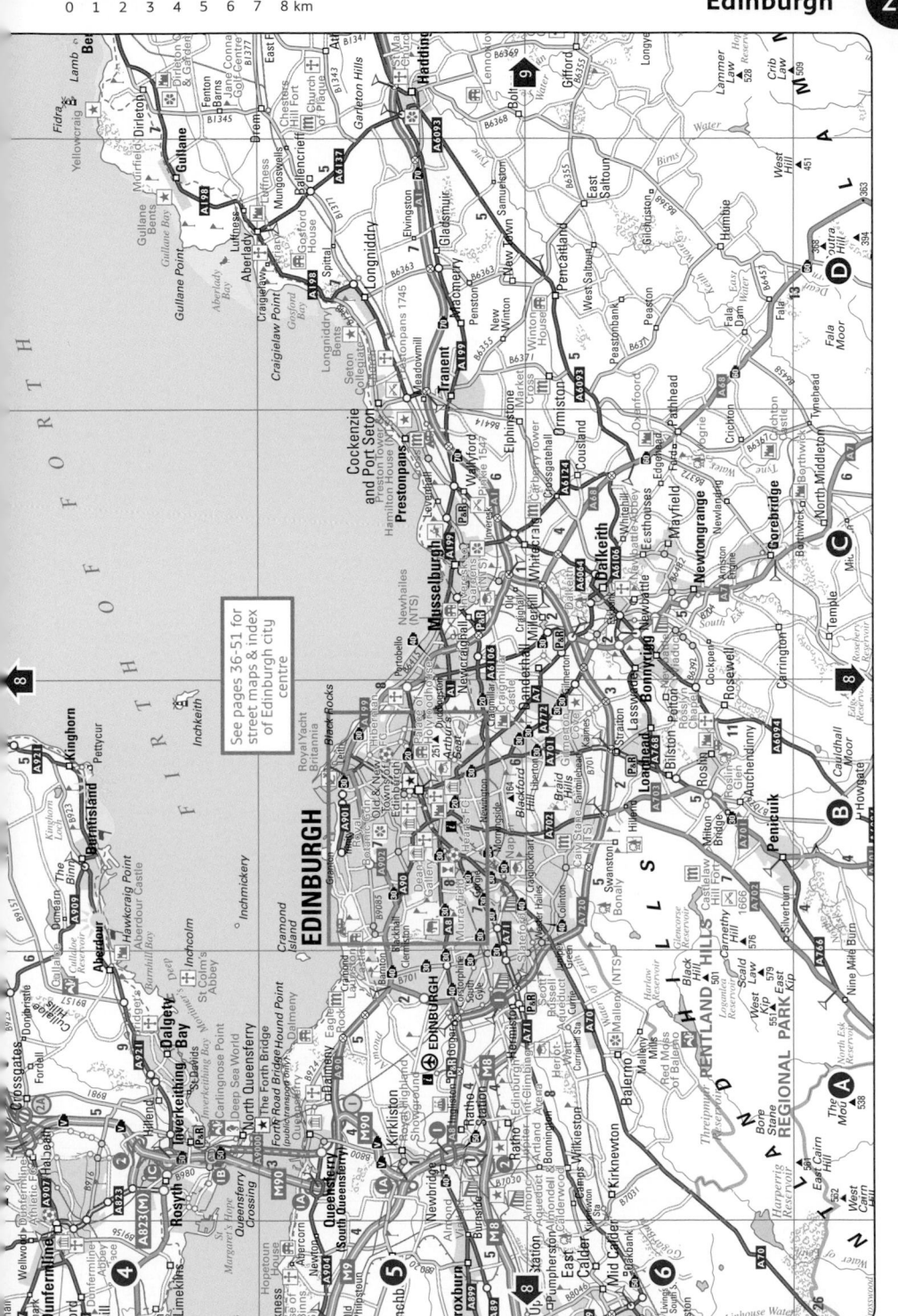

See pages 36–51 for street maps & index of Edinburgh city centre

Administrative area abbreviations

Aber.	Aberdeenshire	*Edin.*	Edinburgh	*Northumb.*	Northumberland	*Shet.*	Shetland
Arg. & B.	Argyll & Bute	*High.*	Highland	*Ork.*	Orkney	*Stir.*	Stirling
Cumb.	Cumbria	*I.o.M.*	Isle of Man	*P. & K.*	Perthshire & Kinross	*T. & W.*	Tyne & Wear
D. & G.	Dumfries & Galloway	*Midloth.*	Midlothian	*R. & C.*	Redcar & Cleveland	*W.Dun.*	West Dunbartonshire
Dur.	Durham	*Na H-E.Siar*	Na H-Eileanan Siar	*Renf.*	Renfrewshire	*W.Loth.*	West Lothian
E.Ayr.	East Ayrshire		(Western Isles)	*S.Ayr.*	South Ayrshire		
E.Loth.	East Lothian	*N.Lan.*	North Lanarkshire	*S.Lan.*	South Lanarkshire		
E.Renf.	East Renfrewshire	*N.Yorks.*	North Yorkshire	*Sc.Bord.*	Scottish Borders		

Index entries shown in **bold** type can be found on the urban area maps, pages 22-23

A

Abbeytown 3 G3
Aberchirder 17 E3
Aberdeen (Obar Dheathain) 17 G5
Aberdour 8 C1
Aberdour 23 A4
Aberfeldy 12 B2
Aberfoyle 7 H1
Aberlady 23 D4
Aberlemno 13 F2
Aberlour (Charlestown of Aberlour) 16 C3
Abernethy 12 D4
Aberuthven 12 C4
Aboyne 17 E6
Abronhill 22 D1
Acharacle 10 D1
Acharn 12 B2
Achiltibuie (Achd-'Ille-Bhuidhe) 18 A5
Achmore 20 E3
Achnasheen 15 F3
Acomb 4 C2
Aird of Sleat 14 C5
Airdrie 8 A2
Airdrie 22 D2
Airidh a' Bhruaich 20 D4
Airth 8 A1
Aiskew 4 D6
Aith 21 H4
Alexandria 7 G3
Alford 17 E5
Allanton *N.Lan.* 8 A3
Allanton *S.Lan.* 22 D3
Allendale Town 4 B3
Alloa 8 A1
Almondbank 12 C3
Alness 15 H2
Alnwick 9 H5
Alston 4 B3
Altnaharra 18 D4
Alva 8 A1
Alyth 12 D2
Amble 9 H5
Ambleside 3 H5
Ancrum 9 E4
Annan 3 G2
Annfield Plain 4 D3
Anniesland 22 B2
Anstruther 13 F4
Appin (An Apainn) 11 F2
Appleby-in-Westmorland 4 A4
Applecross 14 D3
Arbirlot 13 F2
Arbroath 13 F2
Archiestown 16 C3
Ardbeg 6 B4
Ardersier 16 A3
Ardfern 6 D1
Ardgay 15 H1
Ardler 12 D2
Ardminish 6 C4
Ardrishaig 6 D2
Ardrossan 7 F4
Ardvasar 14 C5
Arinagour 10 B2
Arisaig (Àrasaig) 14 C6
Armadale *High.* 19 E2
Armadale *W.Loth.* 8 B2

Arnisdale (Arnasdal) 14 D5
Arniston Engine 23 C6
Arrochar 7 G1
Ashgill 8 A3
Ashgill 22 D3
Ashington 4 D1
Aspatria 3 G3
Auchenback 22 B3
Auchenblae 13 G1
Auchencairn 3 E3
Auchendinny 23 B6
Auchinleck 7 H5
Auchinloch 22 C1
Auchleven 17 E4
Auchmithie 13 F2
Auchnagatt 17 G3
Auchterarder 12 C4
Auchterless 17 F3
Auchtermuchty 12 D4
Auldearn 16 B3
Auldhouse 22 C3
Aultbea (An t-Allt Beithe) 14 D1
Aviemore 16 A5
Avoch 16 A3
Ayr 7 G5

B

Backaland 21 D2
Bail' Ùr Tholastaidh 20 F2
Baile Ailein 20 D3
Baile Mòr 10 B3
Baillieston 22 C2
Balbeggie 12 D3
Balchrick 18 B3
Baldernock 22 B1
Balemartine 10 A2
Balerno 8 C2
Balerno 23 A6
Balfour 21 C3
Balfron 7 H2
Balintore 16 A2
Balivanich (Baile a' Mhanaich) 20 B7
Balla 20 B9
Ballachulish (Baile a' Chaolais) 11 F2
Ballantrae 2 A1
Ballater 16 D6
Ballencrieff 23 D5
Ballingry 8 C1
Ballinluig 12 C2
Balloch *N.Lan.* 22 D1
Balloch *W.Dun.* 16 A3
Balmedie 17 G5
Balmerino 13 E3
Balmore 22 C1
Balmullo 13 E3
Balquhidder 12 A3
Baltasound 21 J1
Balvicar 6 D1
Bamburgh 9 H4
Banchory 17 F6
Banff 17 E2
Bankfoot 12 C3
Banknock 8 A2
Banknock 22 D1
Bannockburn 8 A1
Banton 22 D1
Bardowie 8 A2
Bargeddie 8 A2

Bargeddie 22 C2
Barnard Castle 4 C5
Barnton 23 A5
Barrhead 7 H4
Barrhead 22 A3
Barthol Chapel 17 F4
Barvas (Barabhas) 20 E2
Bathgate 8 B2
Bearpark 4 D3
Bearsden 7 H3
Bearsden 22 B1
Beauly (A' Mhanachainn) 15 H3
Bedale 4 D6
Bedlington 4 D1
Beith 7 G4
Belford 9 H4
Bellingham 4 B1
Bellsbank 7 G6
Bellshill 8 A3
Bellshill 22 D2
Bellsmyre 22 A1
Benderloch (Meadarloch) 11 F3
Bernisdale 14 B3
Berriedale 19 G4
Berwick-upon-Tweed 9 G3
Bettyhill 19 E2
Biggar 8 B4
Billingham 5 E4
Billy Row 4 D4
Bilston 8 C2
Bilston 23 B6
Birdston 22 C1
Birnam 12 C2
Birtley 4 D3
Bishop Auckland 4 D4
Bishopbriggs 22 C1
Bishopton 7 G3
Bishopton 22 A1
Blackburn *Aber.* 17 F5
Blackburn *W.Loth.* 8 B2
Blackford 12 B4
Blackhall *Edin.* 23 B5
Blackhall *Renf.* 22 A2
Blackhall Colliery 5 E4
Blackwaterfoot 6 D5
Blair Atholl 12 B1
Blairgowrie 12 D2
Blanefield 22 B1
Blantyre 7 H4
Blantyre 22 C3
Blaydon 4 D2
Blyth 5 E1
Bo'ness 8 B1
Boarhills 13 F4
Boat of Garten 16 B5
Boddam 17 H3
Boldon 5 E2
Bonar Bridge 15 H1
Bonchester Bridge 9 E5
Bonhill 7 G3
Bonnington 23 A6
Bonnybridge 8 A1
Bonnyrigg 8 D2
Bonnyrigg 23 C6
Borgh (Barra) Na H-E.Siar 20 A9
Borgh (North Uist) Na H-E.Siar 20 C5
Borgue 2 D3

Borrowdale 3 G5
Borve (Borgh) 20 E2
Bothel 3 G4
Bothwell 8 A3
Bothwell 22 D3
Bournmoor 5 E3
Bowburn 5 E4
Bowling 22 A1
Bowness-on-Solway 3 G2
Bowness-on-Windermere 3 H6
Boyndie 17 E2
Braco 12 B4
Brae 21 H3
Braehead 22 B2
Braemar 16 C6
Brampton 4 A2
Brandon 4 D4
Breacleit 20 D3
Breanais 20 C3
Brechin 13 F1
Bridge of Allan 8 A1
Bridge of Cally 12 D2
Bridge of Don 17 G5
Bridge of Earn 12 D4
Bridge of Orchy (Drochaid Urchaidh) 11 H3
Bridge of Weir 7 G3
Bridgend 6 B3
Bridgeton 22 C2
Brig o'Turk 7 H1
Brinian 21 C2
Broadford (An t-Ath Leathann) 14 C4
Brodick 7 E5
Brompton 5 E6
Brompton on Swale 4 D5
Brora 19 F5
Brotton 5 F4
Brough *Cumb.* 4 B5
Brough *Shet.* 21 J3
Broughton in Furness 3 G6
Broxburn 8 B2
Buckhaven 8 D1
Buckie 16 D2
Bunessan 10 C3
Burghead 16 C2
Burnham 17 H3
Burnhope 4 D3
Burnmouth 9 F3
Burnopfield 4 D3
Burntisland 8 C1
Burntisland 23 B4
Burravoe 21 J2
Burrelton 12 D3
Burwick 21 C4
Busby 22 B3
Buttermere 3 G5

C

Cabrach 16 D4
Cadder 22 C1
Cadzow 22 D3
Cairnbaan 6 D2
Cairndow 7 F1
Cairneyhill 8 B1
Cairnryan 2 A2
Caldbeck 3 H4
Calderbank 22 D2
Caldercruix 8 A2

Calderglen 22 C3
Caldwell 22 A3
Callander 7 H1
Cambuslang 22 C2
Cammachmore 17 G6
Campbeltown (Ceann Loch Chille Chiarain) 6 D6
Camps 23 A6
Camserney 12 B2
Canisbay 19 H2
Cannich (Canaich) 15 G4
Caol 11 G1
Caplaw 22 A3
Cappercleuch 8 C4
Caputh 12 C2
Carbeth 22 B1
Carbost 14 B4
Carbrain 22 D1
Cardenden 8 C1
Cardonald 22 B2
Carfin 22 D3
Carinish (Cairinis) 20 B6
Carlisle 3 H3
Carloway (Càrlabhagh) 20 D2
Carlton Miniott 5 E6
Carluke 8 A3
Carmunnock 22 B3
Carmyle 22 C2
Carnbo 12 C4
Carnoustie 13 F3
Carntyne 22 C2
Carnwath 8 B3
Carradale 6 D5
Carrbridge 16 B4
Carrington 23 C6
Carsphairn 2 D1
Castle Douglas 3 E2
Castle Kennedy 2 B3
Castlebay (Bàgh a' Chaisteil) 20 A10
Castlecary 22 D1
Castlemilk 22 C3
Castletown 19 G2
Cathcart 22 B2
Cathkin 22 C3
Catrine 7 H5
Catterick 4 D6
Catterick Garrison 4 D6
Catterline 13 G1
Cawdor 16 A3
Cayton 5 H6
Ceann a' Bhàigh 20 B6
Cearsiadair 20 E4
Ceres 13 E4
Chapel of Garioch 17 F4
Chapelhall 8 A2
Chapelhall 22 D2
Charleston 13 E2
Charlestown 14 D2
Chester-le-Street 4 D3
Chilton 4 D4
Chirnside 9 F3
Chopwell 4 D3
Chryston 7 H3
Chryston 22 C1
Clachan of Campsie 22 C1
Clackmannan 8 B1
Claonaig 6 D4

Clarkston 22 B3
Clashmore 16 A1
Cleator Moor 3 F5
Cleland 22 D3
Clermiston 23 A5
Clochan 16 D2
Clola 17 G3
Clova 13 E1
Clydebank 7 H3
Clydebank 22 A1
Coalburn 8 A4
Coatbridge 8 A2
Coatbridge 22 D2
Cochno 22 A1
Cockenzie and
    Port Seton 8 D2
Cockenzie and
    Port Seton 23 D5
Cockermouth 3 G4
Cockfield 4 D4
Cockpen 23 C6
Colburn 4 D6
Coldstream 9 F4
Colinsburgh 13 E4
Colinton 23 B6
Colintraive 7 E3
Collieston 17 G4
Colliston 13 F2
Comrie 12 B3
Condorrat 22 D1
Coniston 3 IIG
Connel (A' Choingheal)
    11 F3
Conon Bridge (Drochaid
    Sgùideil) 15 H3
Consett 4 D3
Contin (Cunndainn)
    15 G3
Corbridge 4 C2
Cornforth 5 E4
Cornhill 17 E3
Cornhill on Tweed 9 F4
Corpach (A' Chorpaich)
    11 F1
Corran (Ardgour) 11 F1
Corstorphine 23 A5
Coundon 4 D4
Coupar Angus 12 D2
Cousland 23 C6
Cove Bay 17 G5
Cowdenbeath 8 C1
Cowie Aber. 17 F6
Cowie Stir. 8 A1
Coxhoe 5 E4
Coylton 7 G6
Craigellachie 16 C3
Craighouse 6 C3
Craigielaw 23 D5
Craiglockhart 23 B5
Craigmillar 23 B5
Craigneuk 22 D3
Craignure 11 E3
Craigo 13 F1
Craigrothie 13 E4
Craigton (Monikie)
    Angus 13 F3
Craigton (by Kirriemuir)
    Angus 13 E2
Crail 13 F4
Cramlington 4 D2
Cramond 23 A5
Crathes 17 F6
Crawcrook 4 D2
Crianlarich (A' Chrion-
    Làraich) 11 H3
Crichton 23 C6
Crieff 12 B3
Crimond 17 G3
Crinan 6 D2
Crocketford or
    Ninemile Bar 3 E2
Croggan 11 E3

Cromarty (Cromba)
    16 A2
Cromdale 16 B4
Cromore 20 E3
Crook 4 D4
Crook of Devon 12 C4
Crookham 9 G4
Crosbost 20 E3
Crossford 8 B1
Crossgatehall 23 C6
Crossgates 8 C1
Crossgates 23 A4
Crosshouse 7 G5
Crosslee 22 A2
Crossmichael 3 E2
Crovie 17 F2
Croy High. 16 A3
Croy N.Lan. 22 D1
Cruden Bay 17 G4
Crutherland Farm
    22 C3
Culbokie (Cùil Bhàicidh)
    15 H3
Culkein 18 A4
Cullen 17 E2
Cullipool 6 D1
Cullivoe 21 J1
Culloden 16 A3
Cumbernauld 8 A2
Cumbernauld 22 D1
Cuminestown 17 F3
Cummingstown 16 C2
Cumnock 7 H5
Cunningsburgh 21 H5
Cupar 13 E4
Currie 23 A6

D
Dairsie (Osnaburgh)
    13 E4
Dalabrog 20 B8
Dalavich 7 E1
Dalbeattie 3 E2
Dalgety Bay 8 C1
Dalgety Bay 23 A4
Dalhalvaig 19 F3
Dalkeith 8 D2
Dalkeith 23 C6
Dallas 16 C3
Dalmally (Dail Mhàilidh)
    11 G3
Dalmellington 7 G6
Dalmeny 23 A5
Dalmuir 22 A1
Dalry 7 F4
Dalrymple 7 G6
Dalserf 22 D3
Dalston 3 H3
Dalwhinnie 15 H6
Danderhall 23 C6
Darlington 4 D5
Darvel 7 H5
Daviot 17 F4
Deanston 12 B4
Dearham 3 F4
Denholm 9 E5
Denny 8 A1
Dervaig 10 C2
Dingwall (Inbhir
    Pheofharain) 15 H3
Dinnington 4 D2
Distington 3 F4
Dollar 8 B1
Donibristle 23 A4
Dores (Duras) 15 H4
Dornie (An Dòrnaidh)
    14 D4
Dornoch 16 A1
Dougalston 22 B1
Douglas 8 A4
Dounby 21 B2

Doune 12 B4
Dreghorn 7 G5
Drongan 7 G6
Drumbeg 18 B4
Drumchapel 22 B1
Drumlithie 17 F6
Drummore 2 B4
Drumnadrochit (Druim na
    Drochaid) 15 H4
Drumoak 17 F6
Duddingston 23 B5
Dudley 4 D2
Dufftown 16 D3
Duffus 16 C2
Dull 12 B2
Dullatur 22 D1
Dulnain Bridge 16 B4
Dumbarton 7 G3
Dumfries 3 F2
Dunbar 9 E2
Dunbeath 19 G4
Dunbeg (An Dùn Beag)
    11 E3
Dunblane 12 B4
Dundee 13 E3
Dundonald 7 G5
Dunearn 23 B4
Dunecht 17 F5
Dunfermline 8 B1
Dunipace 8 A1
Dunkeld 12 C2
Dunnet 19 G2
Dunning 12 C4
Dunoon 7 F3
Duns 9 F3
Duntocher 22 A1
Dunvegan 14 A3
Durham 4 D3
Durness 18 C2
Duthil 16 B4
Dyce 17 F5
Dyke 16 B3
Dykehead 13 E1

E
Eaglesham 7 H4
Eaglesham 22 B3
Earlston 9 E4
Easington 5 E3
Easington Colliery 5 E3
East Ayton 5 H6
East Calder 8 B2
East Kilbride 7 H4
East Kilbride 22 C3
East Linton 9 E2
East Saltoun 23 D6
East Wemyss 8 D1
Easterhouse 22 C2
Eastfield 5 H6
Easthouses 23 C6
Eastriggs 3 G2
Echt 17 F5
Edderton 16 A1
Edgehead 23 C6
Edinbane 14 B3
Edinbarnet 22 B1
Edinburgh 8 C2
Edinburgh 23 B5
Edinburgh Airport
    23 A5
Edzell 13 F1
Egremont 3 F5
Elderslie 7 G3
Elderslie 22 A2
Elgin 16 C2
Elgol 14 C5
Elie 13 E4
Ellenabeich 6 D1
Ellington 4 D1
Ellon 17 G4
Elphin 18 B5
Elphinstone 23 C5

Elvingston 23 D5
Embo 16 A1
Eòropaidh 20 F1
Errol 12 D3
Erskine 7 G3
Erskine 22 A1
Esh Winning 4 D3
Eskbank 23 C6
Eskdalemuir 3 G1
Ettrick 8 C5
Evanton 15 H2
Evenwood 4 D4
Eyemouth 9 G2

F
Faifley 22 B1
Fairhill 22 D3
Fairholm 22 D3
Fairlie 7 F4
Fairmilehead 23 B6
Fala 23 D6
Fala Dam 23 D6
Falkirk 8 A2
Falkland 12 D4
Fallin 8 A1
Farnell 13 F2
Fauldhouse 8 B2
Fearnan 12 B2
Felling 4 D2
Feolin Ferry 6 B3
Ferguslie Park 22 A2
Ferryden 13 G2
Ferryhill 4 D4
Fetterangus 17 G3
Fettercairn 13 F1
Findhorn 16 B2
Findochty 16 D2
Findon 17 G6
Finstown 21 C3
Fionnphort 10 C3
Fishburn 5 E4
Fishnish 10 D2
Flemington 22 C3
Flimby 3 F4
Fochabers 16 D3
Fodderty 15 H3
Ford Arg. & B. 6 D1
Ford Midloth. 23 C6
Fordell 23 A4
Fordoun 13 G1
Fordyce 17 E2
Forfar 13 E2
Forgandenny 12 C4
Forres 16 B3
Fort Augustus
    (Cille Chuimein) 15 G5
Fort William
    (An Gearasdan) 11 G1
Forth 8 B3
Fortingall 12 B2
Fortrose (A' Chananaich)
    16 A3
Foulden 9 G3
Fowlis Wester 12 C3
Foxbar 22 A2
Foyers (Foithir) 15 G4
Fraserburgh 17 G2
Freuchie 12 D4
Friockheim 13 F2
Frizington 3 F5
Fullwood 22 A3
Furnace 7 E1
Fyvie 17 F4

G
Gabroc Hill 22 A3
Gainford 4 D5
Gairloch (Geàrrloch)
    14 D2
Galashiels 8 D4
Gallowhill 22 A2
Galston 7 H5

Gardenstown 17 F2
Garelochhead 7 F2
Garmond 17 F3
Garmouth 16 D2
Gartcosh 22 C2
Garve (Clachan Ghairbh)
    15 G2
Gatehouse of Fleet 2 D3
Gateshead 4 D2
Gateside 12 D4
Geirinis 20 B7
Georgetown 22 A2
Giffnock 22 B3
Gilchriston 23 D6
Gills 19 H2
Gilmerton Edin. 23 B6
Girvan 2 B1
Gladsmuir 23 D5
Glamis 13 E2
Glasgow (Glaschu) 7 H3
Glasgow (Glaschu)
    22 B2
Glasgow Airport 22 A2
Glenbervie 17 F6
Glenboig 22 D2
Glenburn 22 A2
Glencaple 3 F2
Glencarse 12 D3
Glencoe (A' Chàrnaich)
    11 G2
Gleneig (Gleann Eilg)
    14 D5
Glenfarg 12 D4
Glenfinnan (Gleann
    Fhionnainn) 15 E6
Glenkindie 16 D5
Glenmavis 8 A2
Glenmavis 22 D2
Glenridding 3 H5
Glenrothes 12 D4
Glentrool 2 C2
Gogar 23 A5
Golspie 16 A1
Gordon 9 E3
Gorebridge 8 D2
Gorebridge 23 C6
Gorgie 23 B5
Gosforth Cumb. 3 F5
Gosforth T. & W. 4 D2
Gourdon 13 G1
Gourock 7 F3
Govan 22 B2
Gowkthrapple 22 D3
Grabhair 20 E4
Grandtully 12 C2
Grangemouth 8 B1
Granton 23 B5
Grantown-on-Spey
    16 B4
Grasmere 3 H5
Great Ayton 5 F5
Great Clifton 3 F4
Great Lumley 4 D3
Greatham 5 E4
Greenfaulds 22 D1
Greengairs 22 D1
Greenloaning 12 B4
Greenock 7 F3
Gress (Griais) 20 E2
Gretna 3 H2
Grimshader
    (Griomsiadar) 20 E3
Guardbridge 13 E4
Guide Post 4 D1
Guildtown 12 D3
Guisborough 5 F5
Gullane 8 D1
Gullane 23 D4
Guthrie 13 F2

H
Habost (Tabost) 44 F1

Haddington 9 E2
Hadston 4 D1
Haggs 22 D1
Halbeath 23 A4
Halket 22 A3
Halkirk 19 G3
Hall 22 A3
Haltwhistle 4 B2
Hamilton 8 A3
Hamilton 22 D3
Hamnavoe 21 H5
Haroldswick 21 J1
Harrietfield 12 C3
Harthill 8 B2
Hartlepool 5 F4
Haswell 5 E3
Hatton 17 G4
Hatton of Fintray 17 F5
Haughhead 22 C1
Hawes 4 B6
Hawick 9 E5
Hawkshead 3 H6
Haydon Bridge 4 B2
Heddon-on-the-Wall
    4 D2
Heighington 4 D4
Helensburgh 7 F2
Hellister 21 H4
Helmsdale 19 F5
Helmsley 5 F6
Hermiston 23 A5
Hetton-le-Hole 5 E3
Hexham 4 C2
High Blantyre 22 C3
High Etherley 4 D4
High Lorton 3 G4
Hill of Fearn 16 A2
Hillend Fife 23 A4
Hillend Midloth. 23 B6
Hillington 22 B2
Hillside 13 G1
Hillswick 21 G3
Hilton of Cadboll 16 A2
Holmsgarth 21 H4
Holytown 8 A2
Holytown 22 D2
Hopeman 16 C2
Horden 5 E3
Houghton le Spring 5 E3
Houston 7 G3
Houston 22 A2
Houton 21 C3
Howwood 7 G3
Howwood 22 A2
Humbie 23 D6
Huntly 17 E3
Hurlford 7 G5
Hurworth-on-Tees 5 E5
Hutton Rudby 5 E5

I
Inchinnan 22 A2
Inchture 12 D3
Ingliston 23 A5
Innellan 7 F3
Innerleithen 8 D4
Insch 17 E4
Insh 16 A5
Inver 16 A1
Inveralligin 14 D3
Inverallochy 17 G2
Inveraray (Inbhir Aora)
    7 E1
Inverbervie 13 G1
Inveresk 23 C5
Invergarry
    (Inbhir Garadh) 15 F5
Invergordon 16 A2
Inverie 14 D6
Inverkeilor 13 F2
Inverkeithing 8 C1
Inverkeithing 23 A4

Inverkeithny 17 E3
Inverkip 7 F3
Invermoriston (Inbhir
    Moireasdan) 15 G5
Inverness
    (Inbhir Nis) 15 H3
Inverurie 17 F4
Irvine 7 G5
Isleornsay
    (Eilean Iarmain) 14 C5

J
Jackton 22 B3
Jamestown 7 G2
Jarrow 5 E2
Jedburgh 9 E4
John o'Groats 19 H2
Johnshaven 13 G1
Johnstone 7 G3
Johnstone 22 A2
Johnstone Castle 22 A2
Johnstonebridge 3 F1
Juniper Green 23 A6

K
Kaimes 23 B6
Keig 17 E5
Keiss 19 H2
Keith 16 D3
Kelso 9 F4
Kelty 8 C1
Kelvinside 22 B2
Kemnay 17 F5
Kendal 4 A6
Kenmore 12 B2
Kennacraig 6 D3
Kennethmont 17 E4
Kennoway 13 E4
Keswick 3 G4
Kilbarchan 7 G3
Kilbarchan 22 A2
Kilberry 6 D3
Kilbirnie 7 G4
Kilchoan 10 C1
Kilchrenan
    (Cill Chrèanain) 11 F3
Kilcreggan 7 F2
Killearn 7 H2
Killin 12 A3
Kilmacolm 7 G3
Kilmany 13 E3
Kilmarnock 7 G5
Kilmartin 6 D2
Kilmaurs 7 G4
Kilmelford 6 D1
Kilmorack 15 G3
Kilrenny 13 F4
Kilsyth 8 A2
Kilsyth 22 D1
Kiltarlity 15 H3
Kilwinning 7 G4
Kinbrace 19 E4
Kinbuck 12 B4
Kincardine 8 B1
Kincardine O'Neil 17 E6
Kincraig 16 A5
Kindallachan 12 C2
Kinghorn 8 C1
Kinghorn 23 B4
Kingsbarns 13 F4
Kingsmuir 13 E2
Kingston 16 D2
Kingswells 17 F5
Kingussie 16 A5
Kinkell 22 C3
Kinloch High. 14 B6
Kinloch P. & K. 12 D2
Kinloch Rannoch 12 A2
Kinlochbervie 18 B3
Kinlochewe 15 E2
Kinlochleven (Ceann Loch
    Lìobhann) 11 G1

Kinlochmore 11 G1
Kinloss 16 B2
Kinnaird 12 D3
Kinross 12 D4
Kinrossie 12 D3
Kintore 17 F5
Kirkbean 3 F3
Kirkbride 4 D6
Kirkby Stephen 4 B5
Kirkbymoorside 5 F6
Kirkcaldy 8 C1
Kirkcolm 2 A2
Kirkconnel 8 A5
Kirkcudbright 2 D3
Kirkhill 15 H3
Kirkintilloch 7 H3
Kirkintilloch 22 C1
Kirkliston 8 C2
Kirkliston 23 A5
Kirkmichael 12 C1
Kirkmuirhill 8 A3
**Kirknewton
    W.Loth. 23 A6**
Kirkton of Glenisla
    12 D1
Kirkton of Kingoldrum
    13 E2
Kirkton of Maryculter
    17 F6
Kirkton of Rayne
    17 E4
Kirkton of Skene
    17 F5
Kirktown of Alvah
    17 E2
Kirktown of Deskford
    17 E2
Kirkwall 21 C3
Kirriemuir 13 E2
Kirtomy 19 E2
Knightswood 22 B2
Knockandhu 16 C4
Kyle of Lochalsh (Caol Loch
    Aillse) 14 D4
Kyleakin (Caol Acain)
    14 D4

L
Ladybank 13 E4
Laggan 15 H6
Laide 14 D1
Lairg 18 D5
Lamington 16 A2
Lamlash 7 E5
Lanark 8 A3
Lanchester 4 D3
Langholm 3 H1
Langley Park 4 D3
Langside 22 B2
Larbert 8 A1
Largoward 13 E4
Largs 7 F4
Larkhall 8 A3
Larkhall 22 D3
Lasswade 8 D2
Lasswade 23 C6
Latheron 19 G4
Latheronwheel 19 G4
Lauder 9 E3
Laurencekirk 13 G1
Law 8 A3
Lawers 12 A3
Leeming 4 D6
Leith 23 B5
Lennoxtown 7 H3
Lennoxtown 22 C1
Lenzie 7 H3
Lenzie 22 C1
Lerwick 21 H4
Leslie 12 D4
Lesmahagow 8 A4
Letham Angus 13 F2

Letham Fife 13 E4
Leuchars 13 E3
Leumrabhagh 20 E4
Leven 13 E4
Levenhall 23 C5
Levens 3 H6
Levenwick 21 H5
Leverburgh
    (An T-Òb) 20 C5
Lewiston
    (Blàr na Maigh) 15 H4
Leyburn 4 D6
Lhanbryde 16 C2
Liberton 23 B6
Limekilnburn 22 D3
Lingdale 5 F5
Linksness 21 B3
Linlithgow 8 B2
Lintmill 17 E2
Linwood 7 G3
Linwood 22 A2
Little Brechin 13 F1
Little Dunkeld 12 C2
Livingston 8 B2
Loanhead 8 C2
Loanhead 23 B6
Lochaline
    (Loch Àlainn) 10 D2
Locharbriggs 3 F1
Lochawe
    (Loch Obha) 11 G3
Lochboisdale (Loch
    Baghasdail) 20 B9
Lochbuie 10 D3
Lochcarron
    (Loch Carrann) 14 D4
Lochdon 11 E3
Lochearnhead (Ceann Loch
    Èireann) 12 A3
Lochgelly 8 C1
Lochgilphead (Ceann Loch
    Gilb) 6 D2
Lochgoilhead 7 F1
Lochinver
    (Loch an Inbhir) 18 A4
Lochmaben 3 F1
Lochmaddy 20 C6
Lochranza 7 E4
Lochwinnoch 7 G4
Lockerbie 3 G1
Loftus 5 G5
Logan 7 H5
Logie Coldstone 16 D5
Logie Pert 13 F1
Logierait 12 C2
Longbenton 4 D2
Longcroft 22 D1
Longforgan 13 E3
Longhope 21 B4
Longhoughton 9 H5
Longniddry 8 D2
Longniddry 23 D5
Longside 17 G3
Longtown 3 H2
Lossiemouth 16 C2
Loth 21 D2
Lothbeg 19 F5
Lothmore 19 F5
Loughborough 22 A2
Luffness 23 D4
Luggiebank 22 D1
Lugton 22 A3
Lumphanan 17 E5
Lumsden 16 D4
Lunan 13 F2
Lunanhead 13 E2
Luncarty 12 C3
Lundin Links 13 E4
Lunna 21 H3
Lusta 14 A3
Luthermuir 13 F1
Luthrie 13 E4
Lybster 19 G4
Lymekilns 22 C3

Lynemouth 4 D1
Lyness 21 C4

M
Macduff 17 F2
Machan 22 D3
Machrihanish 6 C5
Macmerry 23 D5
Mallaig (Malaig) 14 C6
Malleny Mills 23 A6
Malletsheugh 22 B3
Markinch 12 D4
Marske-by-the-Sea
    5 F4
Maryburgh
    (Baile Mairi) 15 H3
Maryhill 22 B2
Marykirk 13 F1
Maryport 3 F4
Marywell 13 F2
Mauchline 7 H5
Maud 17 G3
Maybole 7 G6
Mayfield 8 D2
Mayfield 23 C6
Meadowmill 23 D5
Mearns 22 B3
Meigle 12 D2
Meikle Earnock 22 D3
Meikleour 12 D3
Melbost 20 E3
Melrose 9 E4
Melvaig 14 D1
Melvich 19 E2
Memsie 17 G2
Memus 13 E2
Menstrie 8 A1
Methil 8 D1
Methlick 17 F4
Methven 12 C3
Mey 19 G2
Miavaig
    (Miabhaig) 20 C3
Mid Calder 8 B2
Mid Yell 21 J2
Middlesbrough 5 E4
Middleton St. George
    5 E5
Middleton-in-Teesdale
    4 C4
Midtown 14 D1
Millerhill 23 C6
Millikenpark 22 A2
Millom 3 G6
Millport 7 F4
Milltimber 17 F5
Milltown of
    Edinvillie 16 C3
Milltown of
    Rothiemay 17 E3
Milnathort 12 D4
Milngavie 7 H3
Milngavie 22 B1
Milnthorpe 3 H6
Milton High. 16 A2
Milton W.Dun. 22 A1
Milton (Baile a' Mhuilinn)
    15 G4
Milton Bridge 23 B6
Milton of Balgonie
    13 E4
Milton of Campsie
    7 H3
**Milton of Campsie
    22 C1**
Minard 7 E2
Mintlaw 17 G3
Moffat 3 F1
Mollinsburn 22 D1
Moniaive 3 E1
Monifieth 13 E3
Montgarrie 17 E5

Montrose 13 G2
Monymusk 17 E5
Moodiesburn 7 H3
Moodiesburn 22 C1
Morar 14 C6
Moresby Parks 3 F5
Morningside 23 B5
Morpeth 4 D1
Mossbank 21 H3
Mossblown 7 G5
Mossend 22 D2
Mosstodloch 16 D2
Motherwell 8 A3
Motherwell 22 D3
Moulin 12 C2
Mountblow 22 A1
Muchalls 17 G6
Mugdock 22 B1
Muir of Ord
  (Am Blàr Dubh) 15 H3
Muirhead *Angus* 13 E3
Muirhead *N.Lan.* 22 C2
Muirkirk 7 H5
Muirton 12 C4
Mungoswells 23 D5
Munlochy 15 H3
Murthly 12 C3
Murton 5 E3
Musselburgh 8 D2
Musselburgh 23 C5
Muthill 12 B4

N

Nairn 16 A3
Nedd 18 B4
Neilston 7 G4
Neilston 22 A3
Nerston 22 C5
Nether Dallachy 16 D2
Netherton
  ***N.Lan.* 22 D3**
Nethy Bridge 16 B4
New Abbey 3 F2
New Aberdour 17 F2
New Byth 17 F3
New Cumnock 7 H6
New Deer 17 F3
New Galloway 2 D2
New Leeds 17 G3
New Luce 2 B2
New Marske 5 F4
New Pitsligo 17 F3
New Stevenston 8 A3
New Stevenston 22 D3
New Town 23 D5
New Winton 23 D5
Newarthill 8 A3
Newarthill 22 D3
Newbattle 23 C6
Newbiggin-by-the-Sea
  5 E1
Newbridge 23 A5
Newburgh *Aber.* 17 G4
Newburgh *Fife* 12 D4
Newby Bridge 3 H6
Newcastle upon Tyne
  4 D2
Newcraighall 23 C5
Newhouse 22 D2
Newington 23 B5
Newlandrig 23 C6
Newmachar 17 F5
Newmains 8 A3
Newmill 16 D3
Newmilns 7 H5
Newport 19 G4
Newport-on-Tay 13 E3
Newton Aycliffe 4 D4
Newton Mearns 22 B3
Newton Stewart 2 C2
Newtongrange 8 D2
Newtongrange 23 C6

Newtonhill 17 G6
**Newtonmore (Baile Ùr an
  t-Slèibh) 16 A6**
Newtown
  St. Boswells 9 E4
Newtyle 12 D2
Nitshill 22 B2
North Ballachulish
  (Baile a' Chaolais a
  Tuath) 11 F1
North Berwick 9 E1
North Erradale 14 D1
North Kessock 15 H3
**North Queensferry
  23 A4**
North Roe 21 H2
North Shields 5 E2
North Sunderland 9 H4
Northallerton 5 E6
Northbay 20 B9
Northmuir 13 E2
Northton
  (Taobh Tuath) 20 C5

O

Oakley 8 B1
Oathlaw 13 E2
Oban (An t-Òban) 11 E3
Old Craighall 23 C5
Old Deer 17 G3
Old Kilpatrick 7 G3
Old Kilpatrick 22 A1
Old Rayne 17 E4
Oldmeldrum 17 F4
Ollaberry 21 H2
Onich
  (Omhanaich) 11 F1
Ordie 16 D5
Ormiston 8 D2
Ormiston 23 D6
Otterburn 4 B1
Ouston 4 D3
Overbister 21 D1
Overtown 8 A3
Ovingham 4 C2
Oyne 17 E4

P

Painshawfield 4 C2
Paisley 7 G3
Paisley 22 A2
Panbride 13 F3
Parkhead 22 C2
Partick 22 B2
Parton 3 F4
Pathhead 23 C6
Patna 7 G6
Paxton 9 G3
Peaston 23 D6
Peastonbank 23 D6
Peat Inn 13 E4
Peathill 17 G2
Peebles 8 C3
Pegswood 4 D1
Pelton 4 D3
Pencaitland 8 D2
Pencaitland 23 D6
Penicuik 8 C2
Penicuik 23 B6
Pennan 17 F2
Penrith 4 A4
Penshaw 5 E3
Penston 23 D5
Perth (Peairt) 12 D3
Peterculter 17 F5
Peterhead 17 H3
Peterlee 5 E3
Pettycur 23 B4
Pickering 5 G6
Pierowall 21 C1
Pinwherry 2 B1
Pitcairngreen 12 C3

Pitcaple 17 F4
Pitlessie 13 E4
Pitlochry 12 C2
Pitmedden 17 F4
Pitscottie 13 E4
Pittenträit 19 E5
Pittenweem 13 F4
Plains 8 A2
Plains 22 D2
Plockton
  (Am Ploc) 14 D4
Polbain 18 A5
Polbeth 8 B2
Polglass 18 A5
Pollok 22 B2
Pollokshaws 22 B2
Pollokshields 22 B2
Polmont 8 B2
Polnoon 22 B3
Polton 23 B6
Ponteland 4 D2
Pool of Muckhart 12 C4
Poolewe 14 D1
Pooley Bridge 3 H4
Port Appin (Port an
  Apainn) 11 F2
Port Askaig 6 B3
Port Bannatyne 7 E3
Port Ellen 6 B4
Port Erroll 17 G4
Port Glasgow 7 G3
Port William 2 C3
Port of Menteith 7 H1
Port of Ness
  (Port Nis) 20 F1
Portgordon 16 D2
Portknockie 16 D2
Portlethen 17 G6
Portlethen Village 17 G6
Portmahomack 16 B1
Portnacroish
  (Port na Croise) 11 F2
Portnaguran
  (Port nan Giúran) 20 F3
Portnahaven 6 A4
Portobello 23 C5
Portpatrick 2 A3
Portree
  (Port Rìgh) 14 B3
Portskerra 19 E2
Portsonachan 11 F3
Portsoy 17 E2
Potterton 17 G5
Powburn 9 G5
Prestonpans 8 D2
Prestonpans 23 C5
Prestwick 7 G5
Prudhoe 4 D2

Q

Quarff 21 H5
Quarter 22 D3
**Queensferry (South
  Queensferry) 23 A5**
Queenzieburn 22 C1

R

Rafford 16 B3
Rait 12 D3
Rapness 21 D1
Rathen 17 G2
Ratho 8 C2
Ratho 23 A5
Ratho Station 23 A5
Rathven 16 D2
Rawyards 22 D2
Reawick 21 H4
Reay 19 F2
Redcar 5 F4
Redford 13 F2
Reiss 19 H3
Renfrew 7 H3

Renfrew 22 B2
Renton 7 G3
Rhubodach 7 E3
Rhynd 12 D3
Rhynie 16 D4
Richmond 4 D5
Riggend 22 D2
Roadside of
  Kinneff 13 G1
Rora 17 G3
Rosehearty 17 G2
Rosemarkie 16 A3
Rosemount 12 D2
Rosewell 23 B6
Roslin 23 B6
Rosyth 8 C1
Rosyth 23 A4
Rothbury 9 G5
Rothes 16 C3
Rothesay 7 E3
Rothienorman 17 F4
Rowlands Gill 4 D3
Roybridge (Drochaid
  Ruaidh) 15 F6
Rutherend 22 C3
Rutherglen 7 H3
Rutherglen 22 C2
Ruthven 17 E3
Ryton 4 D2

S

Sacriston 4 D3
St. Andrews 13 F4
St. Bees 3 F5
St. Boswells 9 E4
St. Combs 17 G2
St. Cyrus 13 G1
St. Davids 23 A4
St. Fergus 17 H3
St. Fillans 12 A3
St. John's Town of Dalry
  2 D1
St. Margaret's Hope
  21 C4
St. Mary's 21 C3
St. Monans 13 F4
St. Vigeans 13 F2
Salen *Arg. & B.* 10 D2
Salen *High.* 10 D1
Saline 8 B1
Saltburn 16 A2
Saltburn-by-the-Sea 5 F4
Saltcoats 7 F4
Samuelston 23 D5
Sanaigmore 6 A3
Sandend 17 E2
Sandhaven 17 G2
Sandness 21 G4
Sandwick 21 H5
Sandwick (Sanndabhaig)
  Na H-E.Siar 20 E3
Sanquhar 8 A5
Sauchen 17 E5
Scalby 5 H6
Scalloway 21 H5
Scalpay 20 D5
Scarborough 5 H6
Scarinish 10 A2
Scone 12 D3
Sconser 14 C4
Scotby 3 H3
Scotch Corner 4 D5
Scotlandwell 12 D4
Scotstoun 22 B2
Scotton 4 D6
Scourie 18 B3
Scousburgh 21 H6
Scrabster 19 F2
Scremerston 9 G3
Seaham 5 E3
Seahouses 9 H4
Seamer 5 H6

Seascale 3 F5
Seaton 3 F4
Seaton Delaval 5 E2
Seaton Sluice 5 E2
Sedbergh 4 A6
Sedgefield 5 E4
Seghill 4 D2
Selkirk 8 D4
Sgiogarstaigh 20 F1
Shap 4 A5
Shawbost
  (Siabost) 20 D2
Sherburn 5 E3
Shettleston 22 C2
Shieldaig 14 D3
Shieldhill 8 A2
Shilbottle 9 H5
Shildon 4 D4
Shiney Row 5 E3
Shiremoor 5 E2
Shotton Colliery 5 E3
Shotts 8 A2
Silloth 3 G3
Silverburn 23 B6
Skelmorlie 7 F3
Skelton *Cumb.* 3 H4
Skelton *R. & C.* 5 F5
Slamannan 8 A2
Sleights 5 G5
Smailholm 9 E4
Smithton 16 A3
Sollas (Solas) 20 B6
South Dell
  (Dail Bho Dheas) 20 E1
South Gyle 23 A5
South Hetton 5 E3
South Queensferry 8 C2
**South Queensferry
  (Queensferry) 23 A5**
South Shields 5 E2
Southbar 22 A2
Southend 6 C6
Sowerby 5 E6
Spean Bridge (Drochaid an
  Aonachain) 15 F6
Spennymoor 4 D4
Spey Bay 16 D2
Spinningdale 15 H1
Spittal *E.Loth.* 23 D5
Spittalfield 12 D2
Springburn 22 C2
Springfield 13 E4
Springside 7 G5
Springwell 4 D3
Staffin 14 B2
Stainburn 3 F4
Staindrop 4 D4
Stamfordham 4 C2
Stand 22 D2
Stanhope 4 C4
Stanley *Dur.* 4 D3
Stanley *P. & K.* 12 D3
Stannington 4 D2
Startforth 4 C5
Station Town 5 E4
Staveley 3 H6
Staxigoe 19 H3
Stenhousemuir 8 A1
Stepps 7 H3
Stepps 22 C2
Stevenston 7 F4
Stewarton 7 G4
Stirling (Sruighlea) 8 A1
Stockton-on-Tees 5 E4
Stoer 18 A4
Stokesley 5 F5
Stonehaven 17 F6
Stonehouse 8 A3
Stoneyburn 8 B2
Stoneywood 17 F5
Stornoway
  (Steòrnabhagh) 20 E3

Strachan 17 E6
Strachur (Clachan Strachur)
    7 F1
Straiton 23 B6
Stranraer 2 A2
Strathaven 8 A3
Strathblane 7 H3
Strathblane 22 B1
Strathdon 16 D5
Strathpeffer (Strath
    Pheofhair) 15 G3
Strathtay 12 C2
Strathy 19 E2
Strathyre 7 H1
Strichen 17 G3
Stromness 21 B3
Strone 7 F2
Stronmilchan (Sròn nam
    Mialchon) 11 G3
Strontian (Sròn an
    t-Sithein) 11 E1
Stuartfield 17 G3
Sunderland 5 E3
Sunniside 4 D3
Swanston 23 B6
Symbister 21 J3
Symington 7 G5

T
Tain 16 A1
Talmine 18 D2
Tannadice 13 E2
Tannochside 22 C2
Tarbert (Jura)
    Arg. & B. 6 C2
Tarbert (Loch Fyne)
    Arg. & B. 6 D3
Tarbert *Na H-E.Siar*
    20 D4
Tarbet (An Tairbeart)
    7 G1

Tarbolton 7 G5
Tarfside 13 E1
Tarland 16 D5
Tarves 17 F4
Tayinloan 6 C4
Taynuilt (Taigh an Uillt)
    11 F3
Tayport 13 E3
Tayvallich 6 D2
Teangue 14 C5
Teviothead 8 D5
The Murray 22 C3
Thirsk 5 E6
Thornaby-on-Tees 5 E5
Thornhill *D. & G.* 3 E1
Thornhill *Stir.* 7 H1
Thornley 5 E4
Thornliebank 22 B3
Thornton 8 C1
Thorntonhall 22 B3
Thornton-le-Dale 5 G6
Thropton 9 G5
Thrumster 19 H3
Thursby 3 H3
Thurso (Inbhir Theòrsa)
    19 G2
Tillicoultry 8 B1
Tillyfourie 17 E5
Timsgearraidh 20 C3
Tobermory 10 D2
Tolastadh a' Chaolais
    20 D3
Tollcross 22 C2
Tomatin 16 A4
Tomintoul 16 C5
Tomnavoulin 16 C4
Tongue 18 D3
Torphins 17 E5
Torrance 7 H3
Torrance 22 C1
Torrance House 22 C3

Torridon 15 E3
Torver 3 G6
Totaig 14 A3
Tow Law 4 D4
Town Yetholm 9 F4
Townhill 23 A4
Tranent 8 D2
Tranent 23 D5
Tresta 21 H4
Trimdon 5 E4
Trinity 23 B5
Troon 7 G5
Tullibody 8 A1
Tullynessle 17 E5
Tunga 20 E3
Turriff 17 F3
Twatt 21 H4
Twechar 22 D1
Tyndrum (Taigh an
    Droma) 11 H3
Tynemouth 5 E2

U
Uddingston 7 H3
Uddingston 22 C2
Udny Green 17 F4
Udny Station 17 G4
Udston 22 D3
Uig (Uige) 14 B2
Ulbster 19 H3
Ulgham 4 D1
Ullapool (Ullapul) 15 F1
Uplawmoor 22 A3
Upper Bayble
    (Pabail Uarach) 20 F3
Upper Dallachy 16 D2
Upper Largo 13 E4
Urquhart 16 C2
Ushaw Moor 4 D3
Uyeasound 21 J1

V
Valleyfield 8 B1
Veensgarth 21 H4
Vidlin 21 H3
Viewpark 22 D2
Voe 21 H3

W
Walls 21 G4
Wallsend 5 E2
Wallyford 23 C5
Warkworth 9 H5
Washington 5 E3
Waterfoot 7 H4
Waterfoot 22 B3
Waterside 22 C1
Watten 19 G3
Wattston 22 D2
Weem 12 B2
Wemyss Bay 7 F3
West Auckland 4 D4
West Ayton 5 H6
West Calder 8 B2
West Carbeth 22 B1
West Kilbride 7 F4
West Linton 8 C3
West Rainton 5 E3
West Saltoun 23 D6
West Sandwick 21 H2
Wester Hailes 23 B6
Westfield 22 D1
Westhill *Aber.* 17 F5
Westhill *High.* 16 A3
Westmuir 13 E2
Westruther 9 E3
Westwood 22 C3
Whauphill 2 C3
Wheatley Hill 5 E4
Whickham 4 D2
Whifflet 22 D2

Whitburn *T. & W.* 5 E2
Whitburn *W.Loth.* 8 B2
Whitby 5 G5
Whitecraig 23 C5
Whitehall 21 D2
Whitehaven 3 F5
Whitehill 23 C6
Whitehills 17 E2
Whiterashes 17 F4
Whithorn 2 C3
Whiting Bay 7 E5
Whitley Bay 5 E2
Whittingham 9 G5
Wick (Inbhir Ùige)
    19 H3
Widdrington Station
    4 D1
Wide Open 4 D2
Wigton 3 G3
Wigtown 2 C3
Willington 4 D4
Wilkieston 23 A6
Winchburgh 8 B2
Windermere 3 H6
Windygates 13 E4
Windy-Yett 22 A3
Wingate 5 E4
Wishaw 8 A3
Wishaw 22 D3
Witton Gilbert 4 D3
Wolsingham 4 C4
Woodhead 17 F4
Wooler 9 G4
Workington 3 F4

Y
Yarm 5 E5
Yoker 22 B2
Ythanwells 17 E4

Symbol	Description
M8	Motorway
A82	Primary route dual / single carriageway
A70	'A' Road dual / single
B793	'B' Road dual / single
Toll	Other road dual / single carriageway / Toll
→	One way street
	Access restriction
	Pedestrian street
	Minor road / Track
	Railway line / station
	Light Rail / Station
	Railway tunnel / Level crossing
P	Bus (Coach) station / Car Park
rail operated P&R	Park & Ride (operates at least 5 days a week)
	Leisure & tourism
	Shopping
	Administration & law
	Education
	Health & welfare
	Industry & Commerce
	Other notable building
Pol Lib	Police station / Library
Hilton	Major Hotel
	Cinema / Theatre
	Tourist information centre (all year / seasonal)
	Toilet
+ ☾ ✡	Church / Mosque / Synagogue
■	Fire station / Ambulance station / Community centre

Abbreviations used in town plan indexes

All	Alley	Mans	Mansion
App	Approach	Mkt	Market
Arc	Arcade	Ms	Mews
Av	Avenue	Mt	Mount
Bk	Bank	N	North
Bldgs	Buildings	Par	Parade
Boul	Boulevard	Pk	Park
Bri	Bridge	Pl	Place
Cen	Central/Centre	Quad	Quadrant
Cft	Croft	Rd	Road
Ch	Church	Ri	Rise
Circ	Circus	S	South
Clo	Close	Sch	School
Coll	College	Sq	Square
Cor	Corner	St	Street
Cotts	Cottages	St.	Saint
Cres	Crescent	Sta	Station
Ct	Court	Ter	Terrace
Dr	Drive	Twr	Tower
E	East	Vills	Villas
Esp	Esplanade	Vw	View
Est	Estate	W	West
Ex	Exchange	Wd	Wood
Fm	Farm	Wds	Woods
Gdn	Garden	Wf	Wharf
Gdns	Gardens	Wk	Walk
Gra	Grange	Wks	Works
Grn	Green	Yd	Yard
Gro	Grove		
Hts	Heights		
Ho	House		
Hos	Hospital		
Ind	Industrial		
Junct	Junction		
La	Lane		
Ln	Loan		

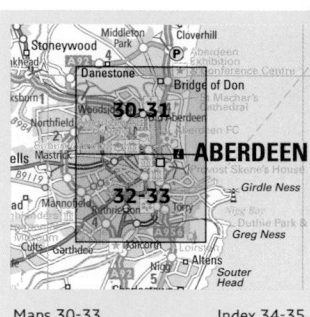

ABERDEEN

Maps 30-33   Index 34-35
Scale 4 inches to 1 mile

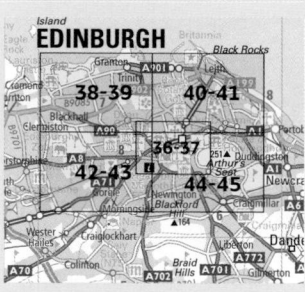

EDINBURGH

Maps 36-45   Index 46-51
Scale 4 inches to 1 mile
City centre map 5.7 inches to 1 mile

GLASGOW

Maps 52-59   Index 60-66
Scale 4 inches to 1 mile

Dundee map & index   67
Inverness map & index   68
Perth map & index   69

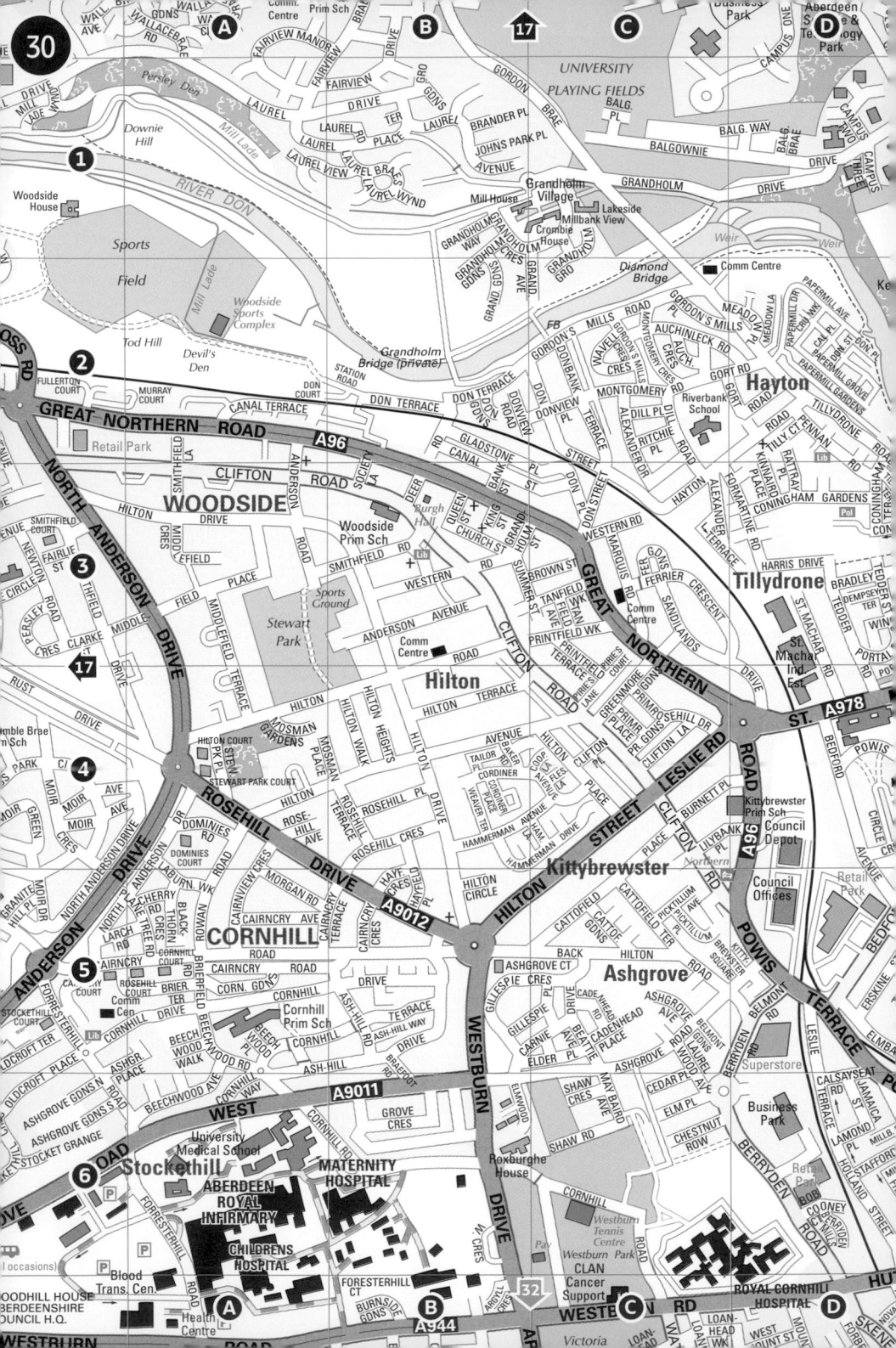

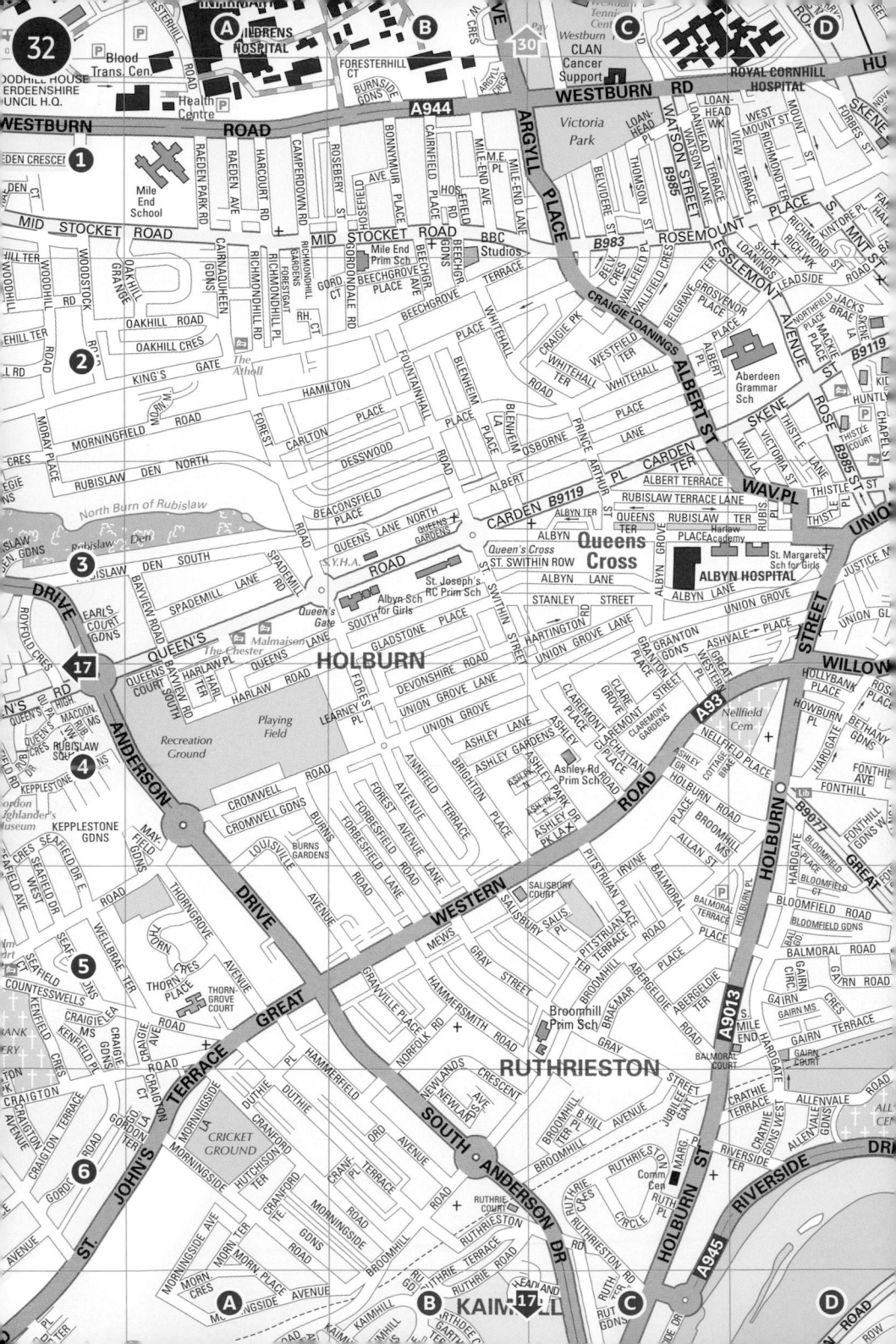

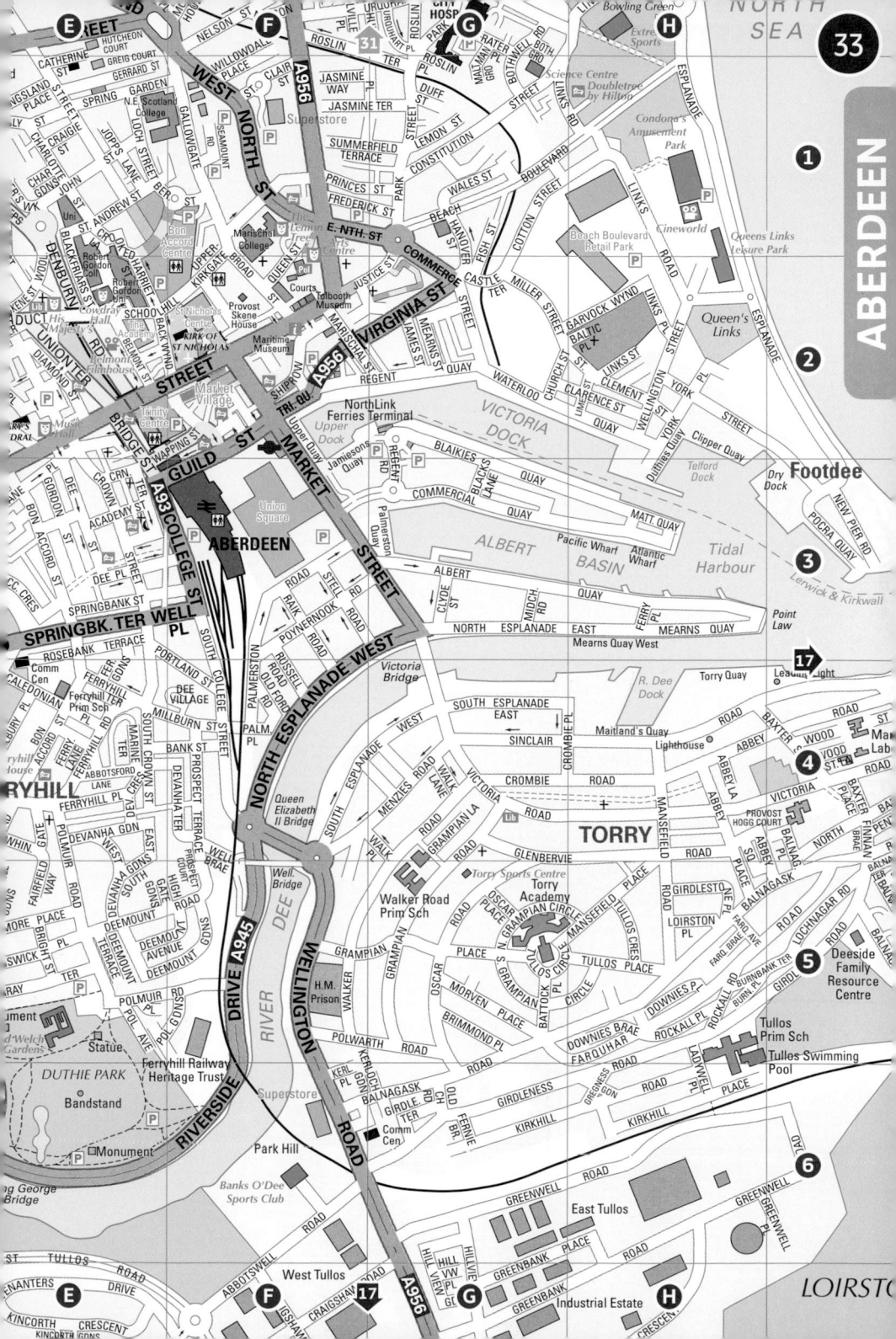

A
Abbey La 33 H4
Abbey Pl 33 H4
Abbey Rd 33 H4
Abbey Sq 33 H4
Abbotsford La 33 E4
Abergeldie Rd 32 C5
Abergeldie Ter 32 C5
Academy St 33 E3
Advocates Rd 31 F6
Albert La 32 B3
Albert Pl 32 C2
Albert Quay 33 G3
Albert St 32 C2
Albert Ter 32 C3
Albury Gdns 32 D4
Albury Pl 33 E4
Albury Rd 32 D4
Albyn Gro 32 C3
Albyn La 32 C3
Albyn Pl 32 C3
Albyn Ter 32 C3
Alexander Dr 30 C2
Alexander Ter 30 C3
Allan St 32 C3
Allenvale Gdns 32 D6
Allenvale Rd 32 D6
Anderson Av 30 B3
Anderson Rd 30 A2
Annfield Ter 32 B4
Ann St 32 D1
Ardarroch Pl 31 G5
Ardarroch Rd 31 F5
Argyll Cres 32 B1
Argyll Pl 32 B1
Ashgrove Av 30 C5
Ashgrove Ct 30 B5
Ashgrove Rd 30 C5
Ash-hill Dr 30 A5
Ash-hill Pl 30 B5
Ash-hill Way 30 B5
Ashley Gdns 32 B4
Ashley Gro 32 C4
Ashley La 32 B4
Ashley Pk Dr 32 B4
Ashley Pk La 32 C4
Ashley Pk N 32 B4
Ashley Pk S 32 C4
Ashley Rd 32 C4
Ashvale Pl 32 C4
Auchinleck Cres 30 C2
Auchinleck Rd 30 C2
Aulton Ct 31 G3

B
Back Hilton Rd 30 C5
Back Wynd 33 E2
Baker St 32 D1
Balgownie Brae 30 D1
Balgownie Ct 31 F3
Balgownie Cres 31 F1
Balgownie Dr 30 C1
Balgownie Gdns 30 C1
Balgownie Pl 30 C1
Balgownie Rd 31 F1
Balgownie Way 30 C1
Balmoral Ct 32 C5
Balmoral Pl 32 C5
Balmoral Rd 32 D5
Balmoral Ter 32 C5
Balnagask Rd 33 H5
Baltic Pl 33 H2
Baltic St 33 G2
Bank St 33 E4
Bank St (Woodside) 30 B3
Battock Pl 33 G5
Baxter St 33 H4
Bayview Ct 31 G4
Bayview Rd 32 A3
Bayview Rd S 32 A4
Beach Boul 33 G1
Beachview Ct 31 G3
Beaconsfield Pl 32 A3
Beattie Av 30 C5
Bedford Av 30 D4
Bedford Pl 30 D5
Bedford Rd 30 D5
Beechgrove Av 32 B2
Beechgrove Gdns 32 B2
Beechgrove Pl 32 B2
Beechgrove Ter 32 B2

Beechwood Av 30 A6
Beechwood Pl 30 A5
Beechwood Rd 30 A5
Beechwood Wk 30 A5
Belgrave Ter 32 C2
Belmont Gdns 30 D5
Belmont Rd 30 D5
Belmont St 33 E2
Belvidere Cres 32 C1
Belvidere St 32 C1
Berryden Rd 30 D6
Berry St 33 F1
Bethany Gdns 32 C4
Blackfriars St 33 E1
Blacks La 33 G3
Blackthorn Cres 30 A5
Blaikies Quay 33 G2
Blenheim La 33 E3
Blenheim Pl 32 B2
Bloomfield Ct 32 D5
Bloomfield Pl 32 D5
Bloomfield Rd 32 D5
Bob Cooney Ct 30 D6
Boddie Pl 31 F6
Bon Accord Cres 33 E3
Bon Accord St 33 E3
Bonnymuir Pl 32 B1
Bradley Ter 30 D3
Braefoot Rd 30 B5
Braemar Pl 32 C5
Brander Pl 30 B5
Bridge of Don 31 G2
Bridge St 33 E2
Brierfield Rd 30 A5
Brighton Pl 32 B4
Bright St 33 E5
Brig o' Balgownie 31 F1
Brimmond Pl 33 G5
Broomhill Av 32 C6
Broomhill Pl 32 C6
Broomhill Rd 32 C5
Broomhill Ter 32 C6
Brown St 30 C3
Brunswick St 33 E5
Burnbank Pl 33 H5
Burnbank Ter 33 H5
Burnett Pl 30 C4
Burns Gdns 32 A4
Burnside Gdns 32 B1
Burns Rd 32 A4

C
Cadenhead Pl 30 C5
Cadenhead Rd 30 C5
Cairnaquheen Gdns 32 A1
Cairncry Av 30 A5
Cairncry Cres 30 A5
Cairncry Rd 30 A5
Cairncry Ter 30 A5
Cairnfield Pl 32 B1
Cairnfold Rd 30 E1
Cairnview Cres 30 A5
Caledonian La 33 E4
Calender Pl 30 D2
Calsayseat Rd 30 D6
Camperdown Rd 30 C5
Campus One 30 D1
Campus Three 30 D1
Campus Two 30 D1
Canal Pl 31 E6
Canal Rd 31 E6
Canal St 31 E6
Canal St (Woodside) 30 B2
Canal Ter 31 E6
Carden Pl 32 B3
Carden Ter 32 B3
Carlton Pl 32 A2
Carnie Dr 30 B5
Castle Ter 33 G2
Catherine St 33 E1
Cattofield Gdns 30 C5
Cattofield Pl 30 C5
Cattofield Ter 30 C5
Causewayend 31 E6
Cedar Pl 30 C6
Chanonry 31 E3
Chapel St 32 C2
Charles St 31 E6
Charlotte Gdns 33 E1
Charlotte St 33 E1
Chattan Pl 32 C4

Cherry Rd 30 A5
Chestnut Row 30 C6
Cheyne Rd 31 F1
Church St 33 G2
Church St (Woodside) 30 B3
Claremont Gdns 32 C4
Claremont Gro 32 C4
Claremont Pl 32 C4
Claremont St 32 C4
Clarence St 33 G2
Clarks La 31 F1
Clifton La 30 C4
Clifton Pl 30 C4
Clifton Rd 30 A3
Clyde St 33 G3
College Bounds 31 E4
College St 33 E3
Colville Pl 31 F6
Commerce St 33 F1
Commercial Quay 33 G3
Coningham Gdns 30 D3
Coningham Rd 30 D3
Coningham Ter 30 D3
Constitution St 33 G1
Cornhill Ct 30 A5
Cornhill Dr 30 A5
Cornhill Gdns 30 A5
Cornhill Rd 30 A6
Cornhill Ter 30 A5
Cornhill Way 30 A6
Corsehill Gdns 30 A5
Corunna Rd 31 G1
Cottage Brae 32 C4
Cotton St 33 G1
Cottown of Balgownie 31 F1
Coull Gdns 31 E1
Craigiela Av 32 A5
Craigie Loanings 32 C2
Craigie Pk 32 C2
Craigie St 32 E1
Craigton Ct 32 A6
Cranford Pl 32 B6
Cranford Rd 32 A6
Cranford St 32 A6
Crathie Gdns W 32 D6
Crathie Ter 32 C6
Crimon Pl 33 E2
Crombie Pl 33 G4
Crombie Rd 33 G4
Cromwell Gdns 32 A4
Cromwell Rd 32 A4
Crooked La 33 E1
Crosier Ctyd 30 D2
Crosier Wk 30 D2
Crown St 33 E3
Crown Ter 33 E3

D
Danestone Pl 31 F1
Danestone Ter 31 F1
Davan Pk 31 F1
Deemount Av 33 E5
Deemount Gdns 33 E5
Deemount Rd 33 E5
Deemount Ter 33 E5
Dee Pl 33 E3
Deer Rd 30 B3
Dee St 33 E3
Dempsey Ter 30 D3
Denburn Rd 33 E2
Denmore Gdns 31 E1
Desswood Pl 32 B2
Devanha Cres 33 E4
Devanha Gdns 33 E5
Devanha Gdns E 33 E5
Devanha Gdns S 33 E5
Devanha Gdns W 33 E5
Devanha Ter 33 E5
Devonshire Rd 32 B4
Diamond St 33 E2
Dill Pl 30 C2
Dill Rd 30 C2
Dominies Ct 30 A4
Dominies Rd 30 A4
Donbank Ter 30 A2
Don Ct 30 A2
Don Gdns 30 B2
Donmouth Ct 31 G1
Donmouth Cres 31 G1
Donmouth Gdns 31 G1
Donmouth Rd 31 G1

Donmouth Ter 31 G1
Don Pl 30 C3
Don St (Old Aberdeen) 31 E3
Don St (Woodside) 30 C3
Don Ter 30 B2
Donside Pl 30 D2
Donview Ho 31 G3
Donview Pl 30 C2
Donview Rd 30 B2
Downies Brae 33 G5
Downies Pl 33 H5
Duff St 33 G1
Dunbar St 31 E4
Duthie Pl 32 A6
Duthie Ter 32 A6

E
East N St 33 F1
East Tullos Ind Est 33 H6
Elder Pl 30 B5
Elmbank Rd 31 E6
Elmbank Ter 30 D5
Elmfield Av 30 D5
Elmfield Pl 30 D5
Elmfield Ter 30 D5
Elm Pl 30 C6
Elphinstone Rd 31 E4
Errol Pl 31 F6
Errol St 31 F6
Erskine St 30 D5
Esplanade 33 H2
Esslemont Av 32 C1
Exchange St 33 F2

F
Fairview Brae 30 A1
Fairview Dr 30 B1
Farmers Hall La 32 D1
Farquhar Av 33 H5
Farquhar Brae 33 H5
Farquhar Rd 33 H5
Fenerty Pl 30 D2
Fernie Brae 33 G6
Ferrier Cres 30 C3
Ferrier Gdns 30 C3
Ferryhill La 33 E4
Ferryhill Pl 33 E4
Ferryhill Rd 33 E4
Ferryhill Ter 33 E4
Ferry Pl 33 H3
Firhill Rd 31 E5
Fish St 33 G2
Fonthill Gdns E 32 D5
Fonthill Gdns W 32 D4
Fonthill Rd 32 D4
Fonthill Ter 32 D4
Forbesfield La 32 B4
Forbesfield Rd 32 B4
Forbes St 32 D1
Forest Av 32 B4
Forest Av La 32 B4
Foresterhill Ct 32 B1
Forestgait 32 A2
Forest Rd 32 A2
Formartine Rd 30 C3
Forresterhill Rd 30 A6
Fountainhall Rd 32 B2
Fowlershill Gdns 31 E1
Fraser Ct 31 E6
Fraserfield Gdns 31 F1
Fraser Pl 30 D6
Fraser Rd 30 D6
Fraser St 30 D6
Frederick St 33 F1
Froghall Av 31 E6
Froghall Gdns 31 E6
Froghall Pl 31 E6
Froghall Rd 31 E6
Froghall Ter 31 E6
Froghall Vw 31 E5

G
Gairn Circle 32 D5
Gairn Ct 32 D5
Gairn Cres 32 D5
Gairn Ms 32 D5
Gairn Rd 32 D5
Gairn Ter 32 D5
Gallowgate 33 F1
Garvock Wynd 33 H2
George St 31 E6

Gerrard St 33 E1
Gilcomston Steps 32 D1
Gillespie Cres 30 B5
Gillespie Pl 30 B5
Girdleness Rd 33 H5
Girdleness Ter 33 G6
Girdlestone Pl 32 B3
Gladstone Pl 32 B3
Gladstone Pl (Woodside) 30 B2
Glenbervie Rd 33 G4
Golf Rd 31 G5
Gordondale Ct 32 A2
Gordondale Rd 32 B1
Gordon La 32 A6
Gordon's Mills Cres 30 C2
Gordon's Mills Pl 30 C2
Gordon's Mills Rd 30 C2
Gordon St 33 E3
Gort Rd 30 C2
Grampian La 33 G4
Grampian Pl 33 G5
Grampian Rd 33 G4
Grandholm Br (Private) 30 B2
Grandholm St 30 B3
Granton Pl 32 C3
Granville Pl 32 B5
Gray St 32 B5
Gray St Ms 32 B5
Great Northern Rd 30 C3
Great Southern Rd 33 D5
Great Western Pl 32 C4
Great Western Rd 32 A4
Greenmore Gdns 30 C4
Greenwell Pl 33 H6
Greenwell Rd 33 H6
Gregness Gdns 33 H6
Greig Ct 33 E1
Grosvenor Pl 32 B5
Grove Cres 30 B6
Guild St 33 F3

H
Hamilton Pl 32 A2
Hammerfield Av 32 A5
Hammersmith Rd 32 B5
Hanover St 33 G1
Harcourt Rd 32 A1
Hardgate 32 D4
Harlaw Pl 32 A4
Harlaw Rd 32 A4
Harlaw Ter 32 A4
Harriet St 33 E2
Harris Dr 30 D3
Harrow Rd 31 F3
Hartington Rd 32 B3
Hayfield Cres 30 B5
Hayfield Pl 30 B4
Hayton Rd 30 C3
Hermitage Av 31 E4
Highgate Gdns 33 F5
High St 31 E4
Hill St 32 D1
Hill Vw Gdns 33 G6
Hillview Rd 33 G6
Hilton Av 30 A4
Hilton Circle 30 B5
Hilton Ct 30 B4
Hilton Dr 30 B4
Hilton Pl 30 A4
Hilton Rd 30 A4
Hilton St 30 B4
Hilton Ter 30 B4
Hilton Wk 30 A4
Holburn Pl 32 D5
Holburn Rd 32 C4
Holburn St 30 D6
Holland Pl 30 D6
Holland St 30 D6
Hollybank Pl 32 D4
Hosefield Av 32 B1
Hosefield Rd 32 B1
Howburn Pl 32 D4
Hunter Pl 31 F6
Huntly St 32 D2
Hutcheon Ct 31 E6
Hutcheon Gdns 31 F1
Hutcheon St 32 D1
Hutchison Ter 32 A6

ABERDEEN

nverdon Ct	31	F2
rvine Pl	32	C5

J

acks Brae	32	D2
amaica St	30	D6
ames St	33	G2
amiesons Quay	33	F3
asmine Pl	33	F1
asmine Ter	33	F1
asmine Way	33	F1
ohns Pk Pl	30	B1
ohn St	33	E1
opps La	33	E1
ubilee Gait	32	C6
ustice Mill La	32	D3
ute St	31	E6

K

Kerloch Gdns	33	F5
Kerloch Pl	33	F6
Kettocks Mill Rd	31	E2
Kidd St	32	D2
King George VI Br	33	E6
Kings Cres	31	F6
King's Gate	32	A2
Kingsland Pl	33	E1
King St	31	F5
King St (Woodside)	30	B3
Kinnaird Pl	30	D2
Kinord Circle	31	E1
Kintore Pl	32	D1
Kirkhill Pl	33	H6
Kirkhill Rd	33	G6
Kittybrewster Sq	30	C5

L

Laburnum Wk	30	A5
Ladywell Pl	33	H5
Lamond Pl	30	D6
Langstane Pl	33	E3
Laurel Av	30	B1
Laurel Braes	30	B1
Laurel Dr	30	A1
Laurel Gdns	30	B1
Laurel Gro	30	B1
Laurel Pl	30	A1
Laurel Rd	30	A1
Laurel Ter	30	B1
Laurel Vw	30	A1
Laurelwood Av	30	C5
Laurel Wynd	30	B1
Leadside Rd	32	D2
Learney Pl	32	A4
Lemon St	33	G1
Leslie Rd	30	C4
Leslie Ter	30	D5
Lilybank Pl	30	C4
Lime St	33	H2
Linksfield Ct	31	G4
Linksfield Gdns	31	F5
Linksfield Pl	31	F5
Linksfield Rd	31	F5
Links Pl	33	H2
Links Rd	33	H1
Links Rd (Bridge of Don)	31	G1
Links St	33	H2
Links Vw	31	G5
Livingstone Ct	31	F3
Loanhead Pl	32	C1
Loanhead Ter	32	C1
Loanhead Wk	32	C1
Loch St	33	E1
Loirston Pl	33	H5
Lord Hay's Ct	31	G2
Lord Hay's Gro	31	F2
Lord Hay's Rd	31	F2
Louisville Av	32	A4

M

Maberly St	33	E1
Mackie Pl	32	D2
Mansefield Pl	33	H5
Mansefield Rd	33	H4
Margaret Pl	32	C6
Marine Ter	33	E4
Marischal St	33	F2
Market St	33	F2

Marquis Rd	30	C3
Matthews Quay	33	H3
May Braid Av	30	C6
Mayfield Gdns	32	A4
Meadow La	30	D2
Meadow Pl	30	C2
Mearns Quay	33	H3
Mearns St	33	G2
Menzies Rd	33	G4
Merkland La	31	G5
Merkland Pl	31	F5
Merkland Rd	31	F5
Merkland Rd E	31	F5
Meston Wk	31	E4
Midchingle Rd	33	G3
Middlefield Cres	30	A3
Middlefield Ter	30	A3
Mile-End Av	32	B1
Mile-End La	32	B1
Mile-End Pl	32	B1
Millbank La	30	D6
Millbank Pl	30	D6
Millburn St	33	E4
Mill Ct	30	A2
Miller St	33	G2
Montgomery Cres	30	C2
Montgomery Rd	30	C2
Morgan Rd	30	A5
Morningfield Ms	32	A2
Morningside Gdns	32	A6
Morningside La	32	A6
Morningside Pl	32	A6
Morningside Rd	32	A6
Morningside Ter	32	A6
Morven Pl	33	G5
Mosman Gdns	30	A4
Mosman Pl	30	A4
Mounthooly	31	F6
Mounthooly Way	31	F6
Mount Pleasant	31	G1
Mount St	32	D1
Murray Ct	30	A2
Murray Ter	33	E5

N

Nellfield Pl	32	C4
Nelson Ct	31	F6
Nelson La	31	F6
Nelson St	31	F6
Newlands Av	32	B6
Newlands Cres	32	B6
Norfolk Rd	32	B5
North Esplanade E	33	G3
North Esplanade W	33	F4
Northfield Pl	32	D2
North Grampian Circle	33	G5
Northsea Ct	31	G3
Novar Pl	32	D1

O

Oakhill Cres	32	A2
Oakhill Grange	32	A2
Oakhill Rd	32	A2
Old Ch Rd	33	G6
Old Ford Rd	33	F4
Orchard Pl	31	E5
Orchard Rd	31	F5
Orchard St	31	E5
Orchard Wk	31	E5
Osborne Pl	32	B2
Oscar Pl	33	G5
Oscar Rd	33	G5

P

Palmerston Pl	33	F4
Palmerston Rd	33	F4
Papermill Gdns	30	D2
Park Rd	31	G6
Park St	33	G1
Pennan Rd	30	D2
Picktillum Av	30	C5
Picktillum Pl	30	C5
Pirie's Ct	30	C4
Pirie's La	30	C4
Pittstruan Pl	32	C4
Pittstruan Ter	32	C5
Pittodrie La	31	F5

Pittodrie Pl	31	F5
Pittodrie St	31	F5
Polmuir Av	33	E5
Polmuir Gdns	32	F5
Polmuir Pl	33	E5
Polmuir Rd	33	E4
Polwarth Rd	33	F5
Portal Cres	30	D3
Portal Ter	30	D4
Portland St	33	E3
Powis Circle	30	D4
Powis Cres	30	D4
Powis La	31	E6
Powis Pl	30	D6
Powis Ter	30	D5
Poynernook Rd	33	F3
Primrosehill Dr	30	C4
Primrosehill Gdns	30	C4
Primrosehill Pl	30	C4
Prince Arthur St	32	C5
Princes St	33	F1
Printfield Ter	30	C3
Printfield Wk	30	C3
Promenade Ct	31	G4
Prospect Ct	33	F4
Prospect Ter	33	F4

Q

Queen Elizabeth II Br	33	F4
Queens Ct	32	B3
Queen's Cross	32	B3
Queens Gdns	32	B3
Queen's Gate	32	A3
Queens La N	32	B3
Queens La S	32	A3
Queens Links Leisure Pk	33	H1
Queens Ter	32	C3
Queen St	33	F2
Queen St (Woodside)	30	B3

R

Raeburn Pl	33	E1
Raeden Av	32	A1
Raeden Pk Rd	32	A1
Raik Rd	33	F3
Rattray Pl	30	D2
Regent Ct	31	G4
Regent Quay	33	G2
Regent Rd	33	G3
Regent Wk	31	F4
Richmondhill Ct	32	A2
Richmondhill Gdns	32	A1
Richmondhill Pl	32	A1
Richmondhill Rd	32	A1
Richmond St	32	D1
Richmond Ter	32	D1
Richmond Wk	32	D1
Ritchie Pl	30	C2
Riverside Dr	32	D6
Riverside Ter	32	C6
Rockall Pl	33	H5
Rockall Rd	33	H5
Rodger's Wk	33	E1
Rosebank Pl	32	D4
Rosebank Ter	33	E4
Rosebery St	32	B1
Rosehill Av	30	A4
Rosehill Ct	30	A5
Rosehill Cres	30	B4
Rosehill Dr	30	A4
Rosehill Pl	30	B4
Rosehill Ter	30	B4
Rosemount Pl	32	C1
Rosemount Viaduct	32	D2
Rose St	32	D2
Roslin Pl	33	G1
Roslin St	31	G6
Roslin Ter	31	F6
Rowan Rd	30	A5
Rubislaw Pl	32	D3
Rubislaw Ter	32	C3
Rubislaw Ter La	32	C3
Russell Rd	33	F4
Ruthrie Ct	32	B6
Ruthrieston Circle	32	C6
Ruthrieston Cres	32	C6
Ruthrieston Pl	32	C6

Ruthrieston Rd	32	B6

S

St. Andrew St	33	E1
St. Clair St	33	F1
St. Clement St	33	G2
St. Machar Dr	30	D4
St. Machar Ind Est	30	D3
St. Machar Pl	31	F3
St. Machar Rd	30	D4
St. Nicholas Cen	33	F2
St. Ninians Ct	31	F3
St. Ninians Pl	31	F2
St. Peter La	31	F6
St. Peter's Gate	31	F5
St. Peter's Pl	31	F5
St. Peter St	31	F6
St. Swithin Row	32	B3
St. Swithin St	32	B3
Salisbury Ct	32	C5
Salisbury Pl	32	C5
Salisbury Ter	32	B5
Sandilands Dr	30	C3
School Av	31	F4
School Dr	31	F4
Schoolhill	33	E2
School Rd	31	F4
School Ter	31	F4
School Wk	31	G4
Scotstown Gdns	31	F3
Seaforth Rd	31	F6
Seamount Rd	33	F1
Seaton Av	31	G3
Seaton Cres	31	G3
Seaton Dr	31	G3
Seaton Gdns	31	G3
Seaton Ho	31	G3
Seaton Pl	31	F3
Seaton Pl E	31	G3
Seaton Rd	31	F4
Seaton Wk	31	F3
Seaview Ho	31	G4
Seaview Rd	31	F1
Shiprow	33	F2
Short Loanings	32	D1
Simpson Rd	31	F1
Sinclair Pl	33	H4
Sinclair Rd	33	G4
Skene La	32	D2
Skene Sq	32	D1
Skene St	32	D2
Skene Ter	33	E2
Smithfield La	30	A3
Smithfield Rd	30	A3
Society La	30	B3
South Anderson Dr	32	B6
South Coll St	33	F3
South Crown St	33	E4
South Esplanade E	33	G4
South Esplanade W	33	F4
South Grampian Circle	33	G5
South Mile End	32	D5
South Mt St	32	D1
Spademill La	32	A3
Spademill Rd	32	A3
Spa St	33	E1
Spital	31	E5
Spital Wk	31	E5
Springbank St	33	E3
Springbank Ter	33	E3
Spring Gdn	33	E1
Stafford St	30	D6
Stanley St	32	C3
Station Rd	30	B2
Stell Rd	33	F3
Stewart Pk Ct	30	A4
Stewart Pk Pl	30	A4
Summerfield Ter	33	F1
Summer St	32	D2
Summer St (Woodside)	30	B3
Sunnybank Pl	31	E5
Sunnybank Rd	31	E5
Sunnyside Av	31	E5
Sunnyside Gdns	31	E5
Sunnyside Rd	30	D5
Sunnyside Ter	31	E5
Sycamore Pl	33	E5

T

Tanfield Av	30	C3
Tanfield Wk	30	C3
Tarbothill Rd	30	D1
Tedder Rd	30	D3
Tedder St	30	D3
Thistle Ct	32	D2
Thistle La	32	D2
Thistle Pl	32	D3
Thistle St	32	D2
Thomas Glover Pl	31	E1
Thomson St	32	C1
Thorngrove Av	32	A5
Thorngrove Ct	32	A5
Thorngrove Cres	32	A5
Thorngrove Pl	32	A5
Tillydrone Av	31	E3
Tillydrone Ct	30	D2
Tillydrone Rd	31	E3
Tillydrone Ter	30	D3
Trinity Quay	33	F2
Tullos Circle	33	G5
Tullos Cres	33	H5
Tullos Pl	33	H5

U

Union Glen	32	D3
Union Gro	32	C3
Union Gro La	32	C4
Union Row	32	D3
Union St	32	D3
Union Ter	33	E2
Union Wynd	32	D2
University Rd	31	E4
Upperkirkgate	33	F2
Urquhart La	31	F6
Urquhart Pl	31	G6
Urquhart Rd	31	F6
Urquhart St	31	G6
Urquhart Ter	31	G6

V

Victoria Br	33	G3
Victoria Rd	33	G4
Victoria St	32	D2
View Ter	32	D1
Virginia St	33	F2

W

Wales St	33	G1
Walker La	33	G4
Walker Pl	33	G4
Walker Rd	33	F5
Wallfield Cres	32	C2
Wallfield Pl	32	C2
Wapping St	33	E2
Waterloo Quay	33	G2
Watson La	32	C1
Watson St	32	C1
Wavell Cres	30	C2
Waverley La	32	D2
Waverley Pl	32	D3
Wellington Brae	33	F4
Wellington Br	33	F5
Wellington Pl	33	E3
Wellington Rd	33	F5
Wellington St	33	H2
Westburn Cres	30	B6
Westburn Dr	30	B5
Westburn Pk	30	C6
Westburn Rd	32	C1
Western Rd	30	C3
Westfield Rd	32	C2
Westfield Ter	32	C2
West Mt St	32	D1
West N St	33	F1
Whinhill Gdns	32	C2
Whinhill Gate	33	E4
Whinhill Rd	32	D5
Whitehall Pl	32	C2
Whitehall Rd	32	B2
Whitehall Ter	32	C2
Willowbank Rd	32	D4
Willowdale Pl	33	F1
Wingate Pl	30	D3
Wingate Rd	30	D3
Woolmanhill	33	E2

Y

York Pl	33	H2
York St	33	H2

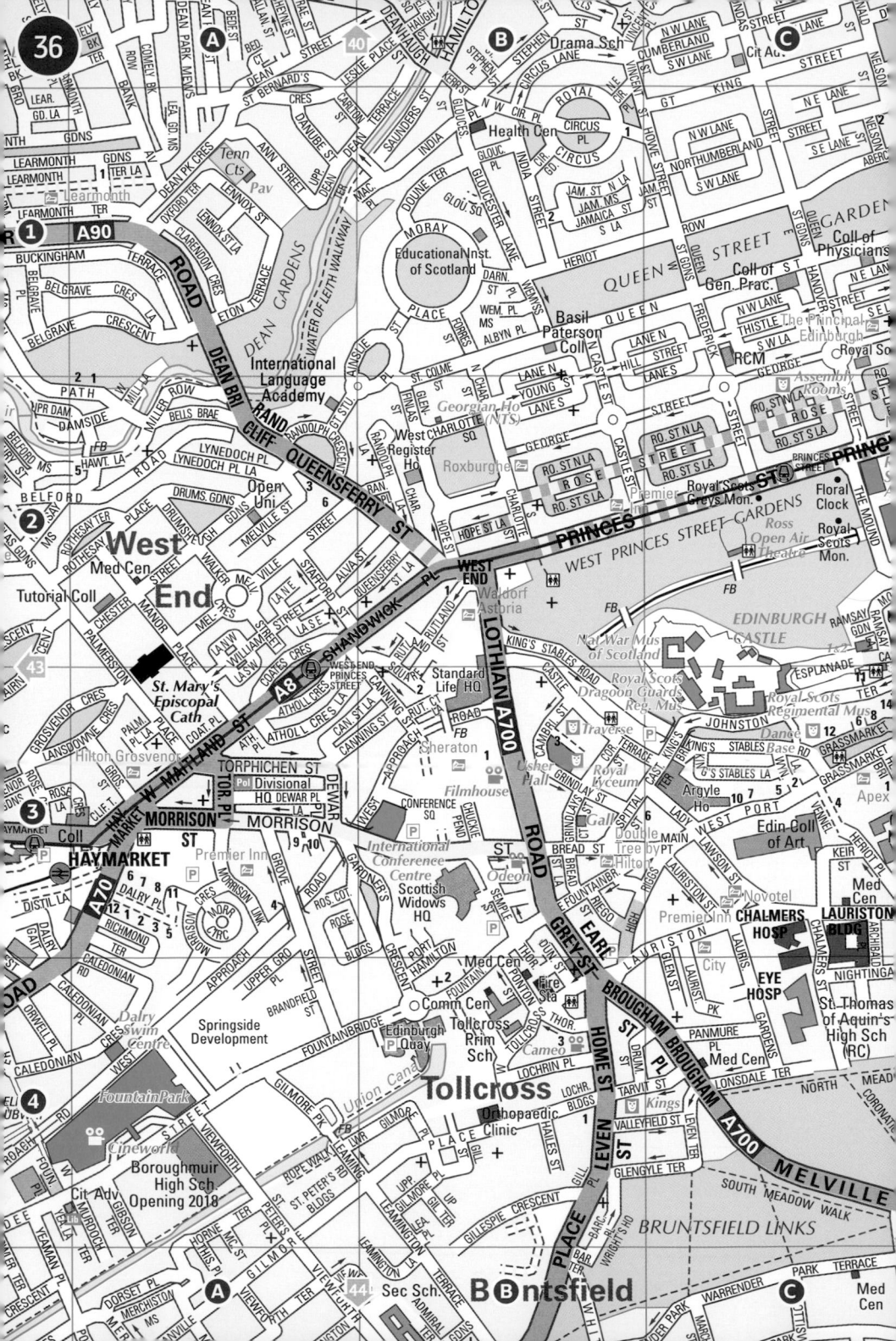

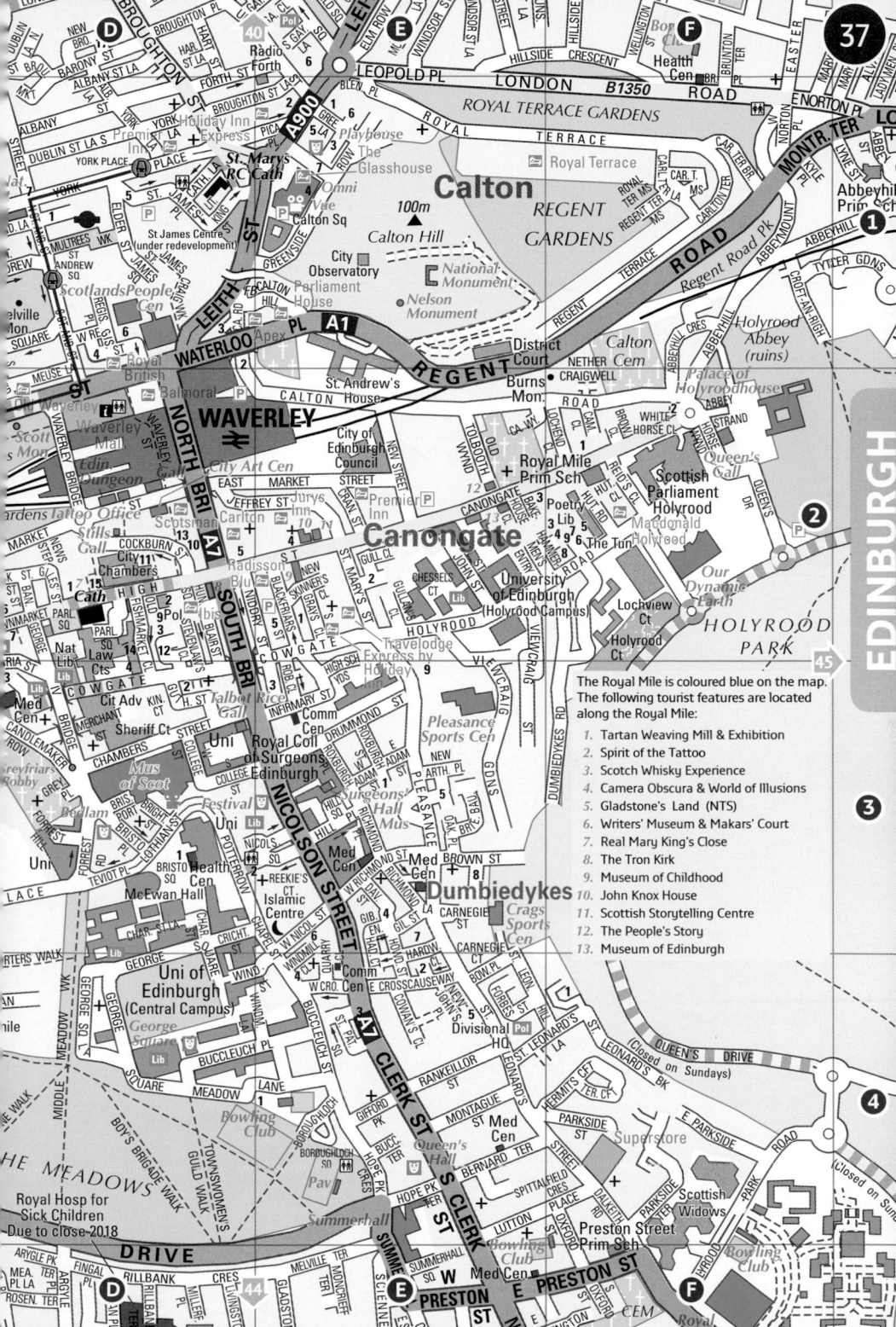

EDINBURGH

The Royal Mile is coloured blue on the map.
The following tourist features are located
along the Royal Mile:

1. Tartan Weaving Mill & Exhibition
2. Spirit of the Tattoo
3. Scotch Whisky Experience
4. Camera Obscura & World of Illusions
5. Gladstone's Land (NTS)
6. Writers' Museum & Makars' Court
7. Real Mary King's Close
8. The Tron Kirk
9. Museum of Childhood
10. John Knox House
11. Scottish Storytelling Centre
12. The People's Story
13. Museum of Edinburgh

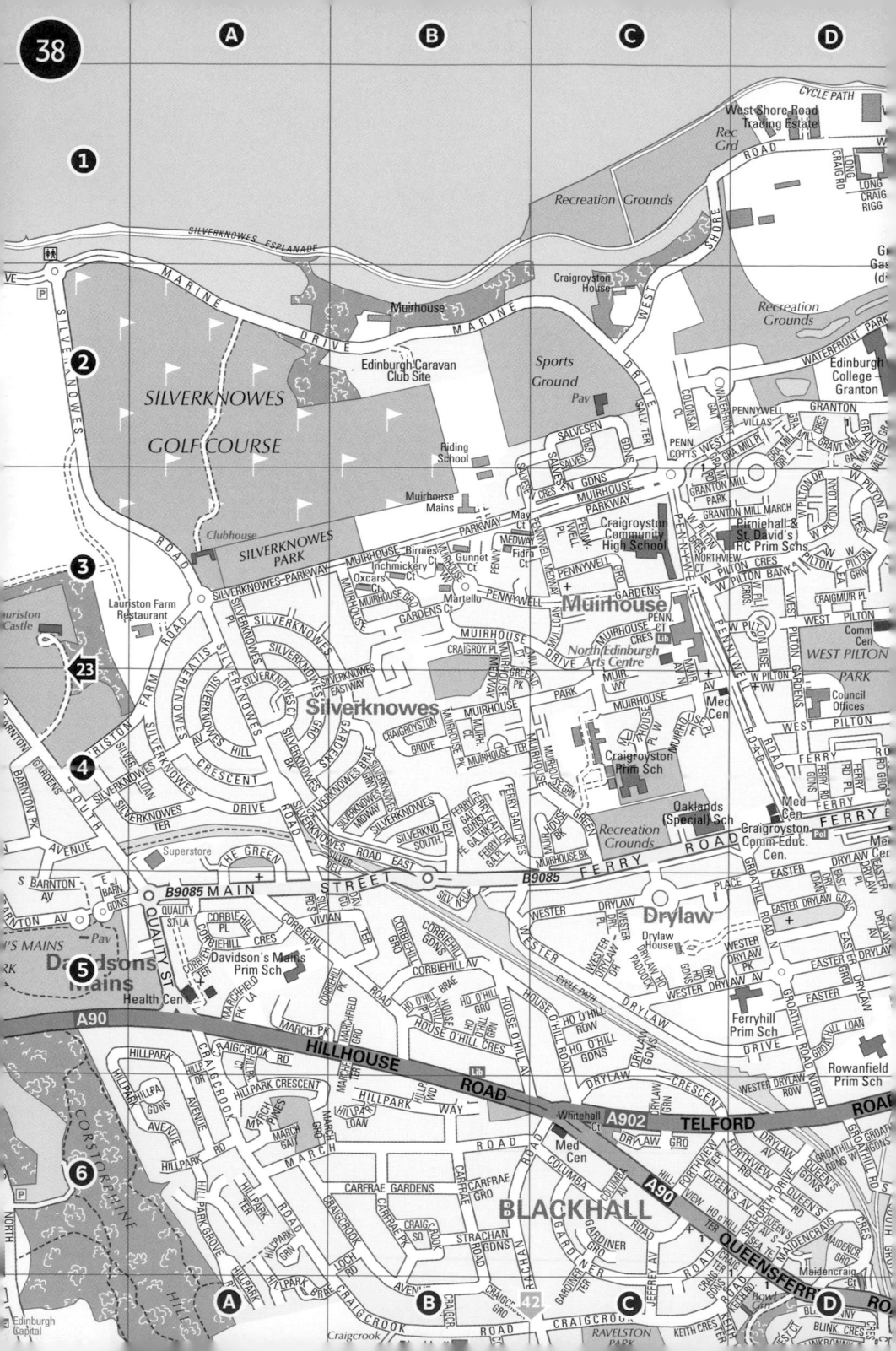

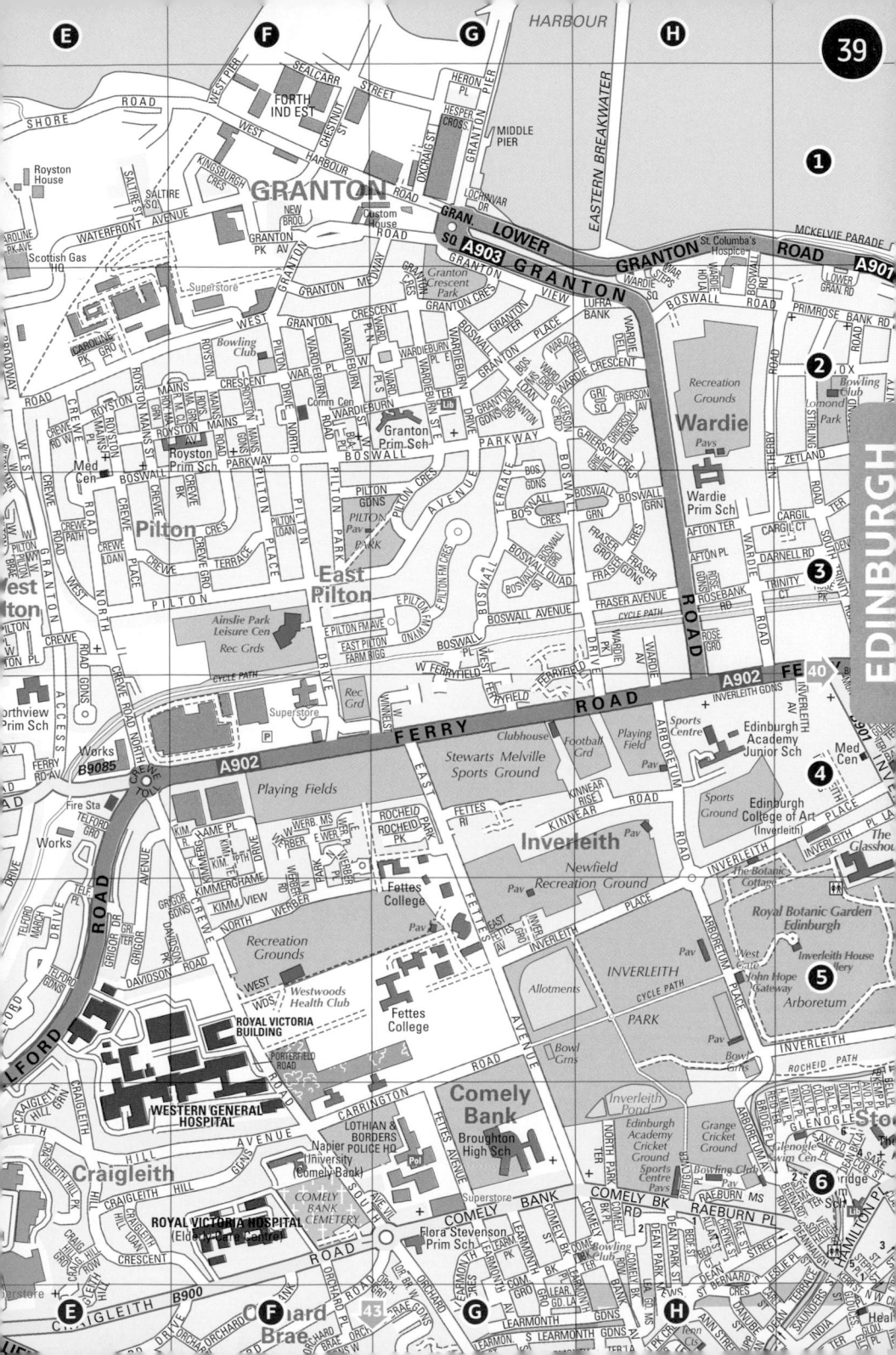

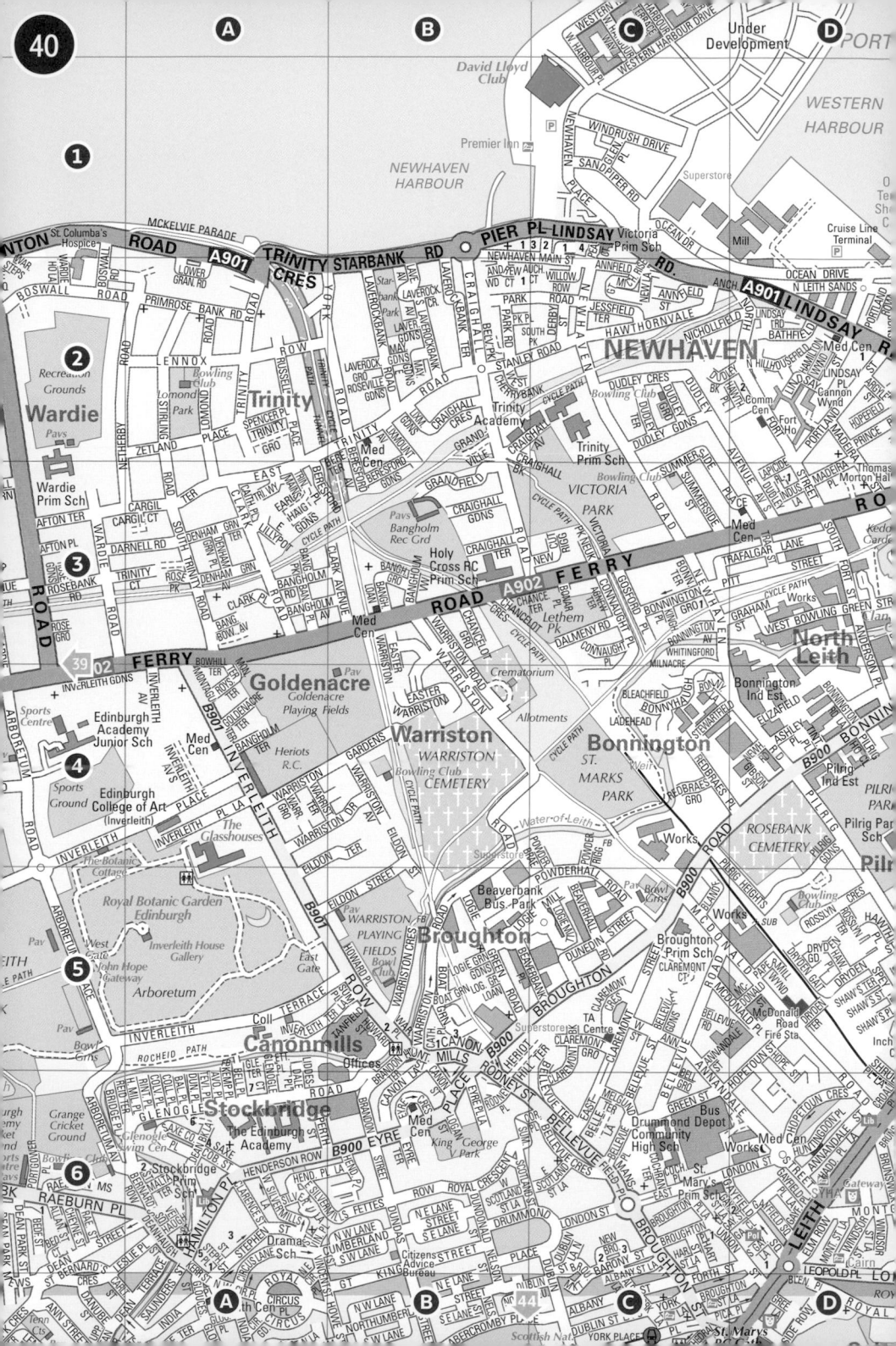

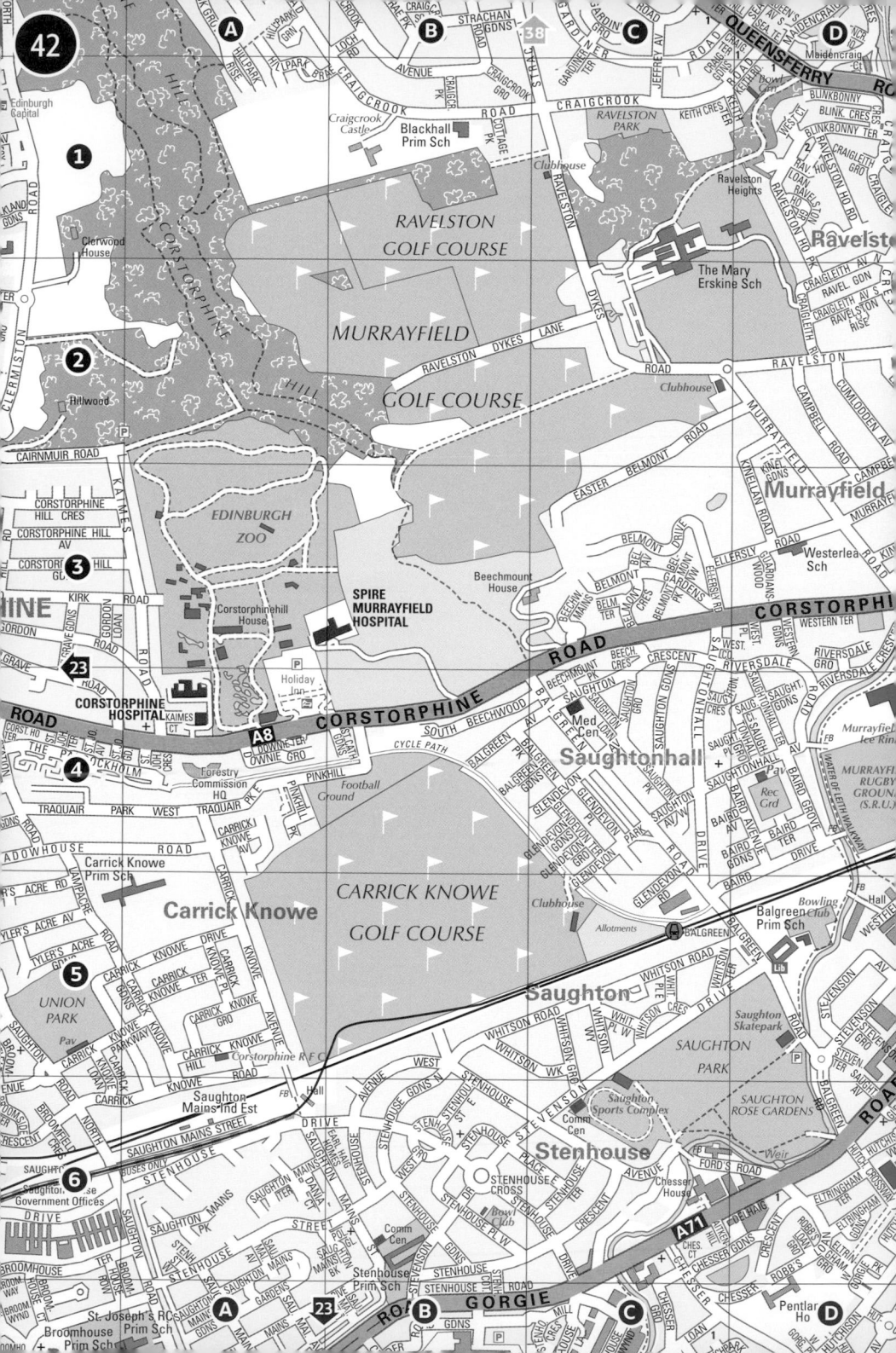

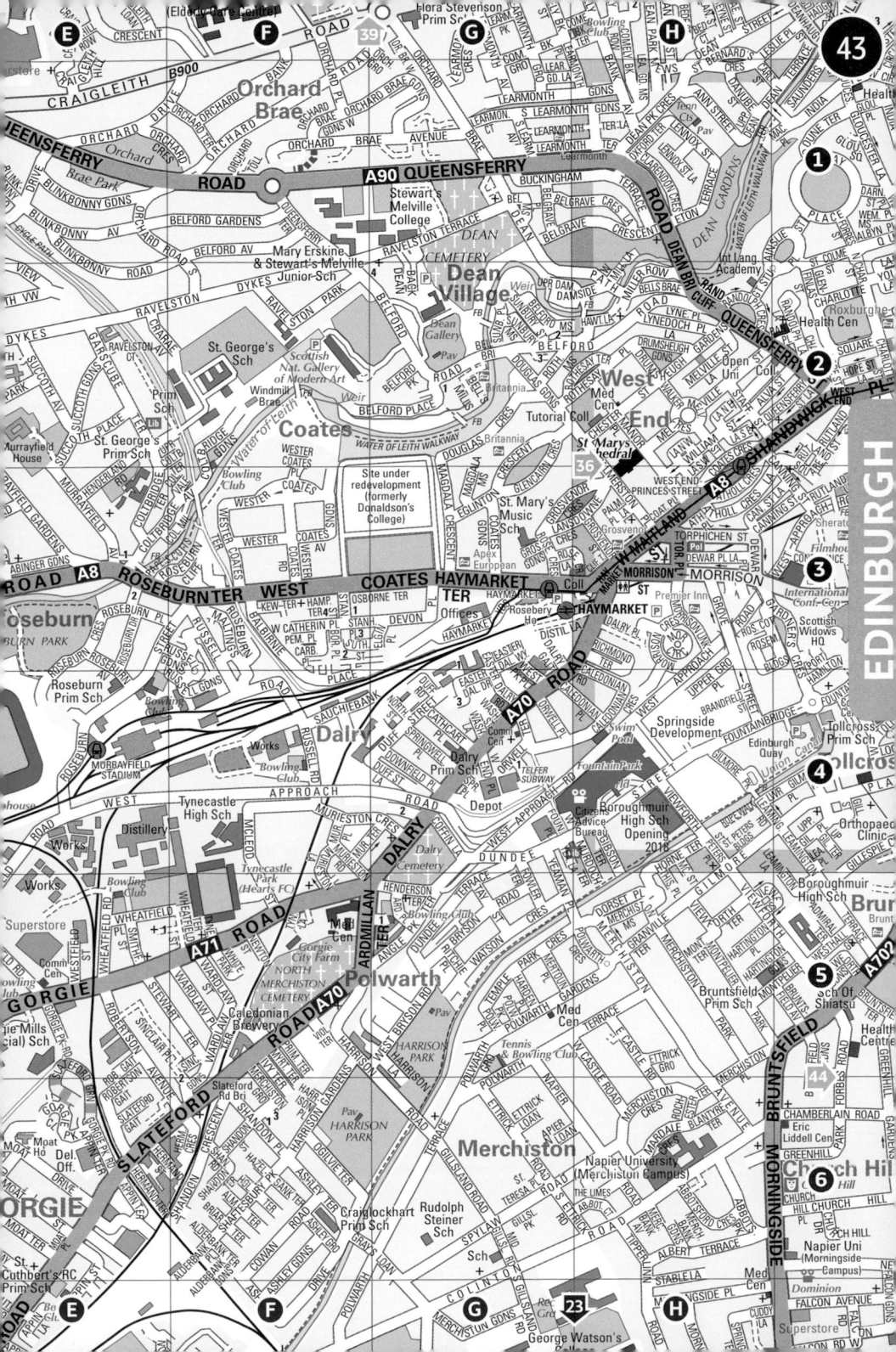

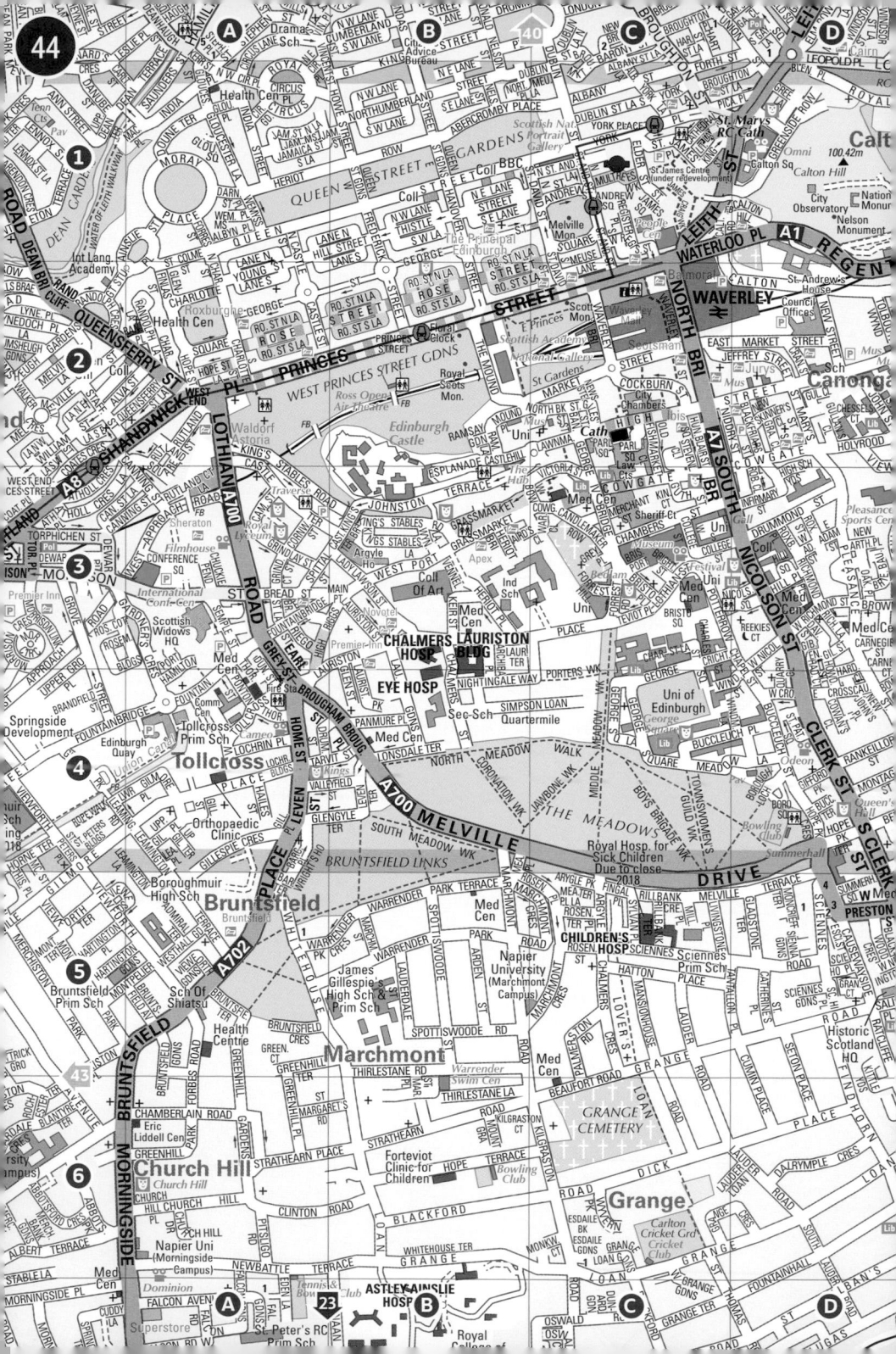

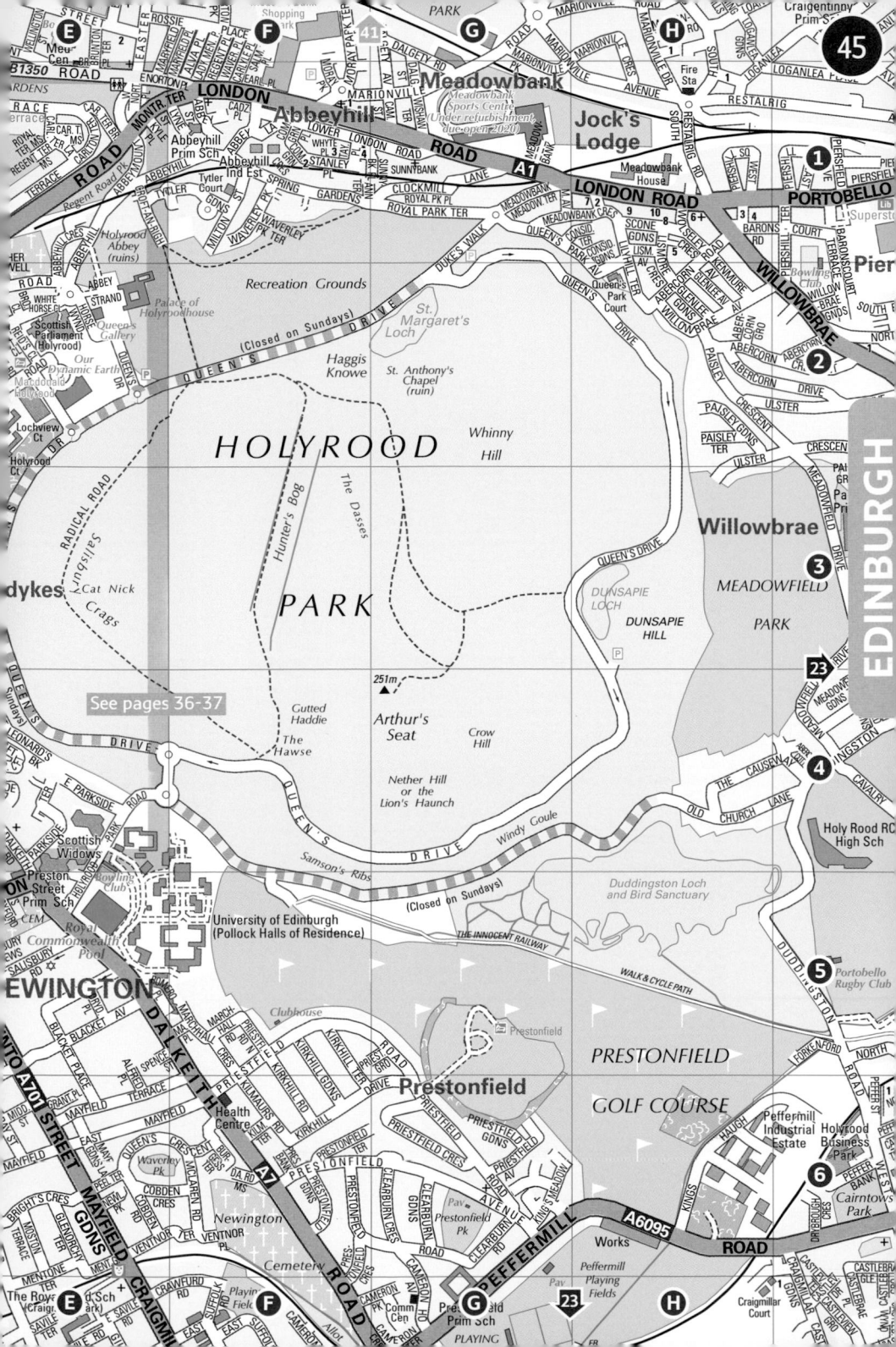

There are street names in this index which are followed by a number in **bold**. These numbers can be found on the map where there is insufficient space to show the street name in full.

A

Abbeyhill	37 F1
Abbeyhill Cres	37 F2
Abbeyhill Ind Est	45 F1
Abbey La	45 F1
Abbeymount	37 F1
Abbey Strand	37 F2
Abbey St	45 F1
Abbotsford Ct	43 H6
Abbotsford Cres	43 H6
Abbotsford Pk	43 H6
Abercorn Cres	45 H2
Abercorn Dr	45 H2
Abercorn Gro	45 H2
Abercorn Rd	45 H2
Abercromby Pl	36 C1
Abinger Gdns	43 E3
Academy Pk	41 F4
Academy St	41 F4
Admiral Ter	44 A5
Admiralty St	41 E2
Advocates Cl 1	37 D2
Afton Pl	39 H3
Afton Ter	39 H3
Agnew Ter	40 C3
Ainslie Pl	36 A1
Aird's Cl	36 C3
Aitkenhill	42 C6
Albany La	37 D1
Albany St	37 D1
Albany St La	37 D1
Albert Dock	41 F2
Albert Pl	40 D6
Albert Rd	41 G3
Albert St	41 E5
Albert Ter	43 H6
Albion Business Cen	41 F6
Albion Gdns	41 F6
Albion Pl	41 F6
Albion Rd	41 F6
Albion Ter	41 F6
Albyn Pl	36 B1
Alderbank Pl	43 F6
Alderbank Ter	43 F6
Alemoor Cres	41 G5
Alemoor Pk	41 G5
Alexander Dr	43 E5
Alfred Pl	45 E5
Allanfield	41 E6
Allanfield Pl	41 E6
Allan St	39 H6
Almondbank Ter	43 F6
Alvanley Ter 1	44 A5
Alva Pl	45 F1
Alva St	36 A2
Anchor Cl 11	37 D2
Anchorfield	40 C2
Anderson Pl	40 D3
Andrew Wd Ct	40 B2
Angle Pk Ter	43 G5
Annandale St	40 C5
Annandale St La	40 D6
Annfield	40 C2
Annfield St	40 C2
Ann St	36 A1
Ann Ter	45 F1
Antigua St 1	40 D6
Appin Ter	43 E6
Arboretum Av	39 H6
Arboretum Pl	39 H5
Arboretum Rd	39 H4
Archibald Pl	36 C3
Arden St	44 B5
Ardmillan Pl	43 G5
Ardmillan Ter	43 F5
Ardmillan Ter La 1	43 F5
Argyle Pk Ter	44 C5
Argyle Pl	44 C5
Argyle St	40 D2
Argyll Ter 2	36 A3
Arthur St	41 E5
Arthur St La	41 E5

Ashley Gro	43 F6
Ashley Pl	40 D4
Ashley Ter	43 F6
Ashville Ter	41 G5
Assembly St	41 F3
Atholl Cres	36 A3
Atholl Cres La	36 A3
Atholl Pl	36 A3
Atholl Ter 3	36 A3
Auchinleck Ct	40 B2
Auchinleck's Brae 1	40 B2
Avenue Vil	39 G6
Avondale Pl	40 A6

B

Back Dean	43 G2
Baird Av	42 D4
Baird Dr	42 C5
Baird Gdns	42 D4
Baird Gro	42 D4
Baird Ter	42 D4
Bakehouse Cl	37 E2
Baker's Pl 1	40 A6
Balbirnie Pl	43 F3
Balfour Pl	40 D5
Balfour St	41 E4
Balgreen Av	42 B4
Balgreen Gdns	42 B4
Balgreen Pk	42 B4
Balgreen Rd	42 C4
Ballantyne La 1	41 E3
Ballantyne Rd	41 E3
Balmoral Pl	40 A6
Baltic St	41 F3
Bangholm Av	40 A3
Bangholm Bower Av	40 A3
Bangholm Gro	40 B3
Bangholm Ln	40 B3
Bangholm Pk	40 A3
Bangholm Pl	40 A3
Bangholm Rd	40 A3
Bangholm Ter	40 A4
Bangholm Vw	40 B3
Bangor Rd	40 D3
Bank St	37 D2
Barclay Pl	36 B4
Barclay Ter	44 A5
Baronscourt Rd	45 H1
Barony Pl 3	40 C6
Barony St	40 C6
Barrie's Cl 14	37 D2
Bathfield	40 D2
Bath Rd	41 G3
Baxter's Pl 1	37 E1
Beaufort Rd	44 C6
Beaverbank Business Pk	40 B5
Beaverbank Pl	40 B5
Beaverhall Rd	40 C5
Bedford Ct	39 H6
Bedford St	39 H6
Beechmount Cres	42 C3
Beechmount Pk	42 C4
Beechwood Mains	42 B3
Beechwood Ter	41 G5
Belford Av	43 F1
Belford Br	43 G2
Belford Gdns	43 F1
Belford Ms	43 G2
Belford Pk	43 G2
Belford Pl	43 F2
Belford Rd	43 G2
Belford Ter 1	43 G2
Belgrave Cres	43 G1
Belgrave Cres La	43 G1
Belgrave Ms	43 G1
Belgrave Pl	43 G1
Bellevue	40 C6
Bellevue Cres	40 C6
Bellevue Gdns	40 C5
Bellevue Gro	40 C6
Bellevue La	40 C6

Bellevue Pl	40 C6
Bellevue Rd	40 C6
Bellevue St	40 C6
Bellevue Ter	40 C5
Bell Pl	40 A6
Bells Brae	36 A2
Bell's Mills	43 G2
Bell's Wynd 2	37 D2
Belmont Av	42 C3
Belmont Cres	42 C3
Belmont Dr	42 C3
Belmont Gdns	42 C3
Belmont Pk	42 C3
Belmont Ter	42 C3
Belmont Vw	42 C3
Belvedere Pk	40 B2
Beresford Av	40 B2
Beresford Gdns	40 B3
Beresford Pl	40 A3
Beresford Ter	40 B3
Bernard St	41 F2
Bernard Ter	37 E4
Bethlehem Way	41 G5
Birnies Ct	38 B3
Blackadder Pl	39 F2
Blacket Av	45 E5
Blacket Pl	45 E5
Blackford Rd	44 B6
Blackfriars St	37 E2
Blackie Rd	41 G4
Blackwood Cres	44 D5
Blair St	37 D2
Blandfield	40 C6
Blantyre Ter	43 H6
Bleachfield	40 C4
Blenheim Pl	37 E1
Blinkbonny Av	43 E1
Blinkbonny Cres	42 D1
Blinkbonny Gdns	43 E1
Blinkbonny Gro	43 E1
Blinkbonny Gro W	43 E1
Blinkbonny Rd	43 E1
Blinkbonny Ter	42 D1
Boat Grn	40 B5
Bonar Pl	40 C3
Bonnington Av	40 C3
Bonnington Business Cen	41 E4
Bonnington Gait 1	40 D4
Bonnington Gro	40 C3
Bonnington Ind Est	40 D4
Bonnington Rd	40 D4
Bonnington Rd La	40 D4
Bonnington Ter	40 C3
Bonnyhaugh	40 C4
Bonnyhaugh La	40 C4
Boothacre Cotts 2	41 H4
Boothacre La	41 H4
Boroughloch	37 E4
Boroughloch Sq	37 E4
Borthwick Pl	43 F3
Borthwick's Cl 3	37 D2
Boswall Av	39 G3
Boswall Cres	39 G3
Boswall Dr	39 G2
Boswall Gdns	39 G3
Boswall Grn	39 H3
Boswall Gro	39 G3
Boswall Ln	39 G3
Boswall Ms	39 G2
Boswall Parkway	39 F2
Boswall Pl	39 G3
Boswall Quad	39 G3
Boswall Rd	39 H2
Boswall Sq	39 G3
Boswall Ter	39 G3
Bothwell St	41 E6
Bowhill Ter	40 A4
Bowie's Cl 1	41 F3
Bowling Grn, The	41 E3
Bowling La 8	41 E3
Bowmont Pl	37 E4
Boyd's Entry 2	37 E2

Boy's Brigade Wk	37 D4
Brandfield St	36 A4
Brandon St	40 B6
Brandon Ter	40 B6
Breadalbane St	40 D3
Breadalbane Ter 5	36 A3
Bread St	36 B3
Bread St La	36 B3
Brewery La 2	41 E3
Briarbank Ter	43 F6
Bridge Pl	39 H6
Briery Bauks	37 E3
Brighton St	37 D3
Bright's Cres	45 E6
Bright Ter 8	36 A3
Bristo Pl	37 D3
Bristo Port	37 D3
Bristo Sq	37 D3
Broad Wynd 7	41 F3
Broomhouse Row	42 A6
Brougham Pl	36 C4
Brougham St	36 B4
Broughton Mkt	40 C6
Broughton Pl	40 C6
Broughton Pl La	40 C6
Broughton Rd	40 C5
Broughton St	40 C6
Broughton St La	37 D1
Brown's Cl	37 F2
Brown's Pl 4	36 C3
Brown St	37 E3
Brown St La 8	37 E3
Brunswick Pl	40 D6
Brunswick Rd	40 D6
Brunswick St	40 D6
Brunswick St La	40 D6
Brunton Gdns 2	41 E6
Brunton Pl	41 E6
Brunton Ter	41 E6
Bruntsfield Av	44 A5
Bruntsfield Cres	44 A5
Bruntsfield Gdns	44 A6
Bruntsfield Pl	43 H6
Bruntsfield Ter	44 A5
Bryson Rd	43 G5
Buccleuch Pl	37 D4
Buccleuch St	37 E4
Buccleuch Ter	37 E4
Buchanan St	41 E5
Buckingham Ter	43 G1
Bull's Cl 5	37 F2
Burgess St	41 F3
Burgess Ter	45 F6
Burlington St	41 E4
Burns St	41 F4

C

Cables Wynd	41 E3
Cables Wynd Ho	41 E3
Cadiz St	41 F3
Cadzow Pl	45 F1
Caithness Pl	40 A3
Caledonian Cres	36 A4
Caledonian Pl	43 G4
Caledonian Rd	36 A3
Calton Hill	37 E1
Calton Rd	37 E2
Calton Sq	37 E1
Cambridge Av	40 D5
Cambridge Gdns	40 D5
Cambridge St	36 B3
Cambridge St La 3	36 B3
Cambusnethan St	45 G1
Cameron Ho Av	45 G6
Campbell Av	42 D3
Campbell Rd	42 D2
Campbell's Cl 7	37 F2
Candlemaker Row	37 D3
Canning St	36 A2
Canning St La	36 A3
Cannon Wynd	40 D2

Canon Ct 3	40 B5
Canongate	37 E2
Canon La	40 B6
Canonmills	40 B5
Canonmills Br 2	40 B5
Canon St	40 B6
Carberry Pl	43 F3
Carfrae Gdns	38 B6
Carfrae Gro	38 B6
Carfrae Pk	38 B6
Carfrae Rd	38 B6
Cargil Ct	39 H3
Cargil Ter	40 A3
Carlton St	36 A1
Carlton Ter	37 F1
Carlton Ter Brae	37 F1
Carlton Ter La	37 F1
Carlton Ter Ms	37 F1
Carlton Wynd	37 E2
Carlyle Pl	45 F1
Carnegie Ct	37 E3
Carnegie St	37 E3
Caroline Pk Av	39 E1
Caroline Pk Gro	39 E2
Carpet La	41 F3
Carrick Knowe Av	42 A5
Carrick Knowe Gdns	42 A5
Carrick Knowe Gro	42 A5
Carrick Knowe Hill	42 A5
Carrick Knowe Pl	42 A5
Carrick Knowe Ter	42 A5
Carrington Rd	39 F6
Carron Pl	41 G3
Carrubber's Cl 5	37 D2
Casselbank St	41 E4
Cassel's La	41 E4
Castlehill	36 C2
Castle St	36 B2
Castle Ter	36 B3
Castle Wynd N 11	36 C3
Castle Wynd S 6	36 C3
Cathcart Pl	43 G4
Cathedral La	37 D1
Catherine Pl	40 B5
Causeway, The	45 H4
Causewayside	44 D5
Chalmers Bldgs 2	36 B4
Chalmers Cl 4	37 E2
Chalmers Cres	44 C5
Chalmers St	36 C3
Chamberlain Rd	44 A6
Chambers St	37 D3
Chancelot Cres	40 B3
Chancelot Gro	40 B3
Chancelot Ter	40 B3
Chapel La 2	41 F3
Chapel St	37 E3
Chapel Wynd 7	36 C3
Charlesfield 1	37 D3
Charles St	37 D3
Charles St La	37 D3
Charlotte La	36 B2
Charlotte Sq	36 B2
Chessels Ct	37 E2
Chesser Av	42 C6
Chesser Cotts 1	42 D6
Chesser Ct	42 C6
Chesser Gdns	42 C6
Chester St	36 A2
Chestnut St	39 F1
Cheyne St	39 H6
Chuckie Pend	36 B3
Church Hill	44 A6
Church Hill Dr	44 A6
Church Hill Pl	44 A6
Circus Gdns	36 B1
Circus La	40 A6
Circus Pl	36 B1
Citadel Ct	41 E2
Citadel Pl	41 E2
Citadel St 2	41 E2
Clarebank Cres	41 G4
Claremont Bk	40 C6

laremont Ct	40 C5
laremont Cres	40 C5
laremont Gdns	41 G4
laremont Gro	40 C5
laremont Pk	41 G4
laremont Rd	41 G4
larence St	40 A6
larendon Cres	36 A1
lark Av	40 B3
lark Pl	40 A3
lark Rd	40 A3
learburn Cres	45 G6
learburn Gdns	45 G6
learburn Rd	45 G6
lerk St	37 E4
lifton Ter	36 A3
linton Rd	44 A6
lockmill La	45 G1
oalhill	41 E3
oates Cres	36 A3
oates Gdns	43 G3
oates Pl	36 A3
oatfield La	41 F3
obden Cres	45 E6
obden Rd	45 E6
obden Ter 7	36 A3
oburg St	41 E3
ochrane Pl 1	41 F4
ochran Pl	40 C6
ochran Ter	40 C6
ockburn St	37 D2
offin La	37 E2
oinyie Ho Cl 1	37 E2
ollege Wynd 2	37 D3
ollins Pl	40 A6
olonsay Cl	38 C2
oltbridge Av	43 E3
oltbridge Gdns	43 F3
oltbridge Millside	43 F3
oltbridge Ter	43 E3
oltbridge Vale	43 F3
olumba Av	38 C6
olumba Rd	38 C6
olville Pl	40 A6
omely Bk	39 G6
omely Bk Av	39 H6
omely Bk Gro	43 G1
omely Bk Pl	39 H6
omely Bk Pl Ms 2	39 H6
omely Bk Rd	39 H6
omely Bk Row	39 H6
omely Bk St	39 G6
omely Bk Ter	39 G6
omely Grn Cres	45 F1
omely Grn Pl	45 F1
ommercial St	41 E2
ommercial Wf 1	41 F2
onference Sq	36 B3
onnaught Pl	40 C3
onsidine Gdns	45 H1
onsidine Ter	45 H1
onstitution St	41 E4
onvening Ct 1	36 A2
ooper's Cl 3	37 F2
orbiehill Av	38 B5
orbiehill Cres	38 A5
orbiehill Gdns	38 B5
orbiehill Gro	38 B5
orbiehill Pk	38 A5
orbiehill Pl	38 A5
orbiehill Rd	38 A5
orbiehill Ter	38 A5
ornhill Ter	41 G4
ornwallis Pl	40 B6
ornwall St	36 B3
oronation Wk	36 C4
orstorphine Rd	42 D3
orunna Pl	41 E3
ottage Pk	42 B1
ouper Fld	41 E2
ouper St	41 E2
owan Rd	43 F6
owan's Cl	37 E4
owgate	37 D3
owgatehead	37 D3
oxfield	42 D6
Coxfield La 2	42 D6
Craigcrook Av	38 B6
Craigcrook Gdns	42 C1
Craigcrook Gro	42 B1
Craigcrook Pk	42 B1
Craigcrook Pl 1	38 D6
Craigcrook Rd	42 C1
Craigcrook Sq	38 B6
Craigcrook Ter	38 C6
Craighall Av	40 B2
Craighall Bk	40 B2
Craighall Cres	40 B2
Craighall Gdns	40 B3
Craighall Rd	40 B2
Craighall Ter	40 B2
Craigleith Av N	42 D2
Craigleith Av S	42 D2
Craigleith Bk	42 D1
Craigleith Cres	42 D1
Craigleith Dr	42 D1
Craigleith Gdns	42 D1
Craigleith Gro	42 D1
Craigleith Hill	43 E1
Craigleith Hill Av	38 D6
Craigleith Hill Cres	39 E6
Craigleith Hill Gdns	39 E6
Craigleith Hill Grn	39 E6
Craigleith Hill Gro	39 E6
Craigleith Hill Ln	39 E6
Craigleith Hill Pk	39 E6
Craigleith Hill Row	39 E6
Craigleith Ri	42 D2
Craigleith Rd	43 E1
Craigleith Vw	42 D2
Craigmuir Pl	42 D1
Craigroyston Gro	38 B4
Craigroyston Pl	38 B4
Cranston St	37 E2
Crarae Av	43 E2
Crawford Br 1	41 F6
Crewe Bk	39 F3
Crewe Cres	39 E3
Crewe Gro	39 F3
Crewe Ln	39 E3
Crewe Path	39 E3
Crewe Pl	39 E3
Crewe Rd Gdns	39 E3
Crewe Rd N	39 E3
Crewe Rd S	39 F5
Crewe Rd W	39 E3
Crewe Ter	39 E3
Crewe Toll	39 E3
Crichton's Cl 4	37 F2
Crichton St	37 D3
Crighton Pl	41 E5
Croall Pl	40 D6
Croft-an-righ	37 F1
Cromwell Pl	41 E2
Crown Pl	41 E4
Crown St	41 E4
Cumberland St	40 B6
Cumberland St N E La	40 B6
Cumberland St N W La	40 B6
Cumberland St S E La	40 B6
Cumberland St S W La	40 B6
Cumin Pl	44 D5
Cumlodden Av	42 D2
Cunningham Pl 1	41 E4

D

Daisy Ter 3	43 FG
Dalgety Av	41 G6
Dalgety Rd	41 G6
Dalgety St	45 G1
Dalkeith Rd	37 F4
Dalkeith Rd Ms	45 F6
Dalmeny Rd	40 C3
Dalmeny St	41 E5
Dalry Gait	43 G3
Dalrymple Cres	44 D6
Dalry Pl	36 A3
Dalry Rd	43 G4
Dalziel Pl 1	45 F1
Damside	43 G2
Dania Ct	42 A6
Danube St	36 A1
Darnaway St	36 B1
Darnell Rd	39 H3
Davidson Gdns	38 B5
Davidson Pk	39 E5
Davidson Rd	39 E5
Davie St	37 E3
Dean Bk La	40 A6
Dean Br	36 A1
Deanery Cl 1	45 H1
Deanhaugh St	40 A6
Dean Pk Cres	36 A1
Dean Pk Ms	39 H6
Dean Pk St	39 H6
Dean Path	43 G1
Dean Path Bldgs 2	36 A2
Dean St	39 H6
Dean Ter	36 A1
Delhaig	42 D6
Denham Grn Av	40 A3
Denham Grn Pl	40 A3
Denham Grn Ter	40 A3
Derby St	40 C2
Devon Pl	43 G3
Dewar Pl	36 A3
Dewar Pl La	36 A3
Dick Pl	44 C6
Dicksonfield	40 D6
Dickson's Cl 5	37 E2
Dickson St	41 E5
Distillery La	43 G3
Dock Pl	41 E2
Dock St	41 E2
Dorset Pl	43 H5
Douglas Cres	43 G2
Douglas Gdns	43 G2
Douglas Gdns Ms 3	43 G2
Douglas Ter 1	36 A3
Doune Ter	36 B1
Downfield Pl	43 G4
Downie Gro	42 A4
Downie Ter	42 A4
Drumdryan St	36 B4
Drummond Pl	40 B6
Drummond St	37 E3
Drumsheugh Gdns	36 A2
Drumsheugh Pl 3	36 A2
Drum Ter	41 F6
Dryden Gait	40 D5
Dryden Gdns	40 D5
Dryden Pl	44 D6
Dryden St	40 D5
Dryden Ter	40 D5
Drylaw Av	38 D6
Drylaw Cres	38 C6
Drylaw Gdns	38 C5
Drylaw Grn	38 C6
Drylaw Gro	38 C6
Drylaw Ho Gdns	38 C5
Drylaw Ho Paddock	38 C5
Dublin Meuse	40 C6
Dublin St	40 C6
Dublin St La N	40 C6
Dublin St La S	37 D1
Dudley Av	40 C2
Dudley Av S	40 D3
Dudley Bk	40 C2
Dudley Cres	40 C2
Dudley Gdns	40 C2
Dudley Gro	40 C2
Dudley Ter	40 C2
Duff Rd	43 G4
Duff St	43 G4
Duff St La	43 G4
Duke Pl	41 F4
Duke St	41 F4
Duke St Glebe	41 F4
Duke's Wk	37 F3
Dumbiedykes Rd	37 F3
Dunbar St	36 B4
Duncan Pl	41 F4
Duncan St	44 D6
Dundas St	40 B6
Dundee St	43 G4
Dundee Ter	43 G5
Dundonald St	40 B6
Dunedin St	40 C5
Dunlop's Ct 12	36 C3
Dunrobin Pl	40 A6

E

Earl Grey St	36 B3
Earl Haig Gdns	40 A3
Earl Haig Homes	42 B6
Earlston Pl	45 F1
East Adam St	37 E3
East Broughton Pl 1	40 C6
East Castle Rd	43 H5
East Claremont St	40 C6
East Ct 2	42 D1
East Cromwell St	41 E2
East Crosscauseway	37 E4
Easter Belmont Rd	42 C3
Easter Dalry Dr	43 G4
Easter Dalry Pl 1	43 G4
Easter Dalry Rigg 3	43 G4
Easter Dalry Rd	43 G3
Easter Dalry Wynd	43 G4
Easter Drylaw Av	38 D5
Easter Drylaw Bk	38 D4
Easter Drylaw Dr	38 D5
Easter Drylaw Gdns	38 D5
Easter Drylaw Gro	38 D5
Easter Drylaw Ln	38 D4
Easter Drylaw Pl	38 D5
Easter Drylaw Vw	38 D4
Easter Drylaw Way	38 D5
Easter Hermitage	41 G5
Easter Rd	41 F5
Easter Warriston	40 B4
East Fettes Av	39 G5
East Fountainbridge	36 B3
East Hermitage Pl	41 F4
East Lillyput	40 A3
East London St	40 C6
East Mkt St	37 D2
East Mayfield	45 E6
East Montgomery Pl	41 E6
East Newington Pl	44 D5
East Norton Pl	37 F1
East Parkside	37 F4
East Pilton Fm Av	39 F3
East Pilton Fm Cres	39 G3
East Pilton Fm Rigg	39 F3
East Pilton Fm Wynd	39 G3
East Preston St	44 D5
East Preston St La 3	44 D5
East Restalrig Ter	41 G4
East Sciennes St	44 D5
East Scotland St La	40 C6
East Silvermills La	40 A6
East Trinity Rd	40 A3
East Werberside	39 F4
East Werberside Pl	39 F4
Edina Pl	41 E6
Edina St	41 E6
Edinburgh Dock	41 G2
Edmonstone Cl 5	37 D3
Eglinton Cres	43 G3
Eglinton St 3	43 F3
Eildon St	40 B5
Eildon Ter	40 A5
Elbe St	41 F3
Elder St	37 D1
Elder St E 5	37 D1
Elgin Pl	43 G3
Elgin St	41 F6
Elgin St N	41 E6
Elgin Ter	41 E6
Elizafield	40 D4
Ellersly Rd	42 C3
Elliot St	41 E6
Elm Pl 2	41 G4
Elm Row	40 D6
Elmwood Ter	41 G4
Eltringham Gdns	42 D6
Eltringham Gro	42 D6
Eltringham Ter	42 D6
Esdaile Bk	44 C6
Esdaile Gdns	44 C6
Esdaile Pk 1	44 C6
Esplanade	36 C3
Eton Ter	36 A1
Ettrickdale Pl	40 A5
Ettrick Gro	43 H5
Ettrick Ln	43 G6
Ettrick Rd	43 G6
Eyre Cres	40 B6
Eyre Pl	40 B6
Eyre Pl La	40 B6
Eyre Ter	40 B6

F

Falcon Gdns	44 A6
Ferryfield	39 G4
Ferry Gait Cres	38 B4
Ferry Gait Dr	38 B4
Ferry Gait Pl	38 B4
Ferry Gait Wk	38 B4
Ferrylee	40 D2
Ferry Rd	40 C3
Ferry Rd Av	39 E4
Ferry Rd Dr	39 E4
Ferry Rd Gdns	38 D4
Ferry Rd Gro	38 D4
Ferry Rd Pl	38 D4
Festival Sq 1	36 B3
Fettes Av	39 G6
Fettes Ri	39 G4
Fettes Row	40 B6
Fidra Ct	38 B3
Findhorn Pl	44 D5
Findlay Av	41 H5
Findlay Cotts	41 H5
Findlay Gdns	41 H5
Findlay Gro	41 H5
Findlay Medway	41 H5
Fingal Pl	44 C5
Fingzies Pl 3	41 G4
Fishmarket Sq 2	40 C1
Fleshmarket Cl 13	37 D2
Forbes Rd	44 A6
Forbes St	37 E4
Ford's Rd	42 C6
Forres St	36 B1
Forrest Hill	37 D3
Forrest Rd	37 D3
Forth Ind Est	39 F1
Fort Ho	40 D2
Forth St	37 D1
Forthview Rd	38 D6
Forthview Ter	38 C6
Fountainbridge	36 B4
Fowler Ter	43 G4
Fox St	41 G3
Fraser Av	39 H3
Fraser Cres	39 H3
Fraser Gdns	39 H3
Fraser Gro	39 H3
Frederick St	36 C1

G

Gabriel's Rd 6	37 D1
Gabriel's Rd (Stockbridge) 6	40 A6
Gardiner Gro	38 C6
Gardiner Rd	38 C6
Gardiner Ter	42 C1
Gardner's Cres	36 A3
Garscube Ter	43 E2
Gayfield Cl	40 D6
Gayfield Pl	40 D6
Gayfield Pl La	40 D6
Gayfield Sq	40 D6
Gayfield St	40 C6
Gayfield St La	40 C6
Gentle's Entry 8	37 F2
George IV Br	37 D2
George Sq	37 D4
George Sq La	37 D4
George St	36 B2

Gibbs Entry 37 E3
Gibson St 40 D4
Gibson Ter 36 A4
Gifford Pk 37 E4
Giles St 41 E3
Gillespie Cres 36 B4
Gillespie Pl 36 B4
Gillespie St 36 B4
Gillsland Pk 43 G6
Gillsland Rd 43 G6
Gilmore Pk 36 A4
Gilmore Pl 43 H5
Gilmour's Entry 7 37 E3
Gilmour St 37 E3
Gladstone Pl 41 G4
Gladstone Ter 44 D5
Glanville Pl 5 40 A6
Glencairn Cres 43 G3
Glendevon Av 42 C4
Glendevon Gdns 42 C5
Glendevon Gro 42 C5
Glendevon Pk 42 C5
Glendevon Pl 42 C4
Glendevon Rd 42 C5
Glendevon Ter 42 C4
Glenfinlas St 36 B2
Glengyle Ter 36 B4
Glenlea Cotts 42 D6
Glenlee Av 45 H2
Glenlee Gdns 45 H2
Glenogle Ct 40 A5
Glenogle Pl 7 40 A6
Glenogle Rd 40 A6
Glenogle Ter 40 A6
Glenorchy Pl 4 37 E1
Glenorchy Ter 45 E6
Glen St 36 C3
Gloucester La 36 B1
Gloucester Pl 36 B1
Gloucester Sq 36 B1
Gloucester St 36 B1
Goldenacre Ter 40 A4
Gordon St 41 F4
Gorgie Cotts 42 D6
Gorgie Pk Cl 43 E6
Gorgie Pk Rd 43 E5
Gorgie Rd 43 E5
Gosford Pl 40 C3
Graham St 40 D3
Grandfield 40 B2
Grandville 40 B2
Grange Ct 44 D5
Grange Cres 44 C6
Grange Ln 44 B6
Grange Ln Gdns 44 C6
Grange Rd 44 C5
Granton Cres 39 G2
Granton Gdns 39 G2
Granton Gro 39 G2
Granton Mains Av 38 D2
Granton Mains Bk 1 38 D2
Granton Mains Brae 38 D2
Granton Mains Ct 39 E2
Granton Mains E 39 E2
Granton Mains Gait 38 D2
Granton Mains Vale 38 D2
Granton Mains Wynd 38 D2
Granton Medway 39 F2
Granton Mill Cres 38 D2
Granton Mill Dr 38 D2
Granton Mill March 38 C3
Granton Mill Pk 38 C3
Granton Mill Pl 38 C2
Granton Mill Rd 38 C2
Granton Mill W 1 38 C3
Granton Pk Av 39 F1
Granton Pier 39 G1
Granton Pl 39 G2
Granton Rd 39 G2
Granton Sq 39 G1
Granton Ter 39 G1
Granton Vw 39 G1
Grantully Pl 45 E6
Granville Ter 43 H5
Grassmarket 36 C3

Grays Ct 6 37 E3
Gray's Ln 43 F6
Great Junct St 41 E3
Great King St 36 C1
Great Michael Cl 4 40 C1
Great Michael Ri 40 C2
Great Michael Sq 1 40 C1
Great Stuart St 36 A2
Green, The 38 A4
Greendale Pk 38 B4
Greenhill Ct 44 A5
Greenhill Gdns 44 A5
Greenhill Pk 44 A6
Greenhill Pl 44 A6
Greenhill Ter 44 A5
Greenside End 6 37 E1
Greenside La 37 E1
Greenside Pl 5 37 E1
Greenside Row 37 E1
Green St 40 C6
Greyfriars Pl 37 D3
Grierson Av 39 H2
Grierson Cres 39 H2
Grierson Gdns 39 H2
Grierson Rd 39 G2
Grierson Sq 39 H2
Grierson Vil 39 H2
Grigor Av 39 E5
Grigor Dr 39 E5
Grigor Gdns 39 E5
Grigor Ter 39 E5
Grindlay St 36 B3
Grindlay St Ct 36 B3
Groathill Av 38 D6
Groathill Gdns E 38 D6
Groathill Gdns W 38 D6
Groathill Ln 38 D5
Groathill Rd N 38 D5
Groathill Rd S 38 D6
Grosvenor Cres 43 G3
Grosvenor Gdns 43 G3
Grosvenor St 36 A3
Grove St 36 A3
Grove Ter 4 36 A3
Guardianswood 42 D3
Gullan's Cl 37 E2
Gunnet Ct 38 B3
Guthrie St 37 D3

H
Haddington Pl 40 D6
Haddon's Ct 37 E3
Hailes St 36 B4
Halmyre St 41 E5
Hamburgh Pl 1 40 D2
Hamilton Pl 40 A6
Hamilton's Folly Ms 5 37 E4
Hamilton Wynd 40 D2
Hammermen's Entry 37 E2
Hampton Pl 4 43 F3
Hampton Ter 43 F3
Hanover St 36 C1
Harden Pl 43 G5
Hardwell Cl 37 E4
Harrismith Pl 41 F6
Harrison Gdns 43 F6
Harrison La 43 G5
Harrison Pl 43 F6
Harrison Rd 43 F6
Hartington Gdns 43 H5
Hartington Pl 43 H5
Hart St 40 C6
Hart St La 40 C6
Hatton Pl 44 C5
Haugh St 40 A6
Hawkhill 41 G5
Hawkhill Av 41 F5
Hawkhill Cl 41 F5
Hawthornbank La 36 A2
Hawthornbank Pl 40 C2
Hawthornbank Ter 2 40 D2
Hawthorn Bldgs 2 43 G2
Hawthornden Pl 40 D5

Hawthorn Ter 5 36 A2
Hawthornvale 40 C2
Haymarket 36 A3
Haymarket Ter 43 G3
Haymarket Yards 43 G3
Hazelbank Ter 43 F6
Henderson Gdns 4 41 E3
Henderland Rd 43 E3
Henderson Pl 40 B6
Henderson Pl La 40 A6
Henderson Row 40 A6
Henderson St 41 E3
Henderson Ter 43 G5
Heriot Br 36 C3
Heriot Cross 1 36 C3
Heriot Hill Ter 40 B5
Heriot Pl 36 C3
Heriot Row 36 B1
Hermand Cres 43 F6
Hermand St 43 E6
Hermand Ter 43 E6
Hermitage Pk 41 G5
Hermitage Pk Gro 41 G5
Hermitage Pk Lea 41 G5
Hermitage Pk S 41 G5
Hermitage Pl 41 F4
Hermits Cft 37 F4
Heron Pl 39 G1
Hesperus Crossway 39 G1
High Riggs 36 C3
High Sch Yards 37 E3
High St 37 D2
Hillend Pl 10 45 H1
Hill Pl 37 E3
Hillside Cres 40 D6
Hillside St 41 E6
Hill Sq 37 E3
Hill St 36 B1
Hill St La N 36 B1
Hill St La S 36 C2
Hillview 38 C6
Hollybank Ter 43 F6
Holyrood Ct 37 F2
Holyrood Pk 45 F2
Holyrood Pk Rd 45 E5
Holyrood Rd 37 E2
Home St 36 B4
Hopefield Ter 40 D2
Hope Pk Cres 37 E4
Hope Pk Sq 1 37 E4
Hope Pk Ter 37 E4
Hope St 36 B2
Hope St La 36 B2
Hope Ter 44 B6
Hopetoun Cres 40 D6
Hopetoun St 40 D6
Horne Ter 36 A4
Horse Wynd 37 F2
House o'Hill Av 38 B5
House o'Hill Brae 38 B5
House o'Hill Cres 38 B5
House o'Hill Gdns 38 C5
House o'Hill Grn 38 B5
House o'Hill Gro 38 B5
House o'Hill Pl 38 B5
House o'Hill Rd 38 B5
House o'Hill Row 38 B5
House o'Hill Ter 38 C6
Howard Pl 40 B5
Howard St 40 B5
Howden St 37 E3

Howe St 36 C1
Hugh Miller Pl 40 A6
Hunter's Cl 13 36 C3
Hunter Sq 37 D2
Huntingdon Pl 40 D6
Huntly St 40 B5
Hutchison Crossway 42 D6
Hutchison Ho 42 D6
Hutchison Medway 43 E6
Hutchison Pk 42 D6
Hutchison Rd 42 D6
Hutchison Vw 42 D6
Hutton Cl 37 F2
Hutton Rd 37 F2

I
Imperial Dock 41 F1
Inchcolm Ct 38 D3
Inchgarvie Ct 38 D4
Inchkeith Ct 40 D5
Inchmickery Ct 38 B3
India Bldgs 3 37 D3
India Pl 36 B1
India St 36 B1
Industrial Rd 41 F4
Industry Home 1 40 D3
Industry La 40 D3
Infirmary St 37 E3
Inglis Ct 2 36 C3
Inverleith Av 40 A4
Inverleith Av S 40 A4
Inverleith Gdns 39 H4
Inverleith Gro 39 G5
Inverleith Pl 39 H4
Inverleith Pl La 40 A4
Inverleith Row 40 A4
Inverleith Ter 40 A5
Inverleith Ter La 40 A5
Iona St 41 E5
Iona St La 41 E5
Ivy Ter 43 F5

J
Jackson's Entry 7 37 F2
Jamaica Ms 36 B1
Jamaica St 36 B1
Jamaica St N La 36 B1
Jamaica St S La 36 B1
Jamaica St W 2 36 B1
James' Ct 4 37 D2
James Craig Wk 37 D1
Jameson Pl 41 E5
Jane St 41 E4
Jane Ter 2 45 F1
Jawbone Wk 37 D4
Jeffrey Av 42 C1
Jeffrey St 37 D2
Jessfield Ter 40 C2
John Cotton Business Cen 41 F6
John's La 41 F3
John's Pl 41 F4
Johnston Ter 36 C3
Junction Pl 41 E4

K
Kaimes Ct 42 A4
Keir St 36 C3
Keith Cres 42 C1
Keith Row 42 D1
Keith Ter 42 C1
Kemp Pl 40 A6
Kenmure Av 45 H2
Kerr St 40 A6
Kew Ter 43 F3
Kilgraston Ct 44 B6
Kilgraston Rd 44 C6
Kilmaurs Rd 45 F6
Kilmaurs Ter 45 F6
Kimmerghame Dr 39 F4
Kimmerghame Ln 39 F4
Kimmerghame Path 39 F4
Kimmerghame Pl 39 F5
Kimmerghame Row 39 F4

Kimmerghame Ter 39 F4
Kimmerghame Vw 39 F5
Kincaid's Ct 37 D3
Kinellan Gdns 42 D3
Kinellan Rd 42 D2
Kinghorn Pl 40 C3
King's Br 36 C3
Kingsburgh Cres 39 F1
Kingsburgh Rd 42 D3
Kings Haugh 45 H6
King's Meadow 45 G6
King's Stables La 36 C3
King's Stables Rd 36 C3
King St 41 E3
Kinnear Ri 39 G4
Kinnear Rd 39 G4
Kirkgate 41 F3
Kirkhill Dr 45 F6
Kirkhill Gdns 45 F5
Kirkhill Rd 45 F5
Kirkhill Ter 45 F5
Kirk St 41 E4
Kirkwood Pl 3 45 F1
Kittle Yards 44 D5
Kyle Pl 37 F1

L
Ladehead 40 C4
Lady Lawson St 36 C3
Lady Menzies Pl 45 F1
Lady Stair's Cl 6 37 D2
Lady Wynd 36 C3
Lamb's Cl 2 37 E4
Lamb's Ct 1 40 B1
Lansdowne Cres 43 G3
Lapicide Pl 40 D3
Largo Pl 40 D3
Lauderdale St 44 B5
Lauder Ln 44 D6
Lauder Rd 44 C5
Laurel Ter 1 43 F5
Laurie St 41 F4
Lauriston Gdns 36 C3
Lauriston Pk 36 C4
Lauriston Pl 36 B4
Lauriston St 36 C3
Lauriston Ter 36 C3
Laverockbank Av 40 B2
Laverockbank Cres 40 B2
Laverockbank Gdns 40 B2
Laverockbank Gro 40 B2
Laverockbank Rd 40 B2
Laverockbank Ter 40 B2
Lawnmarket 37 D2
Leamington La 36 B4
Leamington Pl 36 B4
Leamington Rd 36 A4
Leamington Ter 36 B4
Learmonth Av 39 G6
Learmonth Ct 43 G1
Learmonth Cres 43 G1
Learmonth Gdns 43 G1
Learmonth Gdns La 43 G1
Learmonth Gdns Ms 36 A1
Learmonth Gro 39 G6
Learmonth Pk 39 G6
Learmonth Pl 39 G6
Learmonth Ter 43 G1
Learmonth Ter La 43 G1
Learmonth Vw 1 36 A1
Leith Docks 41 E1
Leith Links 41 F4
Leith St 37 D1
Leith Wk 40 D6
Lennel Av 42 D2
Lennox Row 40 A2
Lennox St 36 A1
Lennox St La 36 A1
Leopold Pl 40 D6
Leslie Pl 39 H6
Leven Cl 1 36 B4
Leven St 36 B4
Leven Ter 36 C4
Lewis Ter 12 36 A3
Liddesdale Pl 40 A5

Name	Grid	Name	Grid	Name	Grid	Name	Grid	Name	Grid
Lilyhill Ter	45 H1	Maidencraig Gro	38 D6	Mill La	41 E3	New Cut Rigg	40 C3	Orchard Rd	43 F1
Lily Ter 1	43 F6	Main Pt	36 C3	Milnacre	40 C4	Newhaven Main St	40 B1	Orchard Rd S	43 E1
Limes, The	43 H6	Main St	38 A5	Milton St	45 F1	Newhaven Pl	40 C1	Orchard Ter	43 F1
Lindean Pl	41 G4	Malta Grn 2	40 A6	Minto St	45 E1	Newhaven Rd	40 D4	Orchard Toll	43 F1
Lindsay Pl	40 D2	Malta Ter	40 A6	Mitchell St	41 F3	Newington Rd	44 D5	Ormidale Ter	42 D3
Lindsay Rd	40 C1	Manderston St	41 E4	Moat Dr	43 E6	New John's Pl	37 E4	Orwell Pl	43 G4
Lindsay St	40 D2	Manor Pl	36 A2	Moat Ho	43 E6	Newkirkgate 2	41 E4	Orwell Ter	43 G4
Links Gdns	41 G3	Mansfield Pl	40 C6	Moat Pl	43 E6	Newlands Pk	45 E6	Osborne Ter	43 F3
Links Gdns La	41 G3	Mansionhouse Rd	44 C5	Moat St	43 E6	New La	40 D4	Oxcars Ct	38 B3
Links 3	41 F3	Marchfield Gro	38 B5	Moat Ter	43 E6	New Orchardfield	41 E4	Oxcraig St	39 G1
Links Pl	41 F3	Marchfield Pk	38 A5	Moncrieff Ter	44 D5	New Skinner's Cl	37 E2	Oxford St	37 F4
Linksview Ho	41 E3	Marchfield Pk La	38 A5	Monkwood Ct	44 C6	News Steps	37 D2	Oxford Ter	36 A1
Lismore Av	45 H1	Marchfield Ter	38 B6	Monmouth Ter	40 A3	New St	37 E2	
Lismore Cres	45 H1	March Gait	38 A6	Montague St	37 E4	Newton St	43 F5	**P**
Little King St	37 D1	March Gro	38 A6	Montagu Ter	40 A4	Nicholfield	40 C2	Paisley Cres	45 H2
Livingstone Pl	44 C5	Marchhall Cres	45 F5	Montgomery St	37 D3	Nicolson Sq	37 D3	Paisley Gdns	45 H2
Lixmount Av	40 B2	Marchhall Pl	45 F5	Montgomery St La	40 D6	Nicolson St	37 E3	Paisley Ter	45 H2
Lixmount Gdns	40 B2	Marchhall Rd	45 F5	Montpelier	43 H5	Niddry St	37 D2	Palmerston Pl	36 A2
Loaning Mills	41 H6	Marchmont Cres	44 B5	Montpelier Pk	43 H5	Niddry St S 3	37 E3	Palmerston Pl La	36 A2
Loaning Rd	41 H6	Marchmont Rd	44 B5	Montpelier Ter	43 H5	Nightingale Way	36 C4	Palmerston Rd	44 C5
Lochend Av	41 G6	Marchmont St	44 B5	Montrose Ter	37 F1	Nisbet Ct	41 G5	Panmure Pl	36 C4
Lochend Castle		March Pines	38 A6	Moray Pk	45 F1	Noble Pl	41 G4	Papermill Wynd	40 D5
Barns	41 G6	March Rd	38 A6	Moray Pk Ter	45 F1	North Bk St	37 D2	Pape's Cotts	43 E3
Lochend Cl	37 F2	Mardale Cres	43 H6	Moray Pl	36 B1	North Br	37 D2	Park Pl	40 B2
Lochend Cres	41 H6	Marine Dr	38 B2	Morningside Rd	43 H6	North Br Arc 10	37 D2	Park Rd	40 B2
Lochend Dr	41 G6	Marine Esplanade	41 H3	Morrison Circ	36 A3	North Castle St	36 B1	Parkside St	37 F4
Lochend Gdns	41 G6	Marionville Av	41 G6	Morrison Cres	36 A3	North Charlotte St	36 B1	Parkside Ter	37 F4
Lochend Gro	41 H6	Marionville Cres	41 H6	Morrison Link	36 A3	North Clyde St La 1	37 D1	Parkvale Pl	41 G4
Lochend Ho	41 H6	Marionville Dr	41 H6	Morrison St	36 A3	Northcote St	43 G4	Parliament Sq	37 D2
Lochend Pk	41 H6	Marionville Gro	41 H6	Moston Ter	45 E6	North E Circ Pl	36 B1	Parliament St	41 E3
Lochend Quad	41 H6	Marionville		Mound, The	36 C2	North Fort St	40 D2	Parsons Grn Ter 2	45 H1
Lochend Rd	41 G5	Medway 1	41 H6	Mound Pl	36 C2	North Hillhousefield	40 D2	Patrick Geddes	
Lochend Rd S	41 G6	Marionville Pk	41 H6	Mount Gra	44 B6	North Junct St	40 D2	Steps 14	36 C3
Lochend Sq	41 G6	Marionville Rd	45 F1	Muirdale Ter 1	38 C6	North Leith Mill 4	40 D2	Patriothall 3	40 A6
Lochinvar Pl	39 G1	Marischal Pl 1	42 D1	Muirhouse Av	38 C4	North Leith Sands	40 D2	Pattison St	41 F3
Lochrin Bldgs	36 B4	Maritime La	41 F3	Muirhouse Av N	38 C3	North Meadow Wk	36 C4	Peacock Ct	40 C1
Lochrin Pl	36 B4	Maritime St	41 F3	Muirhouse Bk	38 B4	North Pk Ter	39 H6	Peel Ter	45 E6
Lochrin Ter 3	36 B4	Market St	37 D2	Muirhouse Cl	38 B3	North Richmond		Peffermill Ind Est	45 H6
Loch Rd	38 B6	Marshall's Ct 3	37 E1	Muirhouse Cres	38 C3	St 1	37 E3	Pembroke Pl	43 F3
Lochview Ct	37 F2	Marshall St 2	37 E3	Muirhouse Ct	38 B3	North St. Andrew La	37 D1	Pennywell Cotts	38 C2
Loganlea Dr	45 H1	Martello Ct	38 B3	Muirhouse Dr	38 B3	North St. Andrew St	37 D1	Pennywell Ct	38 C3
Loganlea Gdns	41 H6	Maryfield	37 F1	Muirhouse Gdns	38 B3	North St. David St	37 D1	Pennywell Gdns	38 B3
Logan St	40 B6	Maryfield Pl	45 F1	Muirhouse Grn	38 C4	Northumberland		Pennywell Gro	38 C3
Logie Grn Gdns	40 B5	Mary's Pl 1	39 H6	Muirhouse Ln	38 C3	Pl 2	36 C1	Pennywell Medway	38 B3
Logie Grn Ln	40 B5	May Ct	38 B3	Muirhouse Ln	38 C3	Northumberland Pl		Pennywell Pl	38 C3
Logie Grn Rd	40 B5	Mayfield Gdns	45 E6	Muirhouse Medway	38 B3	La	36 C1	Pennywell Rd	38 C3
Logie Mill	40 B5	Mayfield Gdns La	45 E6	Muirhouse Pk	38 B4	Northumberland St	36 C1	Pennywell Vil	38 D2
Lomond Rd	40 A2	Mayfield Rd	45 E6	Muirhouse Parkway	38 C3	Northumberland		Persevere Ct	41 E2
London Rd	37 E1	Mayfield Ter	45 E6	Muirhouse Pl E	38 C4	N E La	36 C1	Perth St	40 A6
London St	40 C6	Mayville Gdns	40 B2	Muirhouse Pl W	38 C4	Northumberland Gdns		Picardy Pl	37 E1
Long Craig Rigg	38 D1	Mayville Gdns E	40 B2	Muirhouse Ter	38 B4	N W La	36 C1	Pier Pl	40 B1
Long Craig Rd	38 D1	Meadowbank	45 G1	Muirhouse Vw	38 B3	Northumberland		Piershill La 3	45 H1
Lonsdale Ter	36 C4	Meadowbank Av	45 G1	Muirhouse Way	38 C4	S E La	36 C1	Piershill Pl 4	45 H1
Lord Russell Pl 1	44 D5	Meadowbank Cres	45 G1	Mulberry Pl 1	40 C3	Northumberland St		Piershill Sq W	45 H1
Lorne Pl	41 E5	Meadowbank Pl 7	45 H1	Multrees Wk	37 D1	S W La	36 C1	Pilrig Cotts	41 E5
Lorne Sq	41 E5	Meadowbank Ter	45 G1	Munro Pl 1	40 B5	Northview Ct	38 C3	Pilrig Gdns	40 D4
Lorne St	41 E5	Meadow La	37 D4	Murano Pl	41 E6	North Werber Pk	39 F5	Pilrig Glebe	41 E5
Lothian Rd	36 B2	Meadow Pl	36 C4	Murdoch Ter	36 A4	North Werber Pl	39 F5	Pilrig Ho Cl	40 D4
Lothian St	37 D3	Meadow Pl La	44 C5	Murieston Cres	43 F4	North Werber Rd	39 F5	Pilrig Ind Est	40 D4
Lovers' La	44 C5	Melbourne Pl 7	37 D2	Murieston Cres La 2	43 G4	North W Circ Pl	36 B1	Pilrig Pl	41 E5
Lower Gilmore Pl	36 A4	Melgund Ter	40 C6	Murieston La	43 F4	Norton Pk	41 F6	Pilrig St	40 D4
Lower Granton Rd	39 G1	Melville Cres	36 A2	Murieston Pl	43 F4			Pilton Av	39 E3
Lower London Rd	45 F1	Melville Dr	36 C4	Murieston Rd	43 F4	**O**		Pilton Cres	39 G3
Lufra Bk	39 H2	Melville Pl 6	36 A2	Murieston Ter	43 F4	Oakfield Pl	37 E3	Pilton Dr	39 F3
Lutton Pl	37 E4	Melville St	36 A2	Murrayfield Av	43 E3	Oakville Ter	41 G4	Pilton Dr N	39 F2
Lynedoch Pl	36 A2	Melville St La	36 A2	Murrayfield Dr	42 D3	Ocean Dr	40 D2	Pilton Gdns	39 F3
Lynedoch Pl La	36 A2	Melville Ter	44 C5	Murrayfield Gdns	43 E2	Ocean Way	41 F2	Pilton Ln	39 F3
Lyne St	45 F1	Mentone Gdns	45 E6	Murrayfield Pl 1	43 E3	Ogilvie Ter	43 F6	Pilton Pk	39 F3
		Merchant St	37 D3	Murrayfield Rd	42 D2	Old Assembly Cl 9	37 D2	Pilton Pl	39 F3
M		Merchiston Av	43 H5	Myrtle Ter	43 F5	Old Broughton 2	40 C6	Pinkhill	42 A4
McDonald Pl	40 C5	Merchiston Bk Av	43 H6			Old Ch La		Pinkhill Pk	42 A4
McDonald Rd	40 C5	Merchiston Bk Gdns	43 H6	**N**		Old Fishmarket Cl	37 D2	Pirniefield Bk	41 H4
McDonald St	40 D5	Merchiston Cres	43 H6	Napier Ln	43 G6	Old Tolbooth Wynd	37 E2	Pirniefield Gdns	41 H4
McKelvie Rd	40 A1	Merchiston Gro	43 F5	Napier Rd	43 G6	Orchard Bk	43 F1	Pirniefield Gro	41 H4
Mackenzie Pl	36 B1	Merchiston Ms	43 H5	Nelson Pl 1	36 C1	Orchard Brae	39 G6	Pirniefield Pl	41 H4
McLaren Rd	45 F6	Merchiston Pk	43 H6	Nelson St	36 C1	Orchard Brae Av	43 F1	Pirniefield Ter	41 H4
McLaren Ter 11	36 A3	Merchiston Pl	43 G5	Nether Bakehouse 9	37 F2	Orchard Brae Gdns	43 F1	Pirrie St	41 E4
McLeod St	43 F4	Mertoun Pl	43 G5	Netherby Rd	39 H3	Orchard Brae		Pitlochry Pl	41 F6
McNeill St	36 A4	Meuse La	37 D2	Nether Craigwell	37 F1	Gdns W	43 F1	Pitsligo Rd	44 A6
Madeira Pl	40 D3	Middleby St	45 E6	New Arthur Pl	37 E3	Orchard Brae W	39 G6	Pitt St	40 C3
Madeira St	40 D2	Middlefield	40 D5	New Arthur St 5	37 E3	Orchard Cres	43 E1	Playfair Steps 1	36 C2
Magdala Cres	43 G3	Middle Meadow Wk	37 D4	Newbattle Ter	44 A6	Orchard Dr	43 E1	Pleasance	37 E3
Magdala Ms	43 G3	Middle Pier	39 G1	New Bells Ct 4	41 F3	Orchardfield La	41 E5	Pollard Glebe	42 B6
Maidencraig Ct	38 D6	Mid Gillsland Rd	43 G6	New Broompark	39 F1	Orchard Gro	39 G6	Polwarth Cres	43 H5
Maidencraig Cres	38 D6	Millerfield Pl	44 C5	New Broughton	40 C6	Orchard Pl	39 F6		
		Miller Row	36 A2						

Name	Ref	Name	Ref	Name	Ref	Name	Ref	Name	Ref
Polwarth Gdns	43 G5	Ravelston Dykes La	42 B2	Rosevale Ter	41 F4	Salamander Yards	41 H4	Silverknowes Dr	38 A4
Polwarth Gro	43 G6	Ravelston Dykes Rd	42 C1	Roseville Gdns	40 B2	Salisbury Ms	45 E5	Silverknowes	
Polwarth Pk	43 G5	Ravelston Gdn	42 D2	Rossie Pl	41 E6	Salisbury Pl	44 D5	Eastway	38 A4
Polwarth Pl	43 G5	Ravelston Hts	42 C1	Rosslyn Cres	40 D5	Salisbury Rd	45 E5	Silverknowes Gdns	38 A3
Polwarth Ter	43 G6	Ravelston Ho Gro	42 D1	Rosslyn Ter	40 D5	Salmond Pl	45 F1	Silverknowes Grn	38 B4
Ponton St	36 B4	Ravelston Ho Ln	42 D1	Rothesay Ms	43 G2	Saltire Sq	39 E1	Silverknowes Gro	38 A3
Poplar La	41 F3	Ravelston Ho Pk	42 D1	Rothesay Pl	43 G2	Saltire St	39 E1	Silverknowes Hill	38 A4
Porterfield Rd	39 F5	Ravelston Ho Rd	42 D1	Rothesay Ter	43 G2	Salvesen Cres	38 B2	Silverknowes	
Portgower Pl	39 H6	Ravelston Pk	43 F2	Roxburgh Pl	37 E3	Salvesen Gdns	38 C2	Midway	38 B4
Port Hamilton	36 B3	Ravelston Pl 4	43 G2	Roxburgh St	37 E3	Salvesen Gro	38 C2	Silverknowes Neuk	38 B5
Portland Gdns	40 D2	Ravelston Ri	42 D2	Royal Circ	36 B1	Salvesen Ter	38 C2	Silverknowes	
Portland Row	40 D2	Ravelston Ter	43 G1	Royal Cres	40 B6			Parkway	38 A3
Portland St	40 D2	Redbraes Gro	40 C4	Royal Pk Pl	45 G1	Sand Port	41 F2	Silverknowes Pl	38 A3
Portland Ter 3	40 D2	Redbraes Pl	40 C4	Royal Pk Ter	45 G1	Sandpiper Rd	40 C1	Silverknowes Rd	38 A4
Portsburgh Sq 5	36 C3	Reekie's Ct	37 E3	Royal Ter	37 E1	Sandport Pl	41 E2	Silverknowes Rd E	38 A4
Potterrow	37 D3	Regent Br 2	37 D1	Royal Ter Ms	37 F1	Sandport St	41 E2	Silverknowes Rd S	38 A5
Powderhall Brae	40 C4	Regent Pl	45 F1	Royston Mains Av	39 E2	Sandport Way	41 E3	Silverknowes	
Powderhall Rigg	40 C4	Regent Rd	37 D1	Royston Mains Cl	39 F2	Sauchiebank	43 F4	Southway	38 B4
Powderhall Rd	40 C5	Regent's Ct 1	43 G4	Royston Mains Cres	39 E2	Saughton Av	42 D5	Silverknowes Vw	38 B4
Prestonfield Av	45 F6	Regent Ter	37 F1	Royston Mains Gdns	39 F2	Saughton Cres	42 C4	Silvermills	40 A6
Prestonfield Bk	45 F6	Regent Ter Ms	37 F1	Royston Mains Grn	39 F2	Saughton Gdns	42 C4	Simon Sq 4	37 E3
Prestonfield Cres	45 F6	Register Pl	37 D1	Royston Mains Pl	39 E2	Saughton Gro	42 C4	Simpson Ln	36 C4
Prestonfield Gdns	45 F6	Reid's Cl	37 D2	Royston Mains Rd	39 F2	Saughtonhall Av	42 C4	Sinclair Cl 2	43 F6
Prestonfield Rd	45 F6	Reid's Ct 1	37 F2	Royston Mains St	39 E2	Saughtonhall Av W	42 C4	Sinclair Gdns	43 F5
Prestonfield Ter	45 F6	Reid Ter	39 H6	Royston Ter	40 A4	Saughtonhall Circ	42 D4	Sinclair Pl	43 E5
Priestfield Av	45 G6	Rennie's Isle	41 E2	Russell Gdns	43 F3	Saughtonhall Cres	42 C4	Slateford Gait	43 E6
Priestfield Cres	45 G6	Restalrig Av	45 H1	Russell Pl	40 A2	Saughtonhall Dr	42 C3	Slateford Grn	43 E5
Priestfield Gdns	45 G6	Restalrig Circ	41 H5	Russell Rd	43 F3	Saughtonhall Gdns	42 D4	Slateford Rd	43 F6
Priestfield Gro	45 F5	Restalrig Cres	41 H5	Rutland Ct 2	36 B3	Saughtonhall Gro	42 D4	Slateford Rd Br	43 F6
Priestfield Rd	45 F6	Restalrig Dr	41 H6	Rutland Ct La	36 B3	Saughtonhall Pl	42 C4	Slater's Steps 6	37 F2
Priestfield Rd N	45 F5	Restalrig Gdns	41 H6	Rutland Pl 1	36 B2	Saughtonhall Ter	42 D4	Sleigh Dr	41 G6
Primrose Bk Rd	40 A2	Restalrig Ho	41 H6	Rutland Sq	36 B2	Saughton Ln	42 C4	Sleigh Gdns	41 H6
Primrose St	41 F4	Restalrig Pk	41 G5	Rutland St	36 B2	Saughton Mains Av	42 A6	Sloan St	41 E5
Primrose Ter	43 F5	Restalrig Rd	41 G4	Ryehill Av	41 G4	Saughton Mains Bk	42 A6	Smithfield St	43 E5
Prince of Wales		Restalrig Rd S	45 H1	Ryehill Gdns	41 G4	Saughton Mains		Smith's Pl	41 E4
Dock	41 E1	Restalrig Sq	41 H5	Ryehill Gro	41 G5	Ind Est	42 A6	Solicitor's Bldgs 4	37 D3
Prince Regent St	40 D2	Restalrig Ter	41 F4	Ryehill Pl	41 G4	Saughton Mains Pk	42 A6	Somerset Pl	41 F4
Princes St	36 C2	Richmond La	37 E3	Ryehill Ter	41 G4	Saughton Mains St	42 A6	South Beechwood	42 B4
Prospect Bk Cres	41 G4	Richmond Pl	37 E3			Saughton Mains Ter	42 A6	South Br	37 D2
Prospect Bk Gdns	41 G4	Richmond Ter	36 A3	**S**		Saughton Pk	42 C4	South Charlotte St	36 B2
Prospect Bk Gro	41 H4	Riego St	36 B3			Saughton Rd	42 A6	South Clerk St	37 E4
Prospect Bk Pl	41 H4	Rillbank Cres	44 C5	St. Andrew Pl	41 F4	Saunders St	36 B1	South Coll St	37 D3
Prospect Bk Rd	41 G4	Rillbank Ter	44 C5	St. Andrew Sq	37 D1	Saxe-Coburg Pl	40 A6	South E Circ Pl 1	36 B1
Prospect Bk Ter	41 H4	Rintoul Pl	40 A6	St. Anthony La	41 E3	Saxe Coburg St	40 A6	South Ettrick Rd	43 G6
		Ritchie Pl	43 G5	St. Anthony Pl 5	41 E3	Saxe-Coburg Ter 4	40 A6	South Fort St	40 D3
Q		Riversdale Cres	42 D4	St. Anthony St 6	41 E3	Sciennes	44 D5	South Gayfield La	40 D6
		Riversdale Gro	42 C3	St. Bernard's Cres	36 A1	Sciennes Gdns	44 D5	South Gillsland Rd	43 G6
Quality St	38 A5	Riversdale Rd	42 C3	St. Bernard's Row	40 A6	Sciennes Hill Pl	44 D5	South Gray's Cl	37 E2
Quality St La	38 A5	Robb's Ln	42 D6	St. Catherine's Gdns	42 B4	Sciennes Ho Pl	44 D5	South Gray St	45 E6
Quarry Cl	37 E4	Robb's Ln Gro	42 D6	St. Catherine's Pl	44 D5	Sciennes Pl 2	44 D5	South Groathill Av	38 D6
Quayside Mills 3	41 E3	Robertson Av	43 E5	St. Clair Av	41 F5	Sciennes Rd	44 C5	South Lauder Rd	44 D6
Quayside St	41 E3	Robertson Gait	43 E6	St. Clair Pl	41 F5	Scone Gdns	45 H1	South Laverockbank	
Queen Charlotte La	41 F3	Robertson's Cl	37 E3	St. Clair Rd	41 F5	Scotland St	40 B6	Av	40 B2
Queen Charlotte St	41 F3	Robertson's Ct 2	37 F2	St. Clair St	41 F5	Seacot 1	41 H4	South Learmonth Av	43 G1
Queen's Av	38 C6	Rocheid Pk	39 G4	St. Colme St	36 B2	Seafield Av	41 H4	South Learmonth	
Queen's Av S	38 D6	Rocheid Path	40 A5	St. David's Pl 9	36 A3	Seafield Pl	41 H4	Gdns	43 G1
Queen's Cres	45 E6	Rochester Ter	43 H6	St. David's Ter 10	36 A3	Seafield Rd	41 H4	South Lorne Pl	41 E5
Queen's Dr	37 F2	Rodney Pl	40 B6	St. Giles' St	37 D2	Seaforth Dr	38 D6	South Meadow Wk	44 C5
Queensferry Rd	43 G1	Rodney St	40 B5	St. James' Pl	37 D1	Seaforth Ter	38 D6	South Oxford St	45 E5
Queensferry St	36 A2	Romero Pl	45 E5	St. James Sq	37 D1	Sealcarr St	39 F1	South Pk	40 B2
Queensferry St La	36 A2	Ronaldson's Wf	41 E3	St. John's Cres	42 A4	Seaport St 5	41 F3	South St. Andrew St	37 D1
Queensferry Ter	43 F1	Rope Wk	36 A4	St. John's Hill 9	37 E3	Semple St	36 B3	South St. David St	37 D1
Queen's Gdns	38 D6	Rosebank Cotts	36 A3	St. John St	37 E2	Seton Pl	44 D5	South Sloan St	41 E5
Queen's Pk Av	45 G1	Rosebank Gdns	39 H3	St. Leonard's Bk	37 F4	Shaftesbury Pk	43 F6	South Trinity Rd	40 A3
Queen's Pk Ct	45 H2	Rosebank Gro	39 H3	St. Leonard's Crag 1	37 F4	Shandon Cres	43 F6	Spencer Pl	40 A2
Queen's Rd	38 D6	Rosebank Rd	39 H3	St. Leonard's Hill	37 E4	Shandon Pl	43 F6	Spence St	45 E5
Queen St	36 C1	Rosebery Cres	43 G3	St. Leonard's La	37 E4	Shandon Rd	43 F6	Spey St	40 D5
Queen St Gdns E	36 C1	Rosebery Cres La	43 G3	St. Leonard's St	37 E4	Shandon St	43 F6	Spey St La	40 D5
Queen St Gdns W	36 C1	Roseburn Av	43 E3	St. Leonard's Ter	37 E4	Shandon Ter	43 F6	Spey Ter	40 D5
Quilts, The	40 D3	Roseburn Cliff	43 F3	St. Margaret's Pl	44 B6	Shandwick Pl	36 A3	Spier's Pl 7	41 E3
Quilts Wynd	40 D3	Roseburn Cres	43 E4	St. Margaret's Rd	44 A6	Shaw's Pl	40 D5	Spittalfield Cres	37 E4
		Roseburn Dr	43 E3	St. Mary's St	37 E2	Shaw's Sq 2	40 D6	Spittal St	36 B3
R		Roseburn Gdns 2	43 E3	St. Ninian's Row 3	37 D1	Shaw's St	40 D5	Spittal St La 3	36 C3
		Roseburn Maltings	43 F3	St. Patrick Sq	37 E3	Shaw's Ter	40 D5	Spottiswoode Rd	44 B5
Raeburn Ms	39 H6	Roseburn Pl	43 E4	St. Patrick St 3	37 E4	Sheriff Bk	41 E3	Spottiswoode St	44 B5
Raeburn Pl	39 H6	Roseburn St	43 E4	St. Peter's Bldgs	36 A4	Sheriff Brae	41 E3	Springfield	40 D4
Raeburn St	39 H6	Roseburn Ter	43 E3	St. Peter's Pl	36 A4	Sheriff Pk	41 E3	Springfield Bldgs 3	41 E4
Ramsay Gdn	36 C2	Rosemount Bldgs	36 A3	St. Stephen Pl	40 A6	Shore	41 F3	Springfield La	41 E4
Ramsay La	36 C2	Roseneath Pl	44 B5	St. Stephen St	40 A6	Shore Pl	41 F3	Springfield St	41 E4
Randolph Cliff	36 A2	Roseneath St	44 C5	St. Teresa Pl	43 G6	Shrub Pl	40 D5	Spring Gdns	45 F1
Randolph Cres	36 A2	Roseneath Ter	44 C5	St. Thomas Rd	44 C6	Shrub Pl La	40 D5	Springwell Pl	43 F4
Randolph La	36 B2	Rose Pk	40 A3	St. Triduana's Rest	41 H6	Sienna Gdns	44 D5	Spylaw Rd	43 G6
Randolph Pl	36 B2	Rose St	36 B2	St. Vincent Pl	40 A6	Silverknowes Bk	38 A4	Stafford St	36 A2
Rankeillor St	37 E4	Rose St N La	36 B2	St. Vincent St	40 B6	Silverknowes Brae	38 A4	Stair Pk	42 D3
Ratcliffe Ter	44 D5	Rose St S La	36 B2	Salamander Ct	41 G3	Silverknowes Ct	38 A4	Stanhope Pl	43 F3
Ravelston Ct	43 E2	Rosevale Pl 1	41 G4	Salamander Pl	41 G3	Silverknowes Cres	38 A3	Stanhope St	43 F3
Ravelston Dykes	43 E2			Salamander St	41 F3	Silverknowes Dell	38 B4		

Stanley Pl 45 F1
Stanley Rd 40 B2
Stanwell St 40 D4
Stead's Pl 41 E4
Starbank Rd 40 B2
Stenhouse Av 42 B5
Stenhouse Av W 42 B6
Stenhouse Cotts 42 B6
Stenhouse Cres 42 B6
Stenhouse Cross 42 B6
Stenhouse Dr 42 B6
Stenhouse Gdns 42 B6
Stenhouse Gdns N 42 B6
Stenhouse Gro 42 B6
Stenhouse Pl E 42 B6
Stenhouse Pl W 42 B6
Stenhouse St E 42 B6
Stenhouse St W 42 A6
Stenhouse Ter 42 C6
Stevenlaw's Cl 37 D2
Stevenson Av 42 D5
Stevenson Dr 42 B6
Stevenson Gro 42 D5
Stevenson Rd 42 D5
Stevenson Ter 42 D5
Stewartfield 40 C4
Stewart Ter 43 E5
Stirling Rd 40 A2
Strachan Gdns 38 B6
Strachan Rd 42 C1
Strathearn Pl 44 A6
Strathearn Rd 44 B6
Succoth Av 43 E2
Succoth Ct 43 E2
Succoth Gdns 43 E2
Succoth Pk 42 D2
Succoth Pl 43 E2
Summerbank 40 B6
Summerfield Gdns 41 G4
Summerfield Pl 41 G4
Summerhall 4 44 D5
Summerhall Cres 4 37 E4
Summerhall Pl 5 44 D5
Summerhall Sq 44 D5
Summer Pl 40 B5
Summerside Pl 40 C3
Summerside St 40 C3
Sunbury Ms 43 G2
Sunbury Pl 43 G2
Sunbury St 43 G2
Sunnybank 45 G1
Sunnybank Pl 45 G1
Sunnybank Ter 4 45 F1
Sunnyside 41 F6
Surrey Pl 2 43 F3
Sutherland St 43 F3
Swanfield 41 E3
Sylvan Pl 44 C5

T
Tanfield 40 B5
Tantallon Pl 44 D5
Tarvit St 36 B4
Taylor Gdns 41 E3
Taylor Pl 45 F1
Tay St 43 G5
Telfer Sub 43 G4
Telford Dr 39 E5
Telford Gdns 39 E5
Telford Gro 39 E4
Telford March 39 E5
Telford Pl 39 E5
Telford Rd 39 E6
Temple Pk Cres 43 G5
Tennant St 41 E4
Terrars Cft 37 F4
Teviotdale Pl 40 A6
Teviot Pl 37 D3
Thirlestane La 44 B6
Thirlestane Rd 44 B5
Thistle Ct 3 36 C1
Thistle Pl 36 A4
Thistle St 36 C1
Thistle St N E La 36 C1
Thistle St N W La 36 C1

Thistle St S E La 36 C1
Thistle St S W La 36 C1
Thomson's Ct 8 36 C1
Thorntreeside 41 F4
Thorntreeside Ind Est 41 F5
Thorntree St 41 F5
Thornville Ter 41 F5
Thornybauk 36 B3
Timber Bush 41 F2
Tinto Pl 40 D4
Tipperlinn Rd 43 H6
Tolbooth Wynd 41 E3
Torphichen Pl 36 A3
Torphichen St 36 A3
Tower Pl 41 F2
Tower St 41 F2
Tower St La 41 F2
Tower Wynd 41 F2
Townswomen's Guild Wk 37 D4
Trafalgar La 40 C3
Trafalgar St 40 D3
Traquair Pk E 42 A4
Trinity Cl 39 H3
Trinity Cres 40 A1
Trinity Gro 40 A2
Trinity Mains 40 A3
Trinity Rd 40 A2
Trinity Way 40 A3
Tron Sq 12 37 D2
Tynecastle La 43 F5
Tynecastle Ter 43 F5
Tytler Ct 45 F1
Tytler Gdns 37 F1

U
Ulster Cres 45 H2
Ulster Dr 45 H2
Union Pl 2 37 E1
Union St 40 C6
Upper Bow 8 37 D2
Upper Coltbridge Ter 43 E2
Upper Damside 43 G2
Upper Dean Ter 36 A1
Upper Gilmore Pl 36 B4
Upper Gilmore Ter 36 B4
Upper Gray St 44 D5
Upper Greenside La 7 37 E1
Upper Gro Pl 36 A4
Upper Hermitage 41 F4

V
Valleyfield St 36 B4
Vanburgh Pl 41 F4
Veitch's Sq 40 A6
Vennel 36 C3
Ventnor Pl 45 F6
Ventnor Ter 45 E6
Victoria Dock 41 E2
Victoria Pk Neuk 40 C3
Victoria Quay 41 E2
Victoria St 37 D3
Victoria Ter 9 36 C3
Viewcraig Gdns 37 E2
Viewcraig St 37 E2
Viewforth 36 A4
Viewforth Gdns 44 A5
Viewforth Sq 43 H5
Viewforth Ter 43 H5
Violet Ter 43 F5
Vivian Ter 38 A5

W
Walker St 36 A2
Walker Ter 6 36 A3
Warden's Cl 37 D3
Wardie Av 39 H3
Wardieburn Dr 39 G2
Wardieburn Pl E 39 G2
Wardieburn Pl N 39 G2
Wardieburn Pl S 39 G2

Wardieburn Pl W 39 F2
Wardieburn Rd 39 F2
Wardieburn St E 39 G2
Wardieburn St W 39 F2
Wardieburn Ter 39 F2
Wardie Cres 39 G2
Wardie Dell 39 H1
Wardiefield 39 G2
Wardie Gro 39 G2
Wardie Ho La 39 H1
Wardie Pk 39 H2
Wardie Rd 39 H3
Wardie Sq 39 H2
Wardie Steps 39 H2
Wardlaw Pl 43 F5
Wardlaw St 43 F5
Wardlaw Ter 43 F5
Warrender Pk Cres 44 A5
Warrender Pk Rd 44 B5
Warrender Pk Ter 44 B5
Warriston Av 40 B4
Warriston Cres 40 B5
Warriston Dr 40 A4
Warriston Gdns 40 A4
Warriston Gro 40 A4
Warriston Pl 40 B5
Warriston Rd 40 B3
Warriston's Cl 15 37 D2
Warriston Ter 40 A4
Washington La 43 G4
Washington St 43 G4
Waterfront Av 39 E1
Waterfront Bdy 39 E2
Waterfront Gait 38 C2
Waterfront Pk 38 D2
Waterloo Pl 37 D1
Water's Cl 6 41 F3
Water St 41 F3
Watson Cres 43 G5
Waverley Br 37 D2
Waverley Pk 45 F1
Waverley Pk Ter 45 F1
Waverley Pl 45 F1
Waverley St 37 D2
Websters Land 10 36 C3
Well Ct 4 36 A2
Wellington Pl 41 F3
Wellington St 41 E6
Wemyss Pl 36 B1
Wemyss Pl Ms 36 B1
Werberside Ms 39 F4
West Adam St 37 E3
West Annandale St 40 C5
West App Rd 36 B3
West Bow 37 D3
West Bowl Grn St 40 D3
West Bryson Rd 43 G5
West Castle Rd 43 H5
West Catherine Pl 43 F3
West Cherrybank 40 B2
West Coates 43 F3
West Coll St 37 D3
West Ct 42 D1
West Cromwell St 1 41 E2
West Crosscauseway 37 E4
West End 36 B2
West End Pl 43 G4
Wester Cl 3 40 C1
Wester Coates Av 43 F3
Wester Coates Gdns 43 F3
Wester Coates Pl 43 F2
Wester Coates Rd 43 F3
Wester Coates Ter 43 F3
Wester Drylaw Av 38 C5
Wester Drylaw Dr 38 B5
Wester Drylaw Pk 38 D5
Wester Drylaw Pl 38 C5
Wester Drylaw Row 38 D6
Western Cor 42 C3
Western Gdns 42 D3
Western Harbour 40 D1
Western Harbour Dr 40 C1
Western Pl 42 D3
Western Ter 42 D3
West Ferryfield 39 G3
Westfield Av 42 D5

Westfield Ct 42 D5
Westfield Rd 43 E5
Westfield St 43 E5
West Fountain Pl 43 G4
West Gorgie Pk 42 D6
West Gra Gdns 44 C6
West Granton Access 39 E2
West Granton Rd 39 F2
Westhall Gdns 44 A5
West Harbour Rd 39 F1
West Maitland St 36 A3
West Mayfield 45 E6
West Mill La 36 A2
West Montgomery Pl 40 D6
West Newington St 44 D5
West Nicolson St 37 E3
West Norton Pl 37 F1
West Pk Pl 43 G3
West Pier 39 F1
West Pilton Av 38 D4
West Pilton Bk 38 C3
West Pilton Brae 38 E3
West Pilton Cres 38 C3
West Pilton Crossway 38 D3
West Pilton Dr 38 D3
West Pilton Gdns 38 D3
West Pilton Grn 38 D3
West Pilton Gro 38 D3
West Pilton Lea 38 D3
West Pilton Ln 38 D3
West Pilton March 39 E3
West Pilton Pk 38 D3
West Pilton Pl 39 E3
West Pilton Ri 38 D3
West Pilton Rd 39 E3
West Pilton St 38 D3
West Pilton Ter 38 D3
West Pilton Vw 38 D4
West Pilton Way 39 E3
West Port 36 C3
West Preston St 44 D5
West Register St 37 D1
West Register St La 4 37 D1
West Richmond St 37 E3
West Scotland St La 40 B6
West Shore Business Cen 38 D1
West Shore Rd 38 C2
West Shore Rd Trd Est 38 D1
West Silvermills La 40 A6
West Stanhope Pl 1 43 F3
West Tollcross 36 B4
West Werberside 39 F4
West Winnelstrae 39 G4
West Wds 39 F5
Wheatfield Pl 43 E5
Wheatfield Rd 43 E5
Wheatfield St 43 F5
Wheatfield Ter 1 43 E5
Whitehall Ct 38 C6
White Horse Cl 37 F2
Whitehouse Ln 44 A5
Whitehouse Ter 44 B6
White Pk 43 F5
Whitingford 40 C3
Whitson Cres 42 C5
Whitson Gro 42 C5
Whitson Pl E 42 C5
Whitson Pl W 42 C5
Whitson Rd 42 C5
Whitson Ter 42 C5
Whitson Wk 42 B5
Whitson Way 42 C5
Whyte Pl 45 F1
Wilfrid Ter 5 45 H1
William St 36 A2
William St La N E 36 A2
William St La N W 36 A2
William St La S E 36 A2
William St La S W 36 A3
Willowbank Row 40 C2

Willowbrae Av 45 H2
Willowbrae Rd 45 H2
Wilson's Ct 3 37 E2
Windmill Cl 37 E4
Windmill La 37 D4
Windmill Pl 6 37 E4
Windmill St 37 D4
Windrush Dr 40 C1
Windsor St 40 D6
Windsor St La 40 D6
Wishaw Ter 45 G1
Wolseley Cres 45 H1
Wolseley Gdns 8 45 H1
Wolseley Pl 9 45 H1
Wolseley Ter 6 45 H1
Woodbine Ter 41 F5
Woodville Ter 41 F5
Wright's Hos 44 A5
Wyvern Pk 44 C6

Y
Yardheads 41 E3
Yeaman La 43 G4
Yeaman Pl 43 G4
York Bldgs 7 37 D1
York La 37 D1
York Pl 37 D1
York Rd 40 A2
Young St 36 B2
Young St La N 36 B2
Young St La S 36 B2

Z
Zetland Pl 40 A2

EDINBURGH

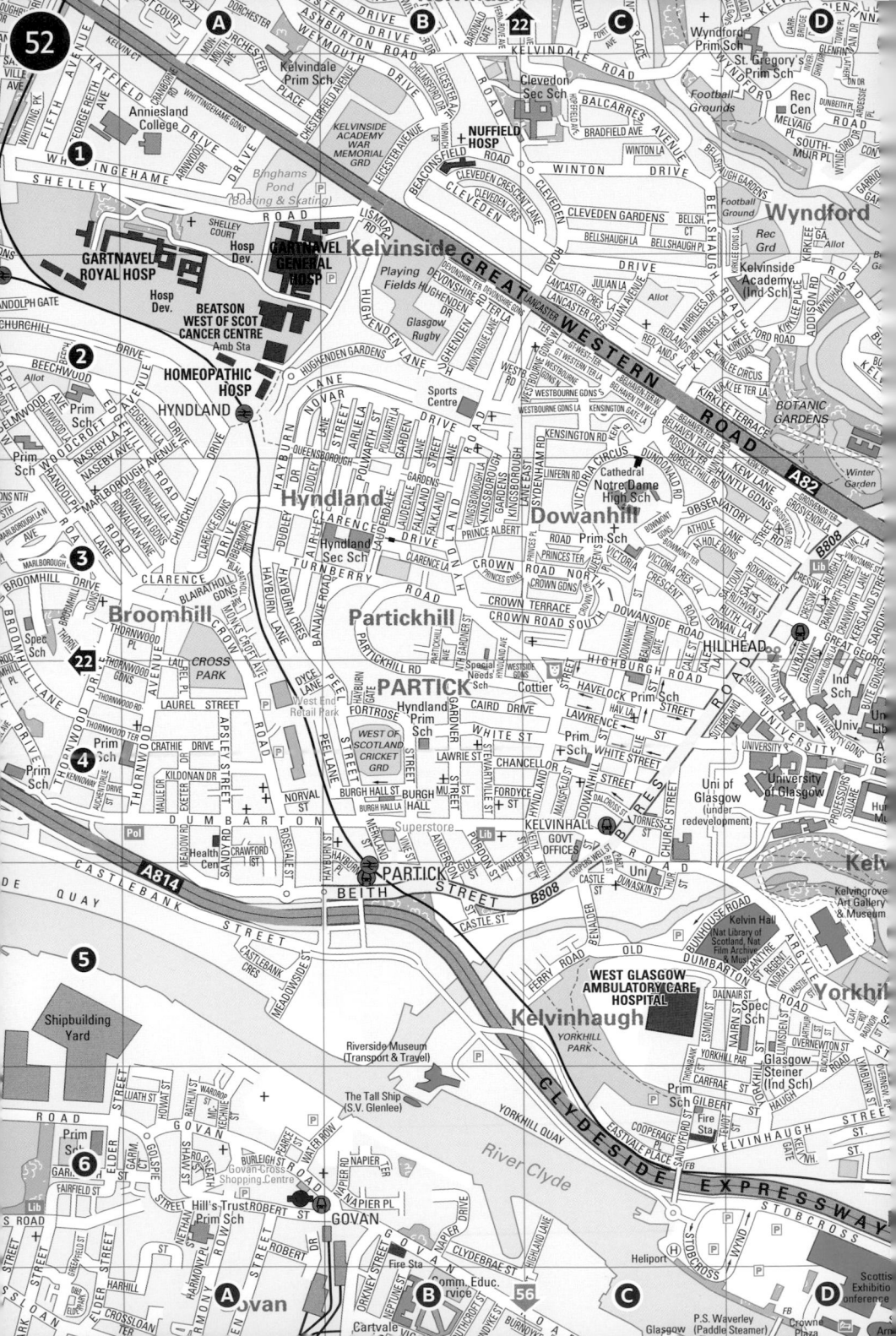

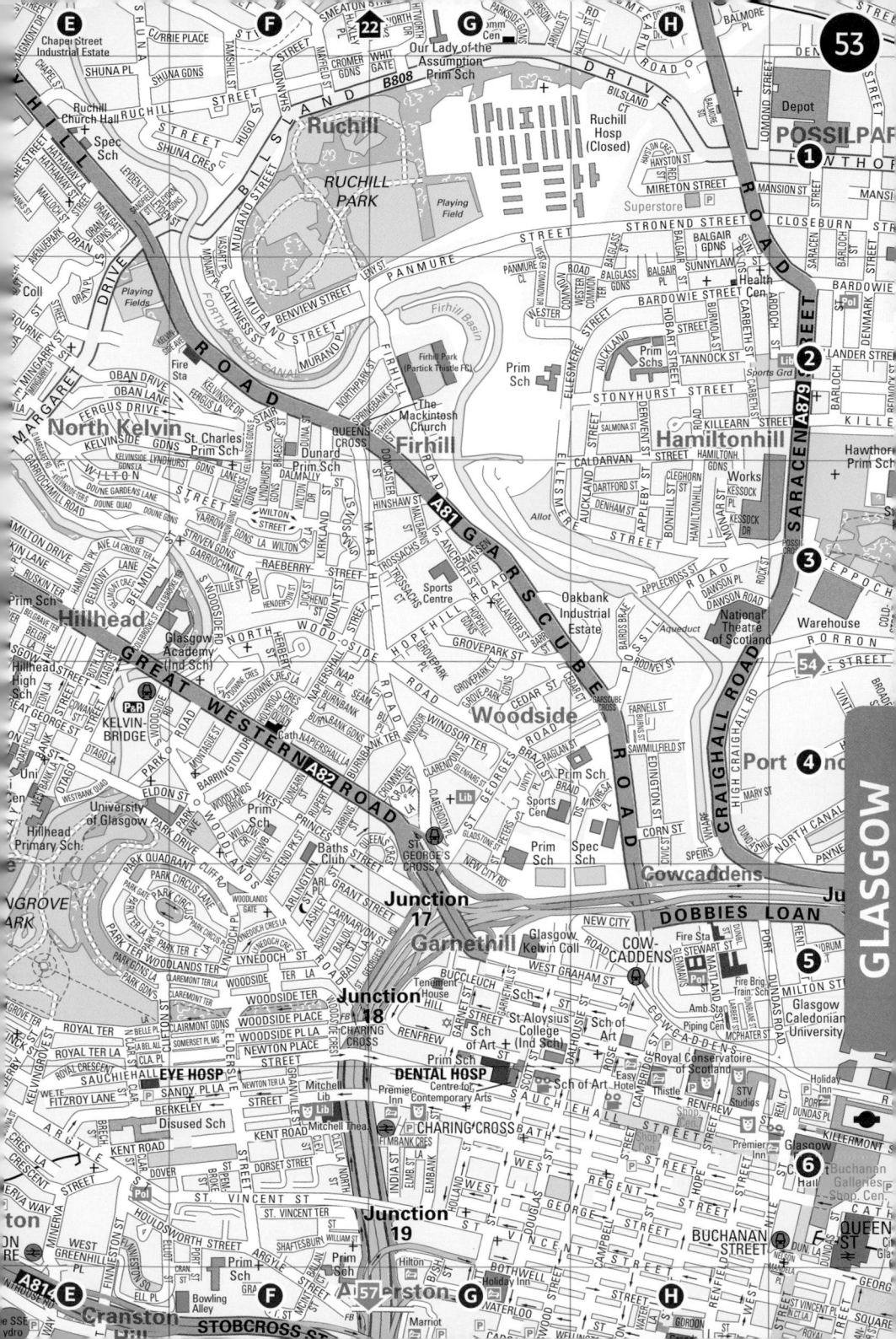

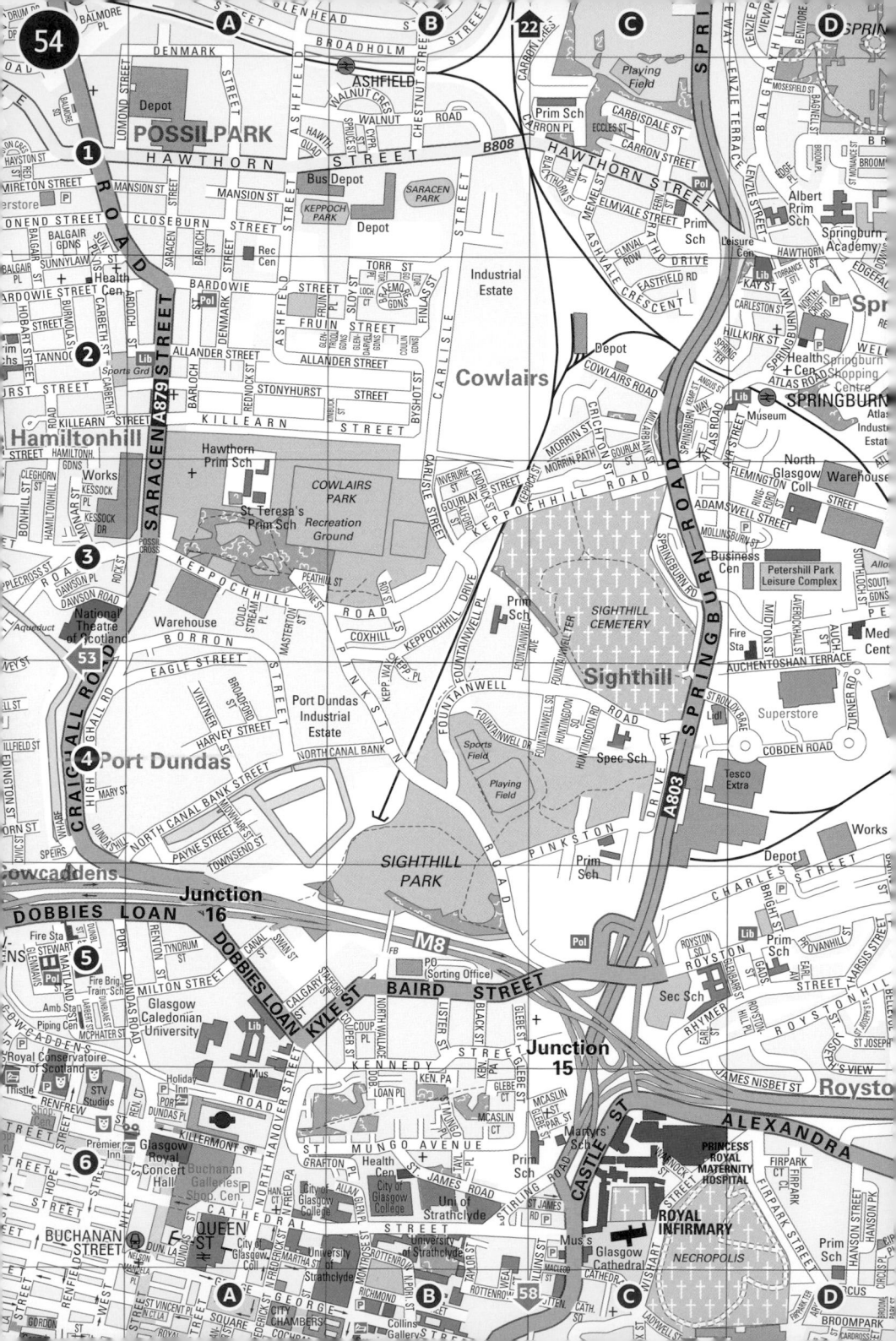

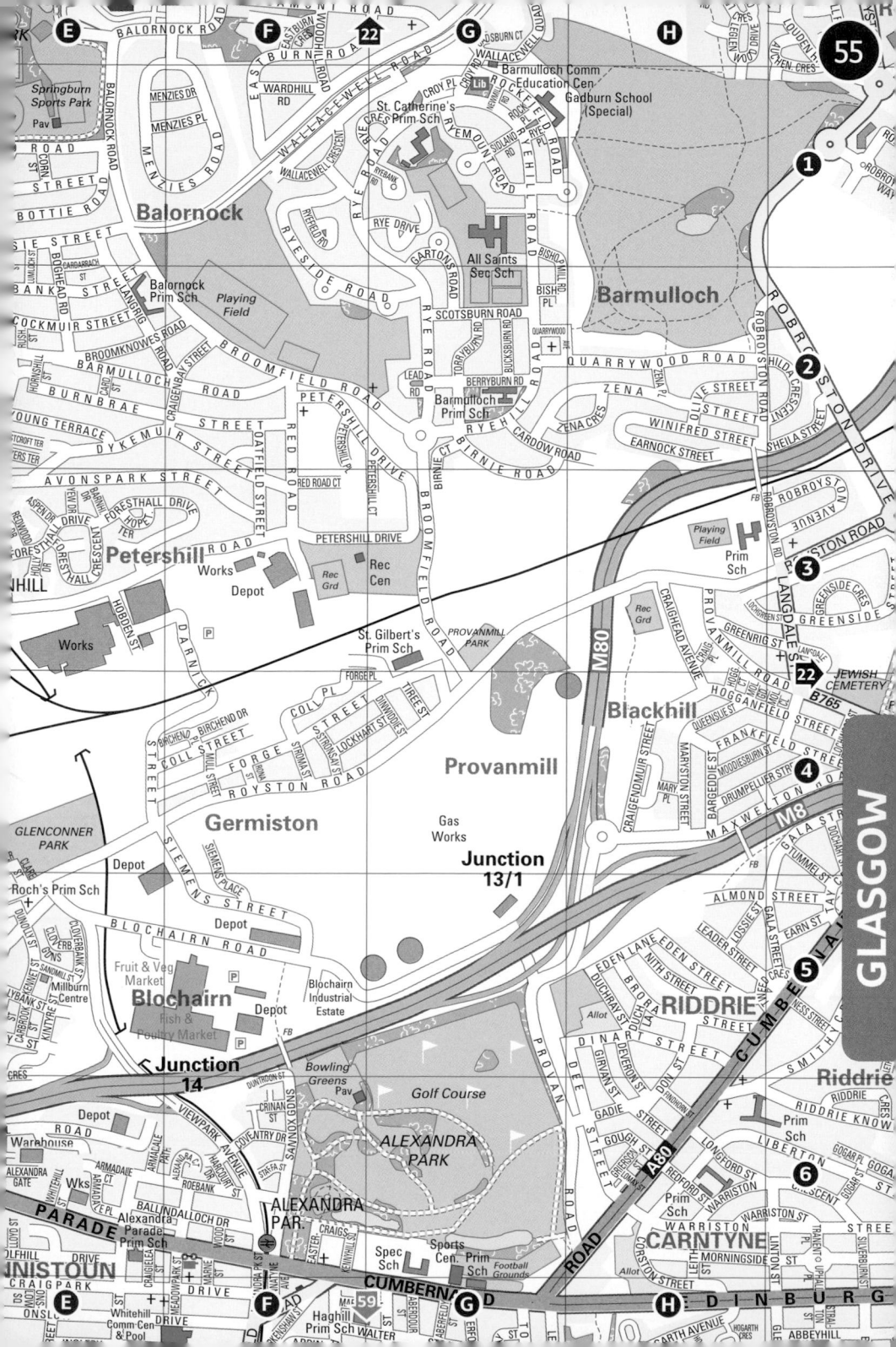

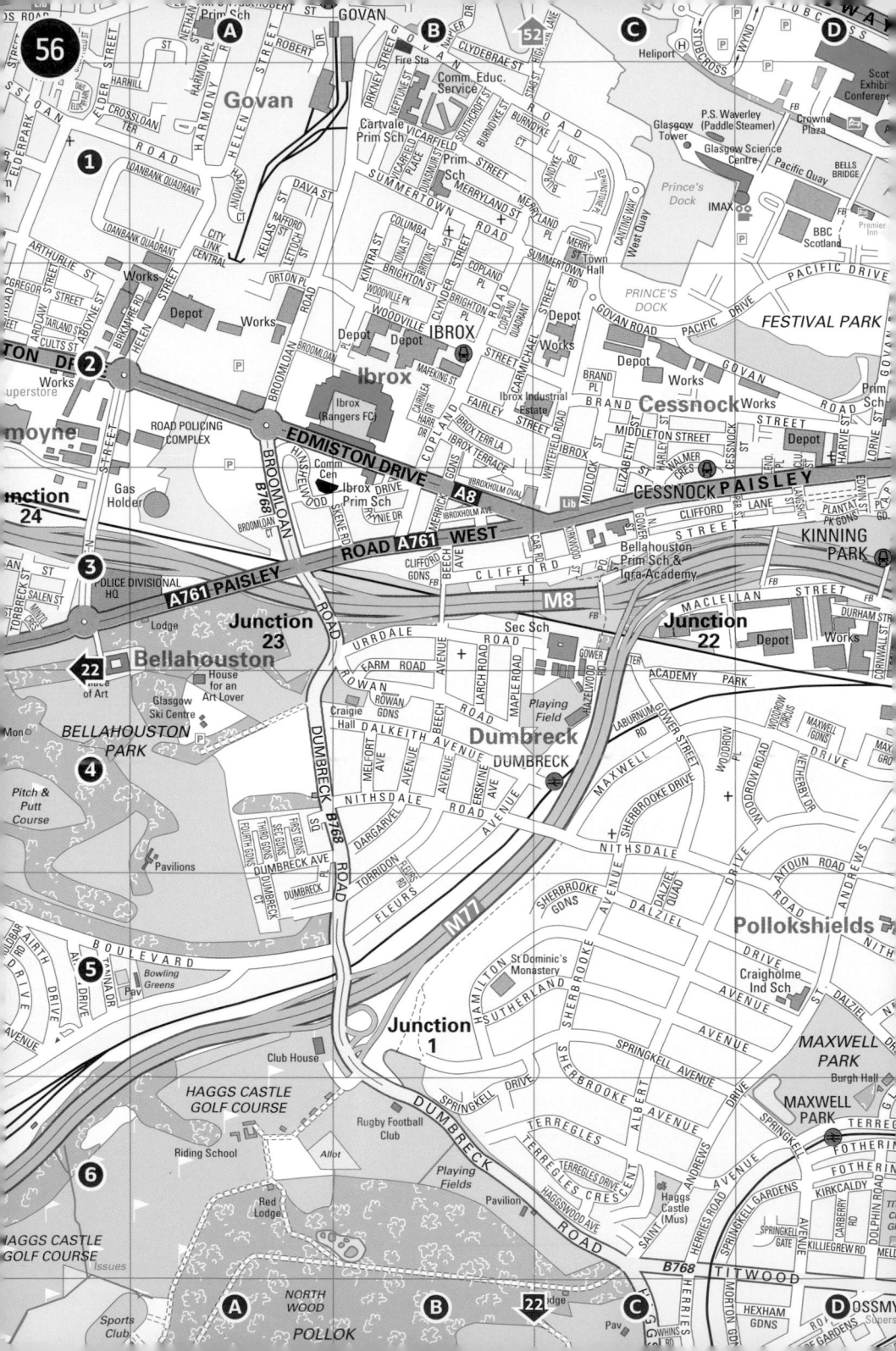

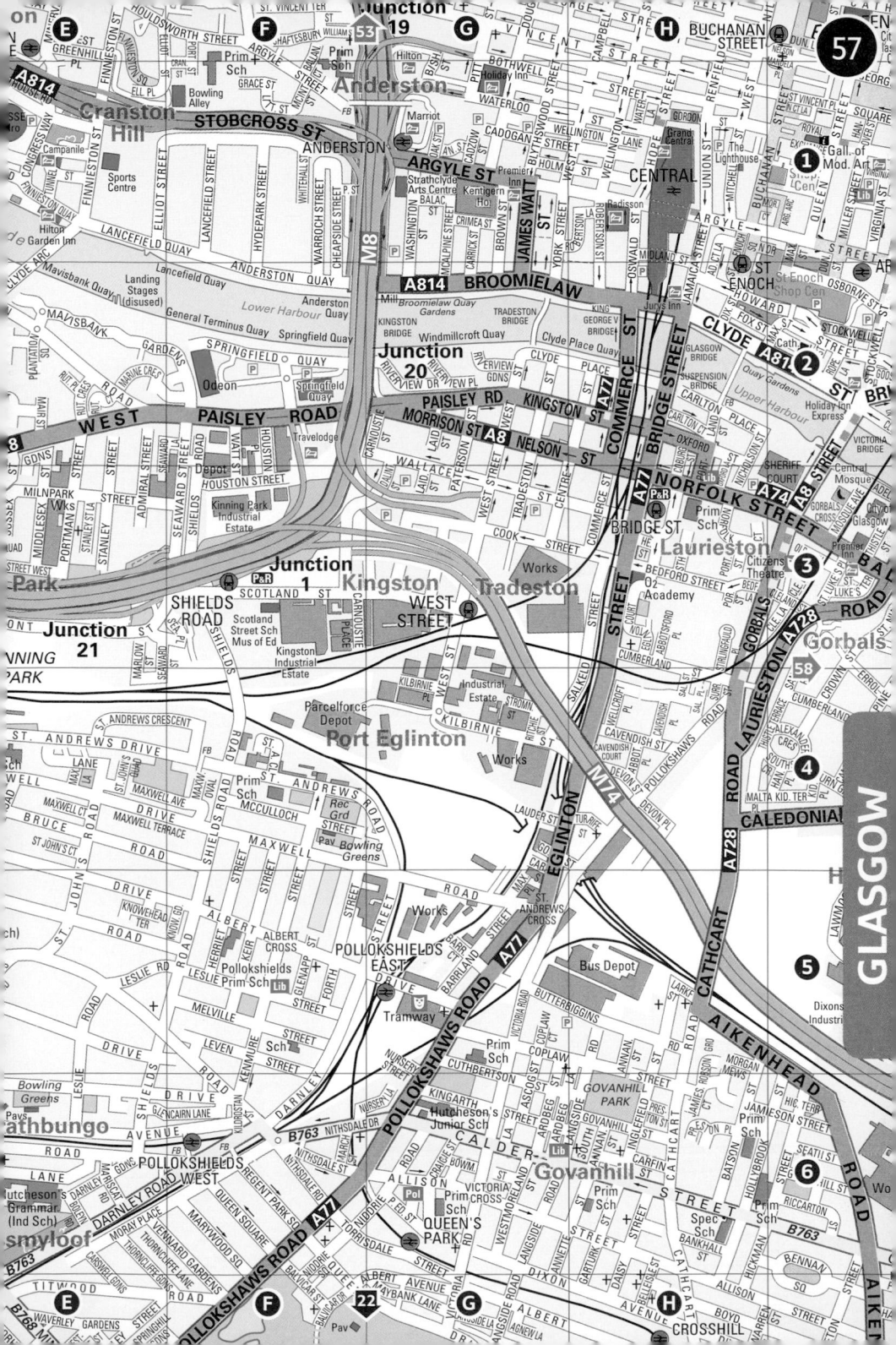

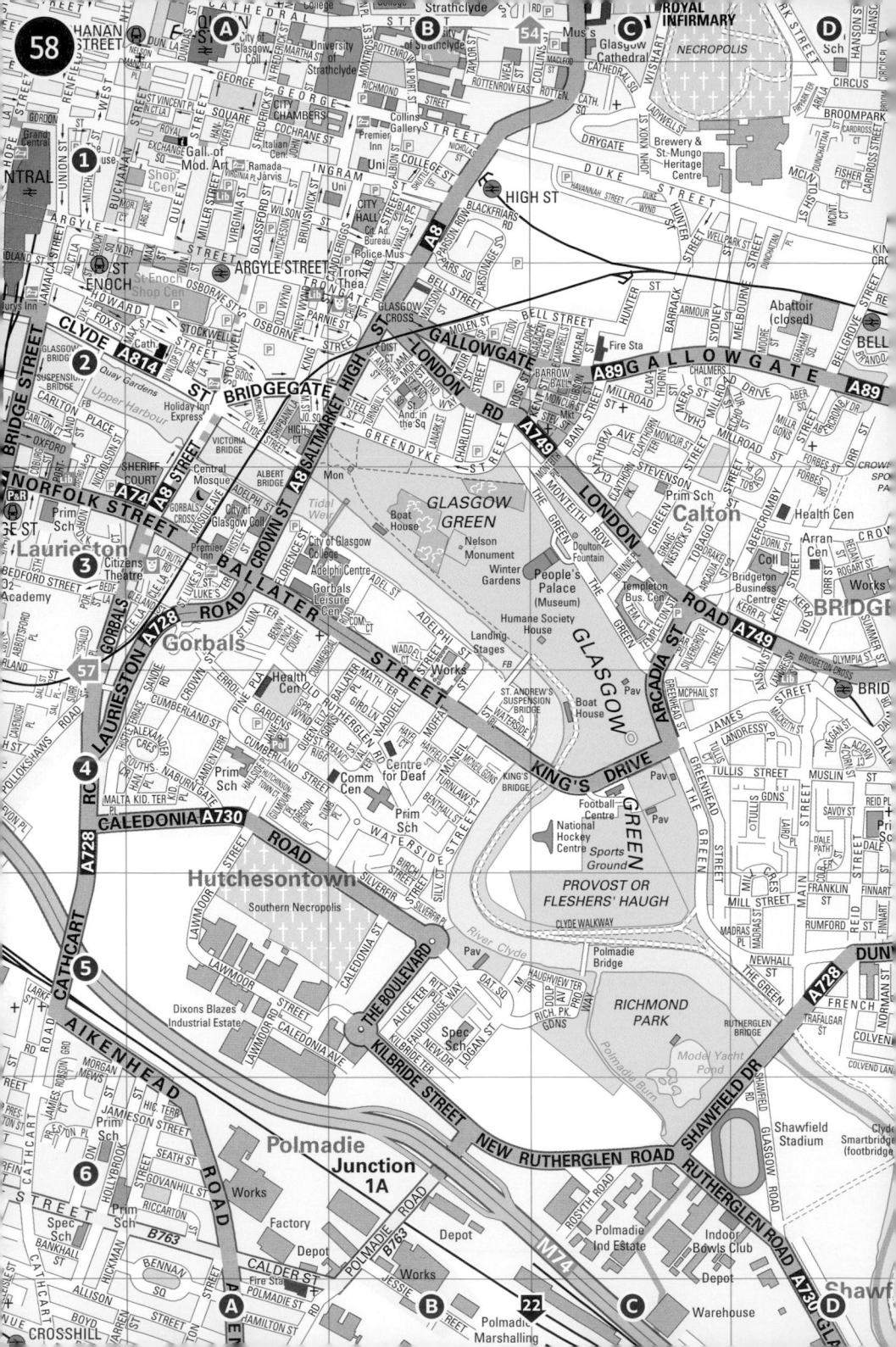

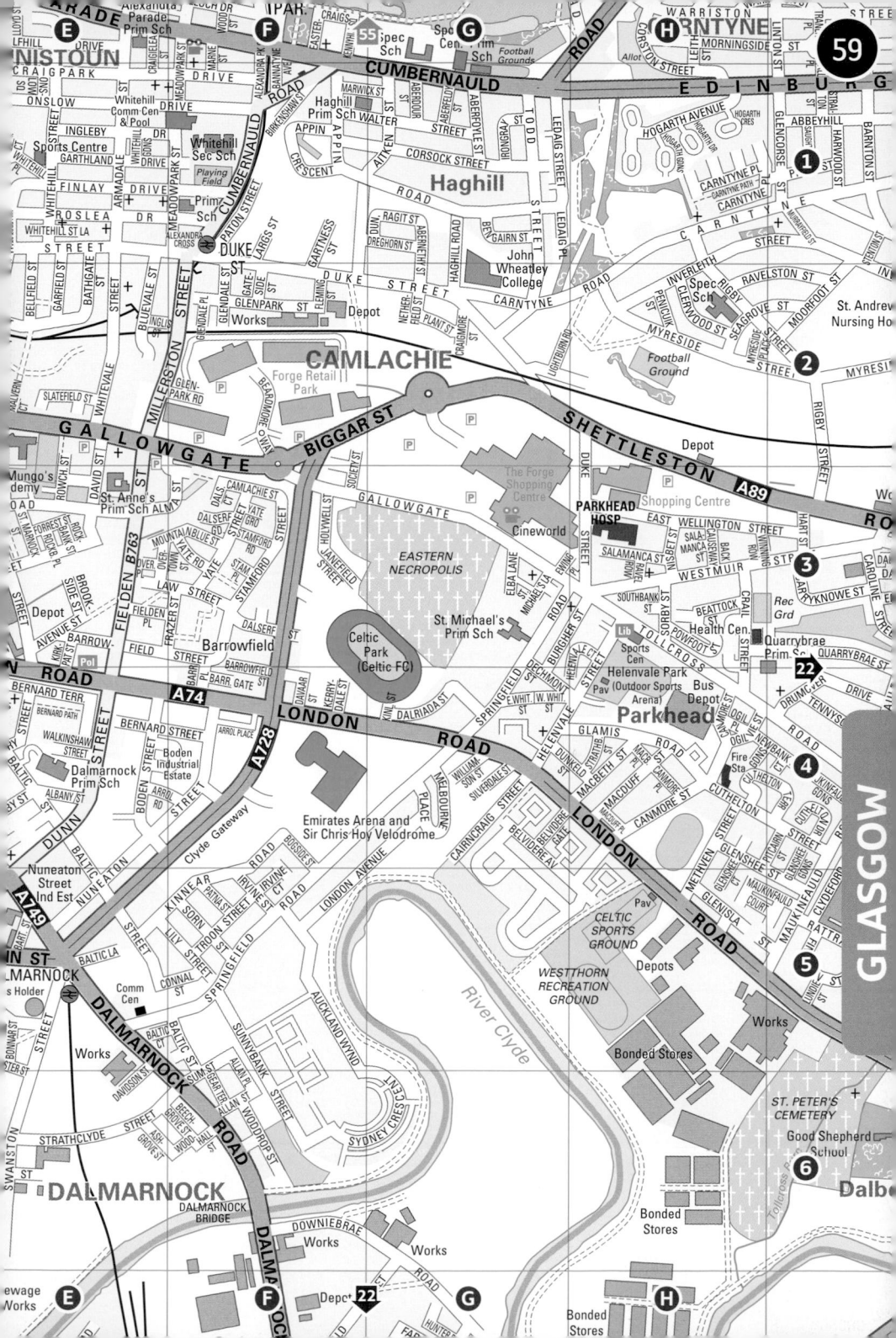

This index contains streets that are not named on the map due to insufficient space. For each of these cases the nearest street that does appear on the map is shown in *italics*.

A

Abbotsford Pl 57 H3
Abercromby Dr 58 D2
Abercromby Sq 58 D2
Abercromby St 58 D3
Aberdour St 59 G1
Aberfeldy St 59 G1
Aberfoyle St 59 G1
Abernethy St 56 C1
Academy Pk 56 C4
Acorn Ct 58 D4
Acorn St 58 D4
Adams Ct La 57 H2
Adamswell St 54 C3
Addison Rd 52 D2
Adelphi St 58 B3
Admiral St 57 E3
Aikenhead Rd 57 H5
Aird's La
  off Bridgegate 58 A2
Airlie La 52 B2
Airlie St 52 A3
Aitken St 59 G1
Albany St 59 E4
Albert Br 58 A3
Albert Cross 57 F5
Albert Dr 56 C6
Albion Gate
  off Albion St 58 B1
Albion St 58 B2
Alexander Cres 58 A4
Alexandra Ct 55 F6
Alexandra Cross 59 F1
Alexandra Par 54 C6
Alexandra Pk St 59 F1
Alford St 54 B3
Alfred La 52 D3
Alfred Ter 53 E3
Allander St 54 A2
Allan Glen Pl 54 B6
Allan Pl 59 F5
Allan St 59 F6
Allison Pl
  off Prince Edward St 57 G6
Allison St 57 G6
Alma St 59 E3
Almond St 55 H5
Alston La
  off Claythorn St 58 C2
Amisfield St 53 E1
Anchor La
  off St. Vincent Pl 58 A1
Ancroft St 53 G3
Anderson St 52 B4
Anderston Cross Cen 57 G1
Anderston Quay 57 F2
Angus St 54 C2
Annandale St 57 H5
Annbank Pl 58 D2
Annbank St 58 D2
Annette St 57 G6
Annfield Pl 58 D1
Anson St 58 D4
Anthony St 57 G1
Appin Cres 59 F1
Appin Rd 59 F1
Appleby St 53 H3
Applecross St 53 H3
Apsley La
  off Apsley St 52 A4
Apsley St 52 A4
Arcadia Pl 58 C3
Arcadia St 58 C3
Ardbeg La 57 G6
Ardbeg St 57 G6

Ardery St
  off Apsley St 52 A4
Ardessie Pl 52 D1
Ardoch St 54 A2
Ardo Gdns
  off Hinshelwood Dr 56 A3
Argyle St 57 G1
Argyll Arc 58 A1
Ark La 58 D1
Arlington Pl 53 F5
Arlington St 53 F5
Armadale Ct 55 E6
Armadale Path 55 E6
Armadale Pl 55 E6
Armadale St 59 E1
Armour St 58 C2
Arnwood Dr 52 A1
Arrol Pl 59 F4
Arrol Rd 59 E4
Arthur St 52 D5
Ascog St 57 G6
Ashfield St 54 A2
Ashgrove St 59 E6
Ashley La 53 F5
Ashley St 53 F5
Ashton La 52 D4
Ashton La N
  off Ashton La 52 D4
Ashton Rd 52 D4
Ashvale Cres 54 C1
Aspen Dr 55 E3
Athole Gdns 52 C3
Athole La 52 C3
Atlas Ind Est 54 D2
Atlas Pl 54 D3
Atlas Rd 54 C2
Atlas Sq
  off Ayr St 54 D2
Auchentoshan Ter 54 D4
Auchinloch St 54 D3
Auckland St 53 H3
Auckland Wynd 59 F5
Avenuepark St 53 E2
Avenue St 59 E3
Avonspark St 55 E3
Ayr St 54 C3
Aytoun Rd 56 D5

B

Back Causeway 59 H3
Bagnell St 54 D1
Bain Sq
  off Bain St 58 C2
Bain St 58 C2
Bairds Brae 53 H3
Baird St 54 B5
Balaclava St
  off McAlpine St 57 G1
Balcarres Av 52 C1
Balgair Pl 53 H2
Balgair St 53 H1
Balglass Gdns 53 H2
Balglass St 53 H2
Balgraybank St 54 D2
Balgrayhill Rd 54 D1
Baliol La 53 F5
Baliol St 53 F5
Ballantrae Ct 57 F1
Ballater Pl 58 B4
Ballater St 58 A3
Ballindalloch Dr 55 E6
Ballindarroch La
  off Armadale St 55 E6
Balmore Sq 53 H1
Balornock Rd 55 E1
Baltic Ct
  off Baltic St 59 E5
Baltic La 59 E5

Baltic Pl 59 E4
Baltic St 59 E4
Banavie La
  off Banavie Rd 52 B3
Banavie Rd 52 A3
Bankhall St 57 H6
Bank St 53 E4
Bannatyne Av 59 F1
Barbreck Rd
  off Pollokshaws Rd 57 G6
Barclay St
  off Lenzie St 54 D1
Bardowie St 53 H2
Bargeddie St 55 H4
Barloch St 54 A2
Barmulloch Rd 55 E2
Barnhill Dr
  off Foresthall Dr 55 E3
Barrack St 58 C2
Barrington Dr 53 F4
Barrland St 57 G5
Barrowfield St 59 E3
Barr St 53 G3
Bartholomew St 59 E5
Bathgate St 59 E2
Bath La
  off Wellington St 53 G6
Bath La W
  off North St 53 F6
Bath St 53 G6
Batson St 57 H6
Beaconsfield Rd 52 B1
Beardmore Way 59 F2
Beaton Rd 57 E6
Beattock St 59 H3
Beaumont Gate 52 C3
Bedford La 57 H3
Bedford St 57 H3
Beech Av 56 B3
Beechgrove St 59 F6
Beith St 52 B5
Belgrave La 53 E3
Belgrave Ter 53 E3
Belhaven Cres La
  off Kensington Rd 52 C2
Belhaven Ter 52 C2
Belhaven Ter La 52 C2
Belhaven Ter W 52 C2
Belhaven Ter W La 52 C2
Bellevue Pl 54 D5
Bellfield St 59 E2
Bellgrove St 58 D2
Bellshaugh Ct 52 C1
Bellshaugh Gdns 52 C1
Bellshaugh La 52 C1
Bellshaugh Pl 52 C1
Bellshaugh Rd 52 C1
Bell St 58 B2
Belmont Cres 53 E3
Belmont La 53 E3
Belmont St 53 E3
Beltane St
  off Dorset St 53 F6
Benalder St 52 C5
Bengairn St 59 G1
Bennan Sq 58 A6
Benny Lynch Ct 58 A3
Benthall St 58 B4
Bentinck St 53 E5
Benview St 53 F2
Berkeley St 53 E6
Berkeley Ter La
  off Elderslie St 53 F6
Bernard Path 59 E4
Bernard St 59 E4

Bernard Ter 59 E4
Berryburn Rd 55 G2
Biggar St 59 F2
Bilsland Ct 53 H1
Bilsland Dr 53 F1
Binnie Pl 58 C3
Birchend Dr 55 F4
Birchend Pl 55 E4
Birch St
  off Silverfir St 58 B5
Birkenshaw St 59 F1
Birkwood St
  off Dalmarnock Rd 59 F6
Birnam Rd
  off London Rd 59 H5
Birnie Ct 55 G3
Birnie Rd 55 G2
Bishopmill Pl 55 G2
Bishopmill Rd 55 G1
Bishop St 57 G1
Blackburn St 56 D2
Blackfriars Rd 58 B1
Blackie St 52 D6
Black St 54 B5
Blackthorn St 54 C1
Blairatholl Av 52 A3
Blairatholl Gdns 52 A3
Blantyre St 52 D5
Blochairn Rd 55 E5
Bluevale St 59 E2
Blythswood Ct
  off Cadogan St 57 G1
Blythswood Sq
  off Blythswood St 53 G6
Blythswood St 57 G1
Boden Ind Est 59 F4
Boden St 59 E4
Boghead Rd 55 E1
Bogside St 59 F4
Boleyn Rd 57 E6
Bonawe St
  off Kirkland St 53 F2
Bonhill St 53 H3
Bonnar St 59 E5
Borron St 54 A3
Botanic Cres 52 D2
Botanic Cres La 52 D2
Bothwell La
  off Blythswood St 57 G1
Bothwell St 53 G6
Boundary Rd
  off Rutherglen Rd 58 C6
Bower St 53 E3
Bowman St 57 G6
Bowmont Gdns 52 C3
Bowmont Ter 52 C3
Bradfield Av 52 C1
Braehead St 58 B5
Braemore Gdns 54 B2
Braeside St 53 F3
Braid Sq 53 G4
Braid St 53 G4
Brandon St 58 D2
Brand Pl 56 C2
Brand St 56 C2
Breadalbane St
  off St. Vincent St 53 F6
Brechin St 53 E6
Bridgegate 58 A2
Bridgegate Path
  off Bridgegate 58 A2
Bridge St 57 H2
Bridgeton Business Cen 58 D3
Bridgeton Cross 58 D3

Brighton Pl 56 B2
Brighton St 56 B2
Bright St 54 D5
Briton St 56 B2
Broadford St 54 A4
Broad St 58 D3
Brodick St 55 E5
Brookside St 59 E3
Brook St 58 D3
Broomfield La 54 D1
Broomfield Pl 54 D1
Broomfield Rd 54 D1
Broomielaw 57 G2
Broomknowes Rd 55 E2
Broomloan Ct 56 A3
Broomloan Pl 56 A2
Broomloan Rd 56 A2
Broompark Circ 54 D6
Broompark Dr 58 D1
Broompark La 58 D1
Broompark St 58 D1
Brora La
  off Brora St 55 H5
Brora St 55 H5
Brown St 57 G1
Bruce Rd 57 E4
Brunswick St 58 A1
Buccleuch La
  off Rose St 53 G5
Buccleuch St 53 G5
Buchanan St 57 H1
Buchan St
  off Norfolk St 57 H3
Buckingham St 52 D3
Buckingham Ter 52 D3
Bucksburn Rd 55 G2
Bunhouse Rd 52 C5
Burgher St 59 G3
Burgh Hall La 52 B4
Burgh Hall St 52 B4
Burgh La 52 D3
Burleigh St 52 A6
Burmola St 53 H2
Burnbank Gdns 53 F4
Burnbank La
  off Napiershall St 53 F4
Burnbank Pl
  off Drygate 58 C1
Burnbank Pl (Woodside)
  off Burnbank Ter 53 G4
Burnbank Ter 53 F4
Burnbrae St 55 E2
Burndyke Ct 56 C1
Burndyke Sq 56 C1
Burndyke St 56 B1
Burns St 53 H4
Burrells La 58 C1
Bute Gdns 52 D4
Bute La
  off Great George St 52 D4
Butterbiggins Rd 57 G5
Butterfield Pl
  off Pollokshaws Rd 57 G5
Byres Rd 52 C4
Byshot St 54 B2

C

Cadogan St 57 G1
Cadzow St 57 G1
Caird Dr 52 B4
Cairncraig St 59 G4
Cairnlea Dr 56 B2
Caithness St 53 F2
Caldarvan St 53 H3

Calder St	57 H6		Chapman St			Clouston Ct			Craigiehall St			Dalmarnock Br	59 F6
Caledonia Av	58 A5		*off Allison St*	57 G6		*off Fergus Dr*	53 E2		*off Craigiehall*			Dalmarnock Dr	58 D4
Caledonia Cres			Charing Cross	53 F5		Clouston La	53 E2		Pl	56 D2		Dalmarnock Rd	58 D4
off Great Western			Charing Cross La			Clouston St	52 D2		Craigielea St	55 E6		Dalnair St	52 C5
Rd	53 E4		*off Granville St*	53 F6		Cloverbank Gdns	55 E5		Craigie St	57 G6		Dalriada St	59 G4
Caledonia Rd	57 H4		Charles St	54 C5		Cloverbank St	55 E5		Craigmaddie Ter La			Dalserf Ct	59 F3
Caledonia St	58 A5		Charlotte La			Clutha St			*off Derby St*	53 E5		Dalserf Gdns	59 F3
Caledon La	52 C3		*off London Rd*	58 B2		*off Paisley Rd*			Craigmont Dr	53 E1		Dalserf St	59 F3
Caledon St	52 C3		Charlotte La S			W	56 D2		Craigmore St	59 G2		Dalziel Dr	56 C5
Calgary St	54 A5		*off Charlotte St*	58 B2		Clydebrae St	52 B6		Craignethan Gdns			Dalziel Quad	56 C5
Caledon St	52 C3		Charlotte La W			Clyde Gateway	59 F4		*off Lawrie St*	52 B4		Dargarvel Av	56 B4
Callander St	53 G3		*off London Rd*	58 B2		Clyde Ind Cen	53 E6		Craigpark	59 E1		Dargarvel Path
Calton Entry			Charlotte St	58 B2		Clyde Pl	57 G2		Craigpark Dr	59 E1		*off Dumbreck*
off Gallowgate	58 C2		Cheapside St	57 F2		Clydeside			Craigpark Ter			Av	56 A5
Cambridge St	53 H6		Chelmsford Dr	52 B1		Expressway	52 C6		*off Craigpark*	59 E1		Darnick St	55 F3
Camden Ter	58 A4		Chesterfield Av	52 A1		Clyde St	57 H2		Crail St	59 H3		Darnley Gdns	57 E6
Camlachie St	59 F3		Chestnut St	54 B1		Clynder St	56 B2		Cranborne Rd	52 A1		Darnley Pl
Campsie St	54 D1		Chisholm St	58 B2		Cobden Rd	54 D4		Cranston St	53 F6		*off Darnley Rd*	57 E6
Canal St	54 A5		Christopher St	55 E4		Coburg St	57 H3		Cranworth La	52 D3		Darnley Rd	57 E6
Candleriggs	58 B2		Churchill Dr	52 A3		Cochrane St	58 A1		Cranworth St	52 D3		Darnley St	57 F6
Canmore Pl	59 H4		Church St	52 C4		Cockmuir St	55 E2		Crathie Dr	52 A4		Dartford St	53 H3
Canmore St	59 H4		Circus Dr	58 D1		Colbert St	58 D5		Crathie La			Davaar St	59 F4
Canting Way	56 C1		Circus Pl	58 D1		Coldstream Pl	54 A3		*off Exeter Dr*	52 A4		Dava St	56 A1
Carberry Rd	56 D6		Circus Pl La	54 D6		Colebrooke La			Crawford La			Davidson St	59 E6
Carbeth St	53 H2		City Link Cen	56 A1		*off Colebrooke*			*off Crawford St*	52 A4		David St	59 E3
Carbrook St	55 E5		Civic St	53 H4		St	53 E3		Crawford Path			Dawson Pl	53 H3
Cardarrach St	55 E1		Clairmont Gdns	53 F5		Colebrooke Pl	53 E3		*off Crawford St*	52 A4		Dawson Rd	53 H3
Cardow Rd	55 G2		Claremont Pas			Colebrooke St	53 E3		Crawford St	52 A4		Deanside La
Cardross Ct	58 D1		*off Claremont*			Colebrooke Ter	53 E3		Cresswell La	52 D3		*off Rottenrow*	58 B1
Cardross St	58 D1		Ter	53 F5		College St	58 B1		Cresswell St	52 D3		Dechmont St	59 G3
Cardwell St			Claremont Pl			Collins St	58 C1		Crichton Pl			Dee St	55 H5
off Eglinton St	57 G4		*off Claremont*			Coll Pl	55 F4		*off Crichton St*	54 C2		Denham St	53 H3
Cardyke St	55 E2		Ter	53 F5		Coll St	55 E4		Crichton St	54 C2		Denmark St	54 A2
Carfin St	57 H6		Claremont St	53 E6		Columba St	56 B1		Crieff Ct			Derby St	53 E6
Carfrae St	52 C6		Claremont Ter	53 F5		Colvend La	58 D5		*off North St*	53 F6		Derby Ter La	53 E5
Carillon Rd	56 C3		Claremont Ter			Colvend St	58 D5		Crimea St	57 G1		Derwent St	53 H2
Carleston St	54 D2		La	53 E5		Comelypark Pl			Crinan St	55 F6		Deveron St	55 H5
Carlisle St	54 B2		Clarence Dr	52 A3		*off Comelypark*			Croftbank St	54 D2		Devon Pl	57 H4
Carlton Ct	57 H2		Clarence Gdns	52 A3		St	59 E2		Cromer Gdns	53 F1		Devonshire Gdns	52 B2
Carlton Pl	57 H2		Clarence La	52 B3		Comelypark St	58 D2		Cromwell La	53 G4		Devonshire Gdns La
Carmichael St	56 B2		Clarendon La			Commerce St	57 H3		Cromwell St	53 G4		*off Hyndland*
Carnarvon St	53 F5		*off Clarendon*			Commercial Ct	58 B3		Crown Circ	52 C3		Rd	52 B2
Carnoustie Pl	57 F3		St	53 G4		Commercial Rd	58 A4		Crown Ct			Devonshire Ter	52 B2
Carnoustie St	57 G2		Clarendon Pl	53 G4		Congress Rd	56 D1		*off Virginia St*	58 A1		Devonshire Ter La	52 B2
Carntyne Path	59 H1		Clarendon St	53 G4		Congress Way	57 E1		Crown Gdns	52 C3		Devon St	57 H4
Carntyne Pl	59 H1		Clare St	55 E4		Connal St	59 F5		Crown Mans			Dick St	53 F3
Carntyne Rd	59 G2		Clayslaps Rd	52 D5		Contin Pl	52 D1		*off North Gardner*			Dinart St	55 H5
Carrick St	57 G2		Claythorn Av	58 C3		Cook St	57 G3		St	52 B3		Dinwiddie St	55 G4
Carrington St	53 F4		Claythorn Circ			Cooperage Pl	52 C6		Crownpoint Rd	58 D3		Dixons Blazes
Carron Cres	54 B1		*off Claythorn*			Coopers Well La			Crown Rd N	52 B3		Ind Est	58 A5
Carron Pl	54 B1		Av	58 C2		*off Dumbarton*			Crown Rd S	52 B3		Dixon St	57 H2
Carron St	54 C1		Claythorn Ct			Rd	52 C5		Crown St	58 A3		Dobbies Ln	53 H5
Carstairs St	59 E6		*off Claythorn*			Coopers Well St	52 C5		Crown Ter	52 B3		Dobbies Ln Pl	54 B6
Castlebank Cres	52 A5		Pk	58 C2		Copland Pl	56 B1		Crow Rd	52 A3		Dolphin Rd	56 D6
Castle Cres N Ct			Claythorn Pk	58 C3		Copland Quad	56 B2		Croy Pl	55 G1		Doncaster St	53 G2
off Royal Ex Sq	58 A1		Claythorn St	58 C2		Copland Rd	56 B2		Croy Rd	55 G1		Don St	55 H6
Castle St	54 C6		Claythorn Ter			Coplaw Ct	57 G5		Cubie St	58 D3		Dora St	58 D5
Castle St			*off Claythorn*			Coplaw St	57 G5		Culloden St	55 F6		Dornoch St	58 D3
(Partick)	52 C5		Pk	58 C2		Cornhill St	55 E1		Cumberland Pl	58 A4		Dorset Sq
Cathedral Sq	58 C1		Clayton Ter	58 D1		Corn St	53 H4		Cumberland St	57 H3		*off Dorset St*	53 F6
Cathedral St	54 A6		Cleghorn St	53 H3		Cornwall St	56 D3		Cumbernauld Rd	59 F1		Dorset St	53 F6
Catherine Pl			Cleland La	58 A3		Cornwall St S	56 D3		Custom Ho Quay			Douglas La
off Hydepark			Cleland St	58 A3		Corsock St	59 G1		*off Clyde St*	58 A2		*off West Regent*
St	57 F1		Clerwood St	59 H2		Corston St	55 H6		Cuthbertson St	57 G6		St	53 G6
Cavendish Ct	57 H4		Cleveden Cres	52 B1		Corunna St	53 E6		Cuthelton St	59 H4		Douglas St	53 G6
Cavendish Pl	57 H4		Cleveden Cres La	52 B1		Cotton St	58 D6		Cuthelton Ter	59 H4		Douglas Ter
Cavendish St	57 H4		Cleveden Dr	52 B1		Coulin Gdns	54 B2		Cypress St	54 B1		*off Glencairn Dr*	57 F5
Cecil St	52 D3		Cleveden Dr La			Couper Pl	54 B5					Doune Gdns	53 E3
Cedar Ct	53 G4		*off Mirrlees Dr*	52 C2		Couper St	54 B5		**D**			Doune Gdns La	53 E3
Cedar St	53 G4		Cleveden Gdns	52 C1		Coventry Dr	55 F6		Dalcross La			Doune Quad	53 E3
Central Sta	57 H1		Cleveland La			Cowan La	53 E4		*off Byres Rd*	52 C4		Dover St	53 E6
Centre St	57 G3		*off Kent Rd*	53 F6		Cowan St	53 E4		Dalcross Pas			Dowanhill St	52 C3
Cessnock St	56 C2		Cleveland St	53 F6		Cowcaddens Rd	53 H5		*off Dalcross St*	52 C4		Dowanside La
Chalmers Ct	58 C2		Clifford Gdns	56 B3		Cowcaddens St			Dalcross St	52 C4		*off Byres Rd*	52 D3
Chalmers Gate			Clifford La	56 C3		*off Renfield St*	53 H5		Dale Path	58 D4		Dowanside Rd	52 C3
off Claython			Clifford Pl			Cowlairs Rd	54 C2		Dale St	58 D4		Downiebrae Rd	59 F6
St	58 C2		*off Clifford St*	56 B3		Coxhill St	54 B3		Dalhousie La			Downs St	54 D2
Chalmers Pl			Clifford St	56 B3		Craigenbay St	55 F2		*off Dalhousie*			Drake St	58 C3
off Claython			Cliff Rd	53 F5		Craigendmuir			St	53 G5		Dreghorn St	59 G1
St	58 C2		Clifton Pl			St	55 H4		Dalhousie St	53 G5		Drem Pl
Chalmers St	58 C2		*off Clifton St*	53 E5		Craighall Rd	53 H4		Dalintober St	57 G3		*off Merkland St*	52 B4
Chancellor St	52 B4		Clifton St	53 E5		Craighead Av	55 H3		Dalkeith Av	56 B4		Drumbottie Rd	55 E1
Chapel St	53 E1		Closeburn St	54 A1		Craigiehall Pl	56 D2		Dalmally St	53 F3		Drumpellier St	55 H4

Drury St
  off Renfield St 57 H1
Dryburgh Gdns
  off Wilton St 53 F3
Drygate 58 C1
Duchray La 55 H5
Duchray St 55 H5
Dudley Dr 52 A3
Dudley La 52 A3
Duke St 58 C1
Duke Wynd 58 C1
Dumbarton Rd 52 A4
Dumbreck Av 56 A4
Dumbreck Ct 56 A5
Dumbreck Path
  off Dumbreck Av 56 A4
Dumbreck Pl 56 A4
Dumbreck Rd 56 B5
Dumbreck Sq 56 A4
Dunard St 53 F2
Dunaskin St 52 C5
Dunbeith Pl 52 D1
Dunblane St 53 H5
Dunchattan Pl 58 D1
Dunchattan St 58 D1
Dundashill 53 H4
Dundas La 54 A6
Dundas St 54 A6
Dundasvale Ct
  off Maitland St 53 H5
Dundasvale Rd
  off Maitland St 53 H5
Dundonald Rd 52 C2
Dunearn St 53 F4
Dunkeld St 59 G4
Dunlop St 58 A2
Dunmore La
  off Norfolk St 57 H3
Dunn St 59 E4
Dunolly St 55 E5
Dunragit St 59 G1
Dunsmuir St 56 B1
Duntroon St 55 F6
Durham St 56 D3
Dyce La 52 A4
Dykemuir Pl
  off Dykemuir St 55 F2
Dykemuir Quad
  off Dykemuir St 55 E2
Dykemuir St 55 E2

E
Eaglesham Ct
  off Blackburn St 57 E2
Eaglesham Pl 57 E2
Eagle St 54 A4
Earlston Av 54 D5
Earlston Pl 54 C5
Earnock St 55 H2
East Bath La
  off Sauchiehall St 54 A6
Eastburn Rd 55 F1
East Campbell St 58 C2
Eastcroft Ter 55 E2
Eastercraigs 55 F6
Eastfield Rd 54 C2
Eastvale Pl 52 C6
East Wellington St 59 H3
East Whitby St 59 G4
Eccles St
  off Carron St 54 C1
Edelweiss Ter
  off Gardner St 52 B4
Eden La 55 H5
Eden St 55 H5
Edgefauld Av 54 D3
Edgefauld Dr 54 D2

Edgefauld Pl 54 D1
Edgefauld Rd 54 D2
Edgehill La 52 A2
Edinburgh Rd 59 H1
Edington St 53 H4
Edwin St 56 D3
Eglinton Ct 57 H3
Eglinton St 57 H3
Elba La
  off Gallowgate 59 G3
Elcho St 58 D2
Elderslie St 53 F5
Eldon Ct
  off Caird Dr 52 B4
Eldon St 53 E4
Elgin St
  off Rowchester St 59 E3
Elie St 52 C4
Elizabeth St 56 C3
Ellesmere St 53 G2
Elliot Pl
  off Finnieston St 53 E6
Elliot St 57 E1
Elmbank Cres 53 G6
Elmbank La
  off North St 53 F6
Elmbank St 53 G6
Elmbank St La 53 G6
Elmvale Row 54 C1
Elmvale Row E
  off Elmvale Row 54 C1
Elmvale Row W
  off Elmvale Row 54 C1
Elmvale St 54 C1
Elphinstone Pl 56 C1
Eltham St
  off Bonhill St 53 H3
Endrick St 54 B3
Errol Gdns 58 A4
Erskine Av 56 B4
Esmond St 52 C5
Eton La 53 E4
Ewing Pl 59 G3
Exchange Pl
  off Buchanan St 58 A1
Exeter Dr 52 A4
Exeter La
  off Exeter Dr 52 A4

F
Fairbairn Path
  off Ruby St 59 E4
Fairbairn St 59 E4
Fairley St 56 B2
Fairlie Pk Dr 52 B4
Falkland La 52 B3
Falkland St 52 B3
Farm Rd 56 B3
Farnell St 53 H4
Fauldhouse St 58 B5
Fergus Ct
  off Fergus Dr 53 E2
Fergus Dr 53 E2
Fergus La 53 F2
Fernbank St 54 C1
Ferry Rd 52 C5
Fielden Pl 59 E3
Fielden St 59 E3
Findhorn St 55 H6
Finlas St 54 B2
Finlay Dr 59 E1
Finnart Sq 58 D5
Finnart St 58 D5
Finnieston Quay 57 E1
Finnieston Sq
  off Finnieston St 53 E6
Finnieston St 57 E1

Firhill Rd 53 G2
Firhill St 53 G2
Firpark Pl
  off Firpark St 54 D6
Firpark St 54 D6
Firpark Ter 58 D1
First Gdns 56 A4
Fisher Ct 58 D1
Fitzroy La 53 E6
Fitzroy Pl
  off Royal Ter 53 E5
Fleming St 59 F2
Flemington St 54 D3
Fleurs Av 56 B4
Fleurs Rd 56 B4
Florence St 58 A3
Forbes Dr 58 D3
Forbes St 58 D2
Fordneuk St 59 E3
Ford Rd 52 D2
Fordyce St 52 B4
Foremount Ter La 52 B3
Foresthall Cres 55 E3
Foresthall Dr 55 E3
Forge Pl 55 F4
Forge Retail Pk 59 F2
Forge Shop Cen, The 59 G3
Forge St 55 F4
Forrestfield St 55 E5
Forrest St 59 E3
Forth St 57 F5
Fortrose St 52 B4
Fotheringay La 56 D6
Fotheringay Rd 56 D6
Foundry St 54 D2
Fountainwell Av 54 B3
Fountainwell Dr 54 B4
Fountainwell Pl 54 B4
Fountainwell Rd 54 B4
Fountainwell Sq 54 C4
Fountainwell Ter 54 C4
Fourth Gdns 56 A4
Fox St 57 H2
Foyers Ter 55 E2
Frankfield St 55 H4
Franklin St 58 D5
Frazer St 59 E3
French St 58 D5
Fruin Pl 54 A2
Fruin St 54 A2

G
Gadie St 55 H6
Gadshill St 54 D5
Gallowgate 58 B2
Gardner St 52 B4
Garfield St 59 E2
Garmouth Ct 52 A6
Garnet Ct
  off New City Rd 53 G5
Garnethill St 53 G5
Garnet St 53 G5
Garnock St 54 D4
Garrioch Cres 52 D1
Garrioch Dr 52 D1
Garrioch Gate
  off Garrioch Rd 53 E1
Garriochmill Rd 53 E2
Garriochmill Way
  off South Woodside Rd 53 F3
Garrioch Quad 52 D1
Garrioch Rd 52 D2
Garscube Cross 53 H4
Garscube Rd 53 G3
Gartferry St 54 D2
Garthland Dr 59 E1
Garth St
  off Glassford St 58 A1

Gartness St 59 F1
Gartons Rd 55 G1
Garvald Ct
  off Baltic St 59 E6
Gateside St 59 F2
Gear Ter 59 F6
General Terminus Quay 57 F2
George Sq 58 A1
George St 58 A1
Gibson St (Calton) 58 C2
Gibson St (Hillhead) 53 E4
Gilbert St 52 C6
Gilmour Pl 58 A4
Girvan St 55 H5
Gladstone St 53 G4
Glamis Rd 59 H4
Glasgow Br 57 H2
Glasgow Cross 58 B2
Glasgow Grn 58 B3
Glasgow Rd 58 D6
Glasgow St 53 E3
Glassford St 58 A1
Glebe Ct 54 B6
Glebe St 54 B5
Glenapp St 57 F5
Glenbarr St 54 D5
Glencairn Dr 56 D6
Glencairn Gdns 57 F6
Glencairn La 57 F6
Glendale Pl 59 F2
Glendale St 59 F2
Glendarvel Gdns 54 B2
Glenfarg St 53 G4
Glenisla St 59 H5
Glenmavis St 53 H5
Glenpark Rd 59 F2
Glenpark St 59 F2
Glenshee Ct 59 H5
Glenshee St 59 H4
Glentrool Gdns 54 A2
Golfhill Dr 55 E6
Golfhill Ter
  off Firpark St 54 D6
Golspie St 52 A6
Goosedubbs
  off Stockwell St 58 A2
Gorbals Cross 58 A3
Gorbals La
  off Oxford St 57 H2
Gorbals St 57 H4
Gordon La
  off Mitchell St 57 H1
Gordon St 57 H1
Gorstan Pl
  off Wyndford Rd 52 C1
Gough St 55 H6
Gourlay Path
  off Endrick St 54 B3
Gourlay St 54 B3
Gourock St 57 G4
  off Eglinton St 57 G4
Govan Cross 52 A6
Govan Cross Shop Cen 52 A6
Govanhill St 57 H6
Govan Rd 56 C2
Gower La
  off North Gower St 56 D3
Gower St 56 C4
Gower Ter 56 C3
Grace St 57 F1
Grafton Pl 54 A6
Graham Sq 58 D2
Graignestock Pl
  off London Rd 58 C3
Graignestock St 58 C3
Granby La 52 D3

Grant St 53 F5
Granville St 53 F6
Gray St 53 E5
Great Dovehill 58 B2
Great George St 52 D3
Great Kelvin La
  off Glasgow St 53 E4
Great Western Rd 53 E3
Great Western Ter 52 C2
Great Western Ter La 52 C2
Green, The 58 C3
Greendyke St 58 B2
Greenhead St 58 C4
Greenlodge Ter
  off Greenhead St 58 C4
Greenrig St 55 H3
Green St 58 C3
Grier Path
  off Crail St 59 H3
Grierson La
  off Lomax St 55 H6
Grierson St 55 H6
Grosvenor Cres 52 D3
Grosvenor Cres La
  off Byres Rd 52 D3
Grosvenor La 52 D3
Grosvenor Ter 52 D3
Grovepark Ct 53 G4
Grovepark Gdns 53 G4
Grovepark Pl 53 G3
Grovepark St 53 G3
Gullane St 52 B5

H
Haggswood Av 56 C6
Haghill Rd 59 G2
Haig St 54 D2
Hallside Pl 58 A4
Hamilton Av 56 D5
Hamilton Dr 53 E3
Hamiltonhill Cres
  off Hamiltonhill Rd 53 H3
Hamiltonhill Rd 53 H3
Hamilton Pk Av 53 E3
Handel Pl 58 A4
Hannover Ct 54 A6
Hanover St 58 A1
Hanson Pk 54 D6
Hanson St 54 D6
Harcourt Dr 55 F6
Harley St 56 C3
Harmony Ct 56 A1
Harmony Pl 56 A1
Harmony Row 56 A1
Harmony Sq
  off Harmony Row 56 A1
Harrison Dr
  off Copland Rd 56 B2
Harvey St 54 A4
Harvie St 56 D2
Hastie St 52 D5
Hathaway La 53 E1
Hathaway St 53 E1
Haugh Rd 52 D6
Havannah St 58 C1
Havelock La 52 C4
Havelock St 52 C4
Hawthorn Quad 54 A1
Hawthorn St 54 A1
Hayburn Ct
  off Hayburn St 52 B4
Hayburn Cres 52 A3
Hayburn Gate 52 B4
Hayburn La
  off Hayburn Pl 52 B4
Hayburn Pl
  off Hayburn St 52 B4
Hayburn St 52 B5
Hayfield Ct 58 B4

Hayfield St 58 B4
Hayston Cres 53 H1
Hayston St 53 H1
Hazelwood Rd 56 C4
Heddle Pl
off Cadogan St 57 G1
Helen St 56 A1
Helenvale Ct 59 H4
Helenvale St 59 G4
Henderson St 53 F3
Herbertson St 57 H3
Herbert St 53 F3
Heron St 58 D4
Herries Rd 56 C6
Herriet St 57 F5
Hickman Ter 58 A6
Hickory St 54 C1
Highburgh Rd 52 C3
High Craighall
Rd 53 H4
Highland La 52 C6
High St 58 B2
Hillfoot St 59 E1
Hillhead Pl
off Bank St 53 E4
Hillhead St 52 D4
Hillhouse St 55 E2
Hillkirk Pl
off Hillkirk St 54 C2
Hillkirk St 54 C2
Hillkirk St La
off Hillkirk St 54 D2
Hillsborough Ter
off Bower St 53 E3
Hillside Gdns La
off North
Gardner St 52 B3
Hill St 53 G5
Hinshaw St 53 G3
Hinshelwood Dr 56 A2
Hobart St 53 H2
Hobden St 55 E3
Hogarth Av 59 H1
Hogarth Cres 59 H1
Hogarth Dr 59 H1
Hogarth Gdns 59 H1
Hogganfield Ct 55 H4
Hogganfield St 55 H4
Holland St 53 G6
Hollybank St 55 E5
Hollybrook Pl
off Hollybrook
St 58 A6
Hollybrook St 58 A6
Holly Dr 55 E3
Holm St 57 G1
Holyrood Cres 53 F4
Holyrood Quad 53 F4
Holywell St 59 F3
Hopefield Av 52 C1
Hopehill Gdns 53 G3
Hopehill Rd 53 G3
Hope St 57 H1
Hopetoun Ter 55 E3
Horne St
off Hawthorn
St 54 C1
Hornshill St 55 E2
Horselethill Rd 52 C2
Hospital St 58 A3
Hotspur St 53 E1
Houldsworth La
off Finnieston
St 53 E6
Houldsworth St 53 E6
Houston Pl 57 F2
Houston St 57 F3
Howard St 57 H2
Howat St 52 A6
Hughenden Dr 52 B2
Hughenden Gdns 52 A2
Hughenden La 52 B2
Hughenden Rd 52 B2

Hughenden Ter
off Hughenden
Rd 52 B2
Hugo St 53 F1
Hunter St 58 C2
Huntingdon Rd 54 C4
Huntingdon Sq 54 C4
Huntly Gdns 52 C3
Huntly Rd 52 C3
Hutcheson St 58 A1
Hutchinsontown
Ct 58 A4
Hydepark St 57 F1
Hyndland Av 52 B4
Hyndland Rd 52 B2
Hyndland St 52 C4

I
Ibroxholm Av 56 B3
Ibroxholm Oval 56 B3
Ibroxholm Pl
off Paisley Rd
W 56 B3
Ibrox Ind Est 56 C2
Ibrox St 56 C2
Ibrox Ter 56 B2
Ibrox Ter La 56 B2
India St 53 G6
Ingleby Dr 59 E1
Inglefield St 57 H6
Inglis St 59 E2
Ingram St 58 A1
Inverleith St 59 H2
Invershin Dr 52 D1
Inverurie St 54 B3
Iona St 56 B1
Irongray St 59 G1
Irvine St 59 F5

J
Jamaica St 57 H2
James Morrison St
off St. Andrews
Sq 58 B2
James Nisbet St 54 C6
James St 58 C4
James Watt La
off James Watt
St 57 G1
James Watt St 57 G1
Jamieson Ct 57 H6
Jamieson Path
off Jamieson St 57 H6
Jamieson St 57 H6
Janefield St 59 F3
Jane Pl 58 A4
Jardine St
off Tillie St 53 F3
Jedburgh Gdns
off Wilton St 53 F3
Jessie St 58 B6
Jocelyn Sq 58 A2
John Knox La
off Drygate 58 C1
John Knox St 58 C1
John St 58 A1
Julian Av 52 C2
Julian La 52 C2

K
Karol Path
off St. Peters St 53 G4
Kay St 54 D2
Keir St 57 F5
Keith Ct 52 C5
Keith St 52 C4
Kelbourne St 53 E2
Kellas St 56 A1
Kelty Pl
off Bedford St 57 H3
Kelvin Dr 52 D2
Kelvingrove St 53 E6
Kelvinhaugh Gate 52 D6

Kelvinhaugh Pl
off Kelvingrove
St 52 D6
Kelvinhaugh St 52 C6
Kelvinside Av 53 E2
Kelvinside Dr 53 F2
Kelvinside Gdns 53 E2
Kelvinside Gdns E 53 F3
Kelvinside Gdns
La 53 E2
Kelvinside Ter S 53 E3
Kelvinside Ter W 53 E3
Kelvin Way 52 D5
Kemp St 54 C2
Kenmure St 57 F6
Kennedy Path
off St. Mungo
Pl 54 B6
Kennedy St 54 B5
Kennet St 55 E5
Kennyhill Sq 55 F6
Kensington Gate
off Kensington
Rd 52 C2
Kensington Gate
La 52 C2
Kensington Rd 52 C2
Kent Rd 53 E6
Kent St 58 C2
Keppochhill Dr 54 B3
Keppochhill Pl 54 B4
Keppochhill Rd 54 A3
Keppochhill Way 54 B4
Keppoch St 54 B3
Kerr Dr 58 D3
Kerr Pl 58 D3
Kerr St 58 D3
Kerrydale St 59 F4
Kersland La 52 D3
Kersland St 52 D3
Kessock Dr 53 H3
Kessock Pl 53 H3
Kew Gdns
off Ruthven St 52 D3
Kew La 52 D3
Kew Ter 52 D3
Kidston Pl 58 A4
Kidston Ter 58 A4
Kilbarchan St
off Bedford St 57 H3
Kilberry St 55 E5
Kilbirnie Pl 57 G4
Kilbirnie St 57 G4
Kilbride St 58 B5
Kildonan Dr 52 A4
Kildrostan St 57 F6
Killearn St 53 H2
Killermont St 54 A6
Killiegrew Rd 56 D6
Kilmair Pl 52 D1
Kinbuck St 54 B2
Kingarth La 57 G6
Kingarth St 57 G6
King George V Br 57 H2
Kingsborough
Gdns 52 B3
Kingsborough Gate
off Prince Albert
Rd 52 B3
Kingsborough La 52 B3
Kingsborough
La E 52 B3
King's Br 58 B4
Kings Cross 58 D1
King's Dr 58 C4
Kingston Br 57 G2
Kingston Ind Est 57 F3
Kingston St 57 G2
King St 58 A2
Kinloch St 59 G4
Kinnear Rd 59 F5
Kinning Pk Ind
Est 57 F3

Kinnoul La
off Dowanside
Rd 52 C3
Kintra St 56 B1
Kintyre St 55 E5
Kirkcaldy Rd 56 D6
Kirkhill Dr 53 E1
Kirkhill Pl
off Kirkhill Dr 52 D1
Kirkland St 53 F3
Kirklee Circ 52 C1
Kirklee Gdns 52 C1
Kirklee Gdns La 52 D2
Kirklee Gate 52 D2
Kirklee Pl 52 D2
Kirklee Quad 52 D2
Kirklee Quad La
off Kirklee Quad 52 D2
Kirklee Rd 52 C2
Kirklee Ter 52 C2
Kirklee Ter La 52 C2
Kirkmichael Av
off Blairatholl
Av 52 A3
Kirkmichael Gdns
off Blairatholl
Av 52 A3
Kirkpatrick St 59 E3
Kirkwood St 56 C3
Knowehead Gdns 57 E5
Knowehead Ter 57 E5
Kyle St 54 A5

L
La Belle Allee 53 E5
La Belle Pl 53 E5
Laburnum Rd 56 C4
La Crosse Ter 53 E3
Ladywell St 58 C1
Laidlaw St 57 G3
Laird Pl 58 D4
Lambhill Quad 57 E3
Lambhill St 56 D3
Lanark St 58 B2
Lancaster Cres 52 C2
Lancaster Cres La 52 C2
Lancaster Ter 52 C2
Lancaster Ter La
off Westbourne
Gdns W 52 C2
Lancefield Quay 57 E1
Lancefield St 57 F1
Landressy Pl 58 C4
Landressy St 58 D4
Lane Gdns
off North Gardner
St 52 B3
Langbank St 57 H3
Langdale St
off Eglinton St 57 H3
Langrig Rd 55 E2
Langshot St 56 D3
Lansdowne Cres 53 F4
Lansdowne Cres
La 53 F4
Larbert St 53 H5
Larch Rd 56 B3
Largs St 59 F1
Latherton Dr 52 D1
Latherton Pl
off Latherton Dr 52 D1
Laudedale La 52 B3
Lauderdale Gdns 52 B3
Laurel Pl 52 A3
Laurel St 52 A4
Launeston Rd 57 H4
Laverockhall St 54 D3
Lawmoor Rd 58 A5
Lawmoor St 58 A5
Lawrence St 52 C4
Lawrie St 52 B4
Law St 59 E3
Leadburn Rd 55 G2
Leader St 55 H5

Ledaig Pl 59 G1
Ledaig St 59 G1
Leicester Av 52 B1
Leith St 55 H6
Lendel Pl
off Paisley Rd
W 56 D3
Leny St 53 F2
Lenzie St 54 D1
Lenzie Ter 54 D1
Leslie Rd 57 E5
Leslie St 57 F5
Lettoch St 56 A1
Leven St 57 F5
Leyden Ct 53 E1
Leyden Gdns 53 E1
Leyden St 53 E1
Liberton St 55 H6
Lightburn Rd 59 G2
Lilybank Gdns 52 D4
Lilybank Gdns La 52 D4
Lilybank La
off Lilybank
Gdns 52 D4
Lilybank Ter
off Great George
St 52 D4
Lily St 59 F5
Lincluden Path
off McCulloch
St 57 F4
Linfern Rd 52 C3
Lismore Rd 52 B1
Lister St 54 B5
Little Dovehill
off Gallowgate 58 B2
Little St
off McIntyre St 57 F1
Lloyd St 55 E6
Lochgreen St 55 H3
Lochsloy Ct 54 B2
Lockhart St 55 F4
Logan St 58 B5
Lomax St 55 H6
Lomond St 53 H1
London Arc
off London Rd 58 B2
London Ave 59 F5
London La
off London Rd 58 B2
London Rd 58 B2
London Way 58 B2
Longford St 55 H6
Lorne St 56 D2
Lorraine Gdns
off Kensington
Rd 52 C2
Lorraine Gdns La
off Westbourne
Gdns La 52 C2
Lorraine Rd
off Kensington
Rd 52 C2
Lossie St 55 H5
Lothian Gdns
off Wilton St 53 E3
Loudon Ter
off Observatory
Rd 52 D3
Lovat St
off Borron St 54 A4
Lowther Ter
off Redlands La 52 C2
Luath St 52 A6
Lumloch St 55 E2
Lumsden St 52 D6
Lymburn St 52 D5
Lyndhurst Gdns 53 F3
Lyndhurst Gdns
La 53 E2
Lynedoch Cres 53 F5
Lynedoch Cres La 53 F5
Lynedoch Pl 53 F5

Lynedoch St	53 F5	Maxwell Oval	57 F4	Monar Dr		Newton Ter		Observatory La
Lynedoch Ter	53 F5	Maxwell Pl	57 G5	*off Monar St*	53 H3	*off Sauchiehall*		*off Observatory*
		Maxwell Rd	57 F4	Monar Pl		*St*	53 F6	*Rd*	52 D3
M		Maxwell St	58 A2	*off Monar St*	53 H3	Newton Ter La	53 F6	Observatory Rd	52 C3
McAlpine St	57 G1	Maxwell Ter	57 F4	Monar St	53 H3	New Wynd	58 A2	Ogilvie Pl	59 H4
McAslin Ct	54 B6	Maxwelton Rd	55 H4	Monart Pl	53 F1	Nicholas St	58 B1	Ogilvie St	59 H4
McAslin St	54 C6	Meadowpark St	59 F1	Moncur St	58 C2	Nicholson La		Old Dalmarnock
Macbeth Pl	59 H4	Meadow Rd	52 A4	Monkscroft Av	52 A3	*off Nicholson*		*Rd*	58 D4
Macbeth St	59 H4	Meadowside St	52 A5	Monkscroft Ct		*St*	57 H2	Old Dumbarton
McCulloch St	57 F4	Megan Gate		*off Crow Rd*	52 A4	Nicholson St	57 H2	*Rd*	52 C5
Macduff Pl	59 H4	*off Megan*		Monkscroft Gdns		Niddrie Rd	57 F6	Old Rutherglen
Macduff St	59 H4	*St*	58 D4	*off Monkscroft*		Niddrie Sq	57 F6	*Rd*	58 A4
McFarlane St	58 C2	Megan St	58 D4	*Av*	52 A3	Nisbet St	59 H3	Old Wynd	58 A2
McIntosh Ct	58 D1	Melbourne Pl	59 G4	Montague La	52 B2	Nisbet St	59 H3	Olive St	55 H2
McIntosh St	58 D1	Melbourne St	58 D2	Montague St	53 F4	Nithsdale Dr	57 F5	Olympia St	58 D3
McIntyre St	57 F1	Meldrum Gdns	56 D6	Monteith Pl	58 C3	Nithsdale Pl		Onslow Dr	59 E1
McKechnie St	52 A6	Melfort Av	56 B4	Monteith Row	58 C3	*off Nithsdale*		Onslow Sq	59 E1
Mackeith St	58 D4	Melrose Gdns	53 F3	Monteith Row La		*Rd*	57 F5	Oran Gdns	53 E1
Mackie St		Melrose St		*off Monteith Pl*	58 C3	Nithsdale Rd	57 F6	Oran Gate	53 E1
off Borron St	54 A4	*off Queens*		Montgomery St	59 E4	Nithsdale St	57 F6	Oran Pl	53 E2
Maclean Sq	56 D2	*Cres*	53 F4	Montrose St	54 B6	Nith St	55 H5	Oran St	53 E1
Maclean St	56 D2	Melvaig Pl	52 D1	Moodiesburn St	55 H4	Norfolk Ct	57 H3	Oregon Pl	58 A4
Maclellan St	56 C3	Melville Ct		Moore St		Norfolk La		Orkney Pl	
Macleod St	54 C6	*off Brunswick*		*off Gallowgate*	58 D2	*off Norfolk St*	57 H3	*off Orkney St*	56 A1
McNeil Gdns	58 B4	*St*	58 B2	Moray Pl	57 E6	Norfolk St	58 A3	Orkney St	56 B1
McNeil St	58 B4	Melville St	57 F5	Morgan Ms	57 H5	Norman St	58 D5	Orr St	58 D3
McPhail St	58 C4	Memel St	54 C1	Morningside St	55 H6	North Canal Bk	54 A4	Orton Pl	56 A2
McPhater St	53 H5	Menzies Dr	55 E1	Morrin Path		North Canal Bk		Osborne St	58 A2
Madras Pl	58 D5	Menzies St	55 E1	*off Crichton*		*St*	54 A4	Oswald St	57 H2
Madras St	58 D5	Menzies Rd	55 E1	*St*	54 C2	North Claremont		Otago La	53 E4
Mafeking St	56 B2	Merchant La	58 A2	Morrin Sq		St *off Royal*		Otago La N	
Main St	58 D5	Merkland Ct		*off Collins St*	54 C6	*Ter*	53 E5	*off Otago St*	53 E4
Mair St	57 E2	*off Vine St*	52 B5	Morrin St	54 C2	North Ct		Otago St	53 E4
Maitland St	53 H5	Merkland St	52 B4	Morrison Ct	57 H1	*off St. Vincent*		Overnewton Pl	
Malloch St	53 E1	Merrick Gdns	56 B3	Morrison St	57 G2	*Pl*	58 A1	*off Kelvinhaugh*	
Malta Ter	57 H4	Merrick Path		Mosesfield St	54 D1	North Ct La		*St*	52 D6
Maltbarns St	53 G3	*off Merrick*		Mosque Av	58 A3	*off Buchanan*		Overnewton Sq	
Malvern Ct	59 E2	*Gdns*	56 B3	Mountainblue St	59 E3	*St*	58 A1	*off Blackie St*	52 D5
Manresa Pl	53 H4	Merryland Pl	56 B1	Mount St	53 F3	Northcroft Rd	54 D2	Overnewton St	52 D5
Mansel St	54 D1	Merryland St	56 B1	Moy St		North Dr	57 H1	Overtown Pl	59 E3
Mansfield St	52 C4	Methven St	59 H5	*off Church St*	52 C4	North Frederick		Overtown St	59 E3
Mansion St	54 A1	Metropole La		Muirhead St		St	58 A1	Oxford La	57 H3
Maple Rd	56 B4	*off Clyde St*	58 A2	*off Purdon*		North Gardner St	52 B4	Oxford St	57 H2
March La		Middlesex Gdns	57 E2	*St*	52 B4	North Gower St	56 C3		
off Nithsdale		Middlesex St	57 E3	Muirpark St	52 B4	North Hanover Pl		**P**	
Dr	57 F6	Middleton St	56 C2	Mull St	55 F4	*off North Hanover*		Pacific Dr	56 C2
Marchmont Ter		Midland St	57 H1	Murano St	53 F2	*St*	54 A6	Pacific Quay	56 D1
off Observatory		Midlock St	56 C3	Murdoch St		North Hanover		Paisley Rd	57 G2
Rd	52 C3	Midton St	54 D3	*off Lenzie St*	54 D1	St	54 A6	Paisley Rd W	56 C3
March St	57 F6	Midwharf St	54 A4	Muslin St	58 D4	Northpark St	53 F2	Palermo St	
Marine Cres	57 E2	Migvie Pl		Myreside Pl	59 H2	North Pl		*off Atlas Rd*	54 C2
Marine Gdns		*off Wyndford*		Myreside St	59 H2	*off North St*	53 F6	Palmerston Pl	
off Mavisbank		*Rd*	52 D1			North Portland		*off Kelvinhaugh*	
Gdns	57 F2	Milan St	57 G5	**N**		St	58 B1	*St*	52 D6
Mariscat Rd	57 E6	Millarbank St	54 C2	Naburn Gate	58 A4	North St	53 F6	Panmure Cl	53 G2
Marlow St	57 E4	Millburn St	54 D5	Nairn St	52 D5	Northumberland		Panmure St	53 G2
Marne St	59 F1	Mill Cres	58 D5	Nansen St	53 G3	St	53 E2	Park Av	53 F4
Martha St	54 A6	Millerston St	59 E2	Napier Dr	52 B6	North Wallace		Park Circ	53 E5
Martin St	58 D5	Miller St	58 A1	Napier Pl	52 B6	St	54 B5	Park Circ La	53 E5
Mart St		Millroad Dr	58 C2	Napier Rd	52 B6	North Woodside		Park Circ Pl	53 F5
off Bridgegate	58 A2	Millroad Gdns	58 D2	Napiershall La	53 F4	Rd	53 F3	Park Dr	53 E4
Marwick St	59 F1	Millroad St	58 C2	Napiershall Pl		Norval St	52 A4	Park Gdns	53 E5
Maryhill Rd	53 F3	Mill St	58 D5	*off Napiershall*		Norwich Dr	52 B1	Park Gdns La	53 E5
Maryhill Shop		Milnbank St	55 E6	*St*	53 F4	Novar Dr	52 A2	Park Gate	53 E5
Cen	53 E1	Milnpark Gdns	56 D3	Napiershall St	53 F4	Nuneaton St	59 E5	Parkgrove Ter	53 E5
Maryston Pl	55 H4	Milnpark St	57 E3	Napier Ter	52 B6	Nuneaton St		Parkgrove Ter La	
Maryston St	55 H4	Milton St	54 A5	Nelson Mandela		*Ind Est*	59 E5	*off Derby St*	53 E5
Mary St	53 H4	Minerva St	53 E6	Pl	54 A6	Nursery La	57 F6	Parkhead Cross	59 H3
Marywood Sq	57 F6	Minerva Way	53 E6	Nelson St	57 G2	Nursery St		Park Quad	53 E5
Masterton St	54 A3	Mingarry La		Neptune St	56 B1	*off Pollokshaws*		Park Rd	53 E4
Matilda Rd	57 E5	*off Clouston*		Nethan St	52 A6	*Rd*	57 G5	Park St S	53 E5
Maukinfauld Ct	59 H5	*St*	53 E2	Netherby Dr	56 D4			Park Ter	53 E5
Maule Dr	52 A4	Mingarry St	53 E2	Netherfield St	59 G2	**O**		Park Ter E La	53 E5
Mavisbank Gdns	57 E2	Mireton St	53 H1	Newark Dr	56 D5	Oakbank Ind Est	53 H3	Park Ter La	53 E5
Maxwell Av	57 E4	Mirrlees Dr	52 C2	Newbank Gdns	59 H4	Oakfield Av	53 E4	Parnie St	58 A2
Maxwell Ct		Mirrlees La	52 C2	New City Rd	53 H5	Oakfield La	53 E4	Parsonage Row	58 B1
off St. John's		Mitchell La	57 H1	Newhall St	58 C4	Oakley Ter	58 D1	Parsonage Sq	58 B1
Rd	57 E4	Mitchell St	57 H1	Newmill Rd	55 G1	Oak St	57 G1	Parson St	54 C6
Maxwell Dr	56 C4	Moffat St	58 B4	New Rutherglen		Oatfield St	55 F2	Partick Br St	52 C4
Maxwell Gdns	56 D4	Moir St	58 B2	Rd	58 B6	Oban Ct		Partickhill Av	52 B4
Maxwell Gro	56 D4	Molendinar Gdns	55 H4	Newton Pl	53 F5	*off Kelvinside*		Partickhill Ct	52 B3
Maxwell La		Molendinar St	58 B2	Newton St		*Gdns*	53 E2	Partickhill Rd	52 B3
off Maxwell Dr	57 E4	Mollinsburn St	54 C3	*off Argyle St*	53 G6	Oban Dr	53 E2	Paterson St	57 G3
						Oban La	53 E2		

Patna St	59 F5
Paton St	59 F1
Payne St	54 A4
Pearce La	
off Pearce St	52 A6
Pearce St	52 A6
Peathill St	54 A3
Peel La	52 B4
Peel St	52 B4
Pembroke St	53 F6
Penicuik St	59 H2
Percy St	
off Clifford St	56 D2
Perth St	
off Argyle St	57 F1
Petershill Ct	55 G2
Petershill Dr	55 F2
Petershill Pl	55 F2
Petershill Rd	54 D3
Phoenix Pk Ter	
off Corn St	53 H4
Phoenix Rd	
off Great Western Rd	53 G5
Piccadilly St	57 F1
Pine Pl	58 A4
Pinkston Dr	54 C4
Pinkston Rd	54 B3
Pitt St	57 G1
Plantation Pk Gdns	
off Clifford La	56 D3
Plantation Sq	57 E2
Plant St	59 G2
Pointhouse Rd	57 E1
Pollokshaws Rd	57 G6
Pollokshields Sq	
off Glencairn Dr	57 F6
Polmadie Ind Est	58 C6
Polmadie Rd	58 B6
Polwarth La	52 B2
Polwarth St	52 B3
Poplar Rd	
off Urrdale Rd	56 B3
Poplin St	58 D5
Port Dundas Ind Est	54 A4
Port Dundas Pl	54 A6
Port Dundas Rd	53 H5
Port Dundas Trd Centres	54 A4
Porter St	56 C3
Portman Pl	
off Cowan St	53 E4
Portman St	57 E3
Port St	53 F6
Portugal La	
off Bedford St	57 H3
Portugal St	57 H3
Possil Cross	54 A3
Possil Rd	53 H4
Powfoot St	59 H3
Preston Pl	57 H6
Preston St	57 H6
Prince Albert Rd	52 B3
Prince Edward St	57 G6
Prince's Dock	56 C1
Princes Gdns	52 B3
Princes Pl	52 C3
Princes Sq	
off Buchanan St	58 A1
Princes Ter	52 C3
Professors Sq	52 D4
Provanhill St	54 D5
Provanmill Pl	
off Provanmill Rd	55 H3
Provanmill Rd	55 H3
Provan Rd	55 G5
Purdon St	52 B4

Q

Quarrybrae St	59 H3
Quarrywood Av	55 G2
Quarrywood Rd	55 H2
Queen Elizabeth Gdns	58 A4
Queen Elizabeth Sq	58 B4
Queen Margaret Ct	
off Fergus Dr	53 E2
Queen Margaret Dr	52 D3
Queen Margaret Rd	53 E2
Queen Mary St	58 D4
Queensborough Gdns	52 A2
Queens Cres	53 F4
Queens Dr	57 F6
Queens Gdns	
off Victoria Cres Rd	52 C3
Queens Gate La	
off Victoria Cres Rd	52 C3
Queenslie St	55 H4
Queens Pl	52 C3
Queen Sq	57 F6
Queen St	58 A1

R

Radnor St	
off Argyle St	52 D6
Raeberry St	53 F3
Rafford St	56 A1
Raglan St	53 G4
Rathlin St	52 A6
Ratho Dr	54 C1
Ravel Row	59 H3
Ravelston St	59 H2
Redan St	58 D3
Redford St	55 H6
Redlands La	52 C2
Redlands Rd	52 C2
Redlands Ter	
off Julian Av	52 C2
Redlands Ter La	52 C2
Redmoss St	53 H1
Rednock St	54 A2
Red Rd	55 F2
Red Rd Ct	55 F3
Redwood Dr	55 E3
Regent Moray St	52 D5
Regent Pk Sq	57 F6
Reidhouse St	54 D2
Reid Pl	58 D4
Reid St	58 D5
Reidvale St	58 D2
Renfield La	
off Hope St	57 H1
Renfield St	57 H1
Renfrew Ct	53 H6
Renfrew La	
off Hope St	53 H6
Renfrew St	53 H6
Renton St	54 A5
Rhymer St	54 C5
Rhynie Dr	56 B3
Riccarton St	58 A6
Richard St	
off Cadzow St	57 G1
Richmond St	58 B1
Rimsdale St	59 E3
Ringford St	54 D3
Ritchie St	57 G4
Riverview Dr	57 G2
Riverview Gdns	57 G2
Riverview Pl	57 G2
Robert Dr	52 A6
Roberton Av	56 C6
Robertson La	57 G1

Robertson St	57 H1
Robert St	52 A6
Robson Gro	57 H5
Rockbank Pl	59 E3
Rockbank St	59 E3
Rockcliffe St	58 D5
Rockfield Pl	55 G1
Rockfield Rd	55 G1
Rock St	53 H3
Rodney St	53 H4
Roebank St	55 F6
Rogart St	58 D3
Rona St	55 F4
Ropework La	
off Clyde St	58 A2
Rosemount Cres	54 D6
Rosemount St	54 D5
Rose St	53 H6
Rosevale St	52 A4
Roslea Dr	59 E1
Rosneath St	52 A6
Rosslyn Ter	52 C2
Ross St	58 B2
Rosyth Rd	58 C6
Rottenrow	54 B6
Rottenrow E	58 B1
Rowallan Gdns	52 A3
Rowallan La E	52 A3
Rowan Gdns	56 B4
Rowan Rd	56 B4
Rowchester St	59 E3
Roxburgh La	
off Saltoun St	52 D3
Roxburgh St	52 D3
Royal Bk Pl	
off Buchanan St	58 A1
Royal Cres	53 E6
Royal Ex Bldgs	
off Royal Ex Sq	58 A1
Royal Ex Ct	
off Queen St	58 A1
Royal Ex Sq	58 A1
Royal Ter	53 E5
Royal Ter La	53 E5
Roystonhill	54 D5
Roystonhill Pl	54 D5
Royston Rd	54 C5
Royston Sq	54 C5
Roy St	54 B3
Ruby St	59 E4
Ruchill Pl	
off Ruchill St	53 F1
Ruchill St	53 E1
Rumford St	58 D5
Rupert St	53 F4
Rushyhill St	55 E2
Ruskin La	53 E3
Ruskin Pl	53 E3
Ruskin Ter	53 E3
Russell St	
off Vine St	52 B4
Rutherglen Br	58 D5
Rutherglen Rd	58 C6
Ruthven La	52 D3
Ruthven St	52 D3
Rutland Ct	
off Govan Rd	57 E2
Rutland Cres	57 E2
Rutland Pl	57 E2
Ryebank Rd	55 G1
Rye Cres	55 F1
Ryefield Rd	55 F1
Ryehill Pl	55 G1
Ryehill Rd	55 G1
Ryemount Rd	55 G1
Rye Rd	55 F1
Ryeside Rd	55 F1

S

St. Andrews Cres	57 E4

St. Andrews Cross	57 G5
St. Andrews Dr	57 E4
St. Andrews La	
off Gallowgate	58 B2
St. Andrews Rd	57 F4
St. Andrews Sq	58 B2
St. Andrews St	58 B2
St. Clair St	
off North Woodside Rd	53 F4
St. Enoch Shop Cen	58 A2
St. Enoch Sq	57 H2
St. Francis Rigg	58 A4
St. Georges Pl	
off St. Georges Rd	53 G5
St. Georges Rd	53 G4
St. James Rd	54 B6
St. John's Ct	57 E4
St. John's Quad	57 E4
St. John's Rd	57 E5
St. Joseph's Ct	54 D5
St. Joseph's Pl	54 D5
St. Joseph's Vw	54 D5
St. Luke's Pl	58 A3
St. Luke's Ter	58 A3
St. Margarets Pl	
off Bridgegate	58 A2
St. Marnock St	59 E3
St. Marys La	
off West Nile St	57 H1
St. Michael's Ct	
off St. Michael's La	59 G3
St. Michael's La	59 G3
St. Monance St	54 D1
St. Mungo Av	54 A6
St. Mungo Pl	54 B6
St. Ninian Ter	
off Ballater St	58 A3
St. Peters La	
off Blythswood St	57 G1
St. Peter's Path	
off Braid St	53 G4
St. Peters St	53 G4
St. Rollox Brae	54 C4
St. Valentine Ter	58 B4
St. Vincent Cres	52 D6
St. Vincent Cres La	52 D6
St. Vincent La	
off Hope St	53 G6
St. Vincent Pl	58 A1
St. Vincent St	53 G6
St. Vincent Ter	53 F6
Salamanca St	59 H3
Salisbury Pl	57 H4
Salisbury St	57 H4
Salkeld St	57 H4
Salmona St	53 H2
Saltmarket	58 A2
Saltmarket Pl	
off Bridgegate	58 A2
Saltoun Gdns	
off Roxburgh St	52 D3
Saltoun La	52 D3
Saltoun St	52 C3
Sanda St	53 E2
Sandfield St	53 E1
Sandiefield Rd	58 A4
Sandmill St	55 E5
Sandringham La	
off Kersland St	52 D3
Sandyford Pl	
off Sauchiehall St	53 F6
Sandyford Pl La	53 E6
Sandyford St	52 C6

Sandy La	
off Crawford St	52 A4
Sandy Rd	52 A5
Sannox Gdns	55 F6
Saracen Head La	
off Gallowgate	58 C2
Saracen St	54 A3
Sardinia La	52 D3
Sardinia Ter	
off Cecil St	52 D3
Sauchiehall La	
off Sauchiehall St	53 G6
Sauchiehall St	53 G6
Savoy St	58 D4
Sawmillfield St	53 H4
Schipka Pas	
off Gallowgate	58 B2
Scone St	54 A3
Scotland St	57 F3
Scotland St W	57 E3
Scotsburn Rd	55 G2
Scotstoun Mill Rd	
off Partick Br St	52 C5
Scott St	53 G6
Seagrove St	59 H2
Seamore St	53 F4
Seath St	58 A6
Seaward La	57 E2
Seaward Pl	57 E4
Seaward St	57 F3
Second Gdns	56 A4
Seton Ter	58 D1
Shaftesbury St	53 F6
Shakespeare St	53 E1
Shamrock St	53 G5
Shanks St	53 E1
Shannon St	53 F1
Shawfield Dr	58 C6
Shawfield Ind Est	58 D6
Shawfield Rd	58 D5
Shaw St	52 A6
Shearer St	
off Paisley Rd	57 F2
Shelley Ct	52 A1
Sheppard St	
off Cowlairs Rd	54 C2
Sherbrooke Av	56 C5
Sherbrooke Dr	56 C4
Sherbrooke Gdns	56 C5
Shettleston Rd	59 G2
Shields Rd	57 F3
Shipbank La	
off Clyde St	58 A2
Shore St	58 D6
Shortridge St	53 E1
Shuna Gdns	53 F1
Shuna Pl	53 E1
Shuttle La	
off George St	58 B1
Shuttle St	58 B1
Sidland Rd	55 G1
Siemens Pl	55 F4
Siemens St	55 F4
Silverdale St	59 G4
Silverfir Ct	58 B5
Silverfir Pl	58 B5
Silverfir St	58 B5
Silvergrove St	58 C3
Simpson St	53 F3
Skene Rd	56 B3
Slatefield Ct	
off Slatefield St	59 E2
Slatefield St	59 E2
Sloy St	54 B2
Snowdon Pl	
off Benthall St	58 B4
Snowdon St	
off Benthall St	58 B4
Society St	59 F3
Solway St	58 D6

Somerset Pl 53 F5
Somerset Pl Ms 53 F5
Sorby St 59 H3
Sorn St 59 F5
South Annandale
St 57 H6
Southbank St 59 H3
Southcroft St 56 B1
South Ex Ct
off Queen St 58 A1
South Frederick
St 58 A1
Southloch Gdns 54 D3
Southloch St 54 D3
Southmuir St 54 D3
Southpark Av 52 D4
Southpark La 53 E4
Southpark Ter
off Southpark
Av 53 E4
South Portland
St 57 H3
Southside Cres 57 H4
South Woodside
Rd 53 F3
Spiers Wf 53 H4
Spoutmouth
off Gallowgate 58 B2
Springbank St 53 F2
Springburn Rd 54 C4
Springburn Shop
Cen 54 D2
Springburn Way 54 C2
Springfield Ct
off Buchanan
St 58 A1
Springfield Quay 57 F2
Springfield Rd 56 C5
Springkell Av 56 C5
Springkell Dr 56 B6
Springkell Gdns 56 C6
Springkell Gate 56 D6
Spring La
off Lawmoor
St 58 A5
Springvale Ter 54 C2
Spring Wynd 58 A4
Spruce St 54 B1
Staffa St 55 F6
Stafford St 54 B5
Stag St 56 B1
Stair St 53 F2
Stamford Pl 59 F3
Stamford Rd 59 F3
Stamford St 59 F3
Stanley St 57 E3
Stanley St La 57 E3
Steel St 58 B2
Stevenson St 58 C2
Stewart St 53 H5
Stewartville St 52 B4
Stirlingfauld Pl 57 H3
Stirling Rd 54 B6
Stobcross Rd 52 D6
Stobcross St 57 F1
Stobcross Wynd 52 C6
Stockwell Pl 58 A2
Stockwell St 58 A2
Stonyhurst St 53 H2
Stratford St 52 D1
Strathbran St 59 H4
Strathclyde St 59 E6
Striven Gdns 53 F3
Stroma St 55 F4
Stromness St 57 G4
Stronend St 53 H1
Stronsay St 55 F4
Suffolk St
off Kent St 58 C2
Summerfield St 59 F6
Summer St 58 D3
Summertown Rd 56 B1
Sunnybank St 59 F5

Sunnylaw St 53 H2
Surrey St 57 H4
Sussex St 57 E3
Sutherland Av 56 B5
Sutherland La 52 C4
Swanston St 59 E6
Swan St 54 A5
Sword St 58 D2
Sydenham La
off Crown Rd S 52 B3
Sydenham Rd 52 C3
Sydney Cres 59 G6
Sydney St 58 C2
Syriam Pl
off Syriam St 54 D2
Syriam St 54 D2

T
Tamworth St
off Rimsdale
St 59 E3
Tannock St 53 H2
Taransay St 52 A6
Taylor Pl 54 B6
Taylor St 58 B1
Telephone La 52 C3
Templetons
Business Cen 58 C3
Templeton St 58 C3
Terregles Av 56 B6
Terregles Cres 56 B6
Terregles Dr 56 C6
Teviot St 52 C6
Teviot Ter
off Sanda St 53 E2
Tharsis St 54 D5
Third Gdns 56 A4
Thistle St 58 A3
Thistle Ter 58 A3
Thomson St 59 E2
Thornbank St 52 C5
Thornbridge Av
off Balcarres
Av 52 C1
Thorncliffe Gdns 57 E6
Thorncliffe La 57 E6
Thornhill Path
off Crail St 59 H4
Thornwood Av 52 A4
Thornwood Gdns 52 A4
Thornwood Pl 52 A3
Thurso St 52 C5
Tibbermore Rd 52 A3
Tillie St 53 F3
Tiree St 55 G4
Tobago Pl 58 D3
Tobago St 58 C3
Todd St 59 G1
Toll Ct 57 E2
Tollcross Rd 59 H3
Tontine La 58 B2
Torness St 52 C4
Torrance St 54 D2
Torr Gdns 54 B2
Torridon Av 56 B5
Torridon Path
off Dumbreck
Av 56 A5
Torrisdale St 57 F6
Torr Pl 54 B2
Torr St 54 B2
Torryburn Rd 55 G2
Tower St 57 E3
Townmill Rd 54 D6
Townsend St 54 A5
Tradeston St 57 G3
Trafalgar St 58 D5
Trongate 58 A2
Troon St 59 F5
Trossachs Ct
off Trossachs
St 53 G3
Trossachs St 53 G3

Tullis Ct 58 C4
Tullis St 58 C4
Tunnel St 57 E1
Tureen St 58 D2
Turnberry Av
off Turnberry
Rd 52 B3
Turnberry Rd 52 A3
Turnbull St 58 B2
Turner Rd 54 D4
Turnlaw St 58 B4
Turriff St 57 H4
Tweed Cres 55 H5
Tyndrum St 54 A5

U
Union Pl
off Gordon St 57 H1
Union St 57 H1
Unity Pl 53 G4
University Av 52 D4
University Gdns 52 D4
University of
Glasgow 52 D4
University Pl 52 D4
Urrdale Rd 56 B3

V
Valleyfield St
off Ayr St 54 C3
Vasart Pl 53 F1
Vennard Gdns 57 E6
Vermont St 57 E3
Vicarfield Pl
off Vicarfield
St 56 B1
Vicarfield St 56 B1
Victoria Br 58 A2
Victoria Circ 52 C3
Victoria Cres
off Dowanside
Rd 52 C3
Victoria Cres La 52 C3
Victoria Cres Pl
off Bowmont
Ter 52 C3
Victoria Cres Rd 52 C3
Victoria Cross 57 G6
Viewfield La 53 E4
Viewpark Av 55 F6
Vine St 52 B4
Vinicombe La 52 D3
Vinicombe St 52 D3
Vintner St 54 A4
Virginia Bldgs
off Virginia St 58 A1
Virginia Ct
off Virginia St 58 A1
Virginia Pl 58 A1
Virginia St 58 A1
Vulcan St
off Springburn
Way 54 C2

W
Waddell Ct 58 B3
Waddell St 58 B4
Walker Ct 52 B5
Walker St 52 B5
Walkinshaw St 59 E4
Wallace St 57 G2
Wallacewell Cres 55 F1
Wallacewell Pl 55 F1
Wallacewell Rd 55 F1
Walls St 58 B1
Walmer Cres 56 C2
Walnut Cres 54 B1
Walnut Pl 54 B1
Walnut Rd 54 B1
Walter St 59 F1
Wanlock St 52 A6
Wardhill Rd 55 F1
Wardrop St 52 A6

Warnock St 54 C6
Warriston Cres 55 H6
Warriston St 55 H6
Warroch St 57 F1
Washington St 57 G1
Waterloo La
off Waterloo
St 57 H1
Waterloo St 57 G1
Water Row 52 A6
Waterside Pl 58 B4
Waterside St 58 B4
Watson St 58 B2
Watt St 57 F2
Waverley Ter
off Whitevale
St 59 E2
Weaver St 58 B1
Webster St 59 E5
Wellcroft Pl 57 H4
Wellfield St 54 D2
Wellington La 57 G1
Wellington St 57 H1
Wellpark St 58 C1
Westbank Ct 53 E4
Westbank La 53 E4
Westbank Quad 53 E4
Westbourne
Gdns La 52 C2
Westbourne
Gdns N 52 C2
Westbourne
Gdns S 52 C2
Westbourne
Gdns W 52 C2
Westbourne Rd 52 B2
Westbourne Ter La
off Westbourne
Rd 52 B2
West Campbell
St 57 G1
West End Pk St 53 F5
Wester Common
Dr 53 G1
Wester Common
Rd 53 G2
Wester Common
Ter 53 H2
Westercraigs 58 D1
Westercraigs Ct
off Westercraigs 58 D1
West George La
off Pitt St 53 G6
West George St 53 G6
West Graham St 53 G5
West Greenhill Pl 53 E6
Westminster Gdns
off Kersland
St 52 D3
Westminster Ter
off Royal Ter 53 E6
Westmoreland St 57 G6
Westmuir St 59 H3
West Nile St 57 H1
West Princes St 53 F4
West Regent La
off Hope St 53 H6
West Regent St 53 G6
Westside Gdns 52 B4
West St 57 G3
West Whitby St 59 G4
Whitefield Rd 56 C3
Whitehall St 57 F1
Whitehill Ct 59 E1
Whitehill Gdns 59 E1
Whitehill Pl 59 E1
Whitehill St 59 E1
Whitehill St La 59 E1
White St 52 B4
Whitevale St 59 E2
Whittingehame
Gdns 52 A1
Whitworth Gate 53 G1

Williamson St 59 G4
William St 53 F6
Willowbank Cres
off Woodlands
Rd 53 F4
Willowbank St 53 F4
Wilson St 58 A1
Wilton Cres 53 F3
Wilton Cres La 53 F3
Wilton Dr 53 F3
Wilton Gdns 53 F3
Wilton St 53 E3
Windmillcroft
Quay 57 G2
Windsor St 53 G4
Windsor Ter 53 G4
Winifred St 55 H2
Winning Row 59 H3
Winton Dr 52 C1
Winton La 52 C1
Wishart St 58 C1
Woddrop St 59 F6
Woodhall St 59 F6
Woodlands Dr 53 F4
Woodlands Gate 53 F5
Woodlands Rd 53 F4
Woodlands Ter 53 E5
Woodrow Circ 56 D4
Woodrow Pl 56 C4
Woodrow Rd 56 D4
Woodside Cres 53 F5
Woodside Pl 53 F5
Woodside Pl La 53 F5
Woodside Ter 53 F5
Woodside Ter La 53 F5
Wood St 55 F6
Woodville Pk 56 B2
Woodville St 56 B2
Wyndford Dr 52 D1
Wyndford Pl
off Wyndford
Rd 52 D1
Wyndford Rd 52 C1
Wyndham Ct
off Wyndham
St 52 D2
Wyndham St 52 D2
Wyper Pl 59 E2

Y
Yarrow Gdns 53 F3
Yarrow Gdns La
off Yarrow
Gdns 53 F3
Yate Gro 59 F3
Yate Rd 59 F3
Yate St 59 F3
Yew Dr 55 E3
Yorkhill Par 52 C5
Yorkhill Quay 52 B6
Yorkhill St 52 D6
York St 57 G2
Young Ter 55 E2

Z
Zena Cres 55 G2
Zena Pl 55 H2
Zena St 55 H2

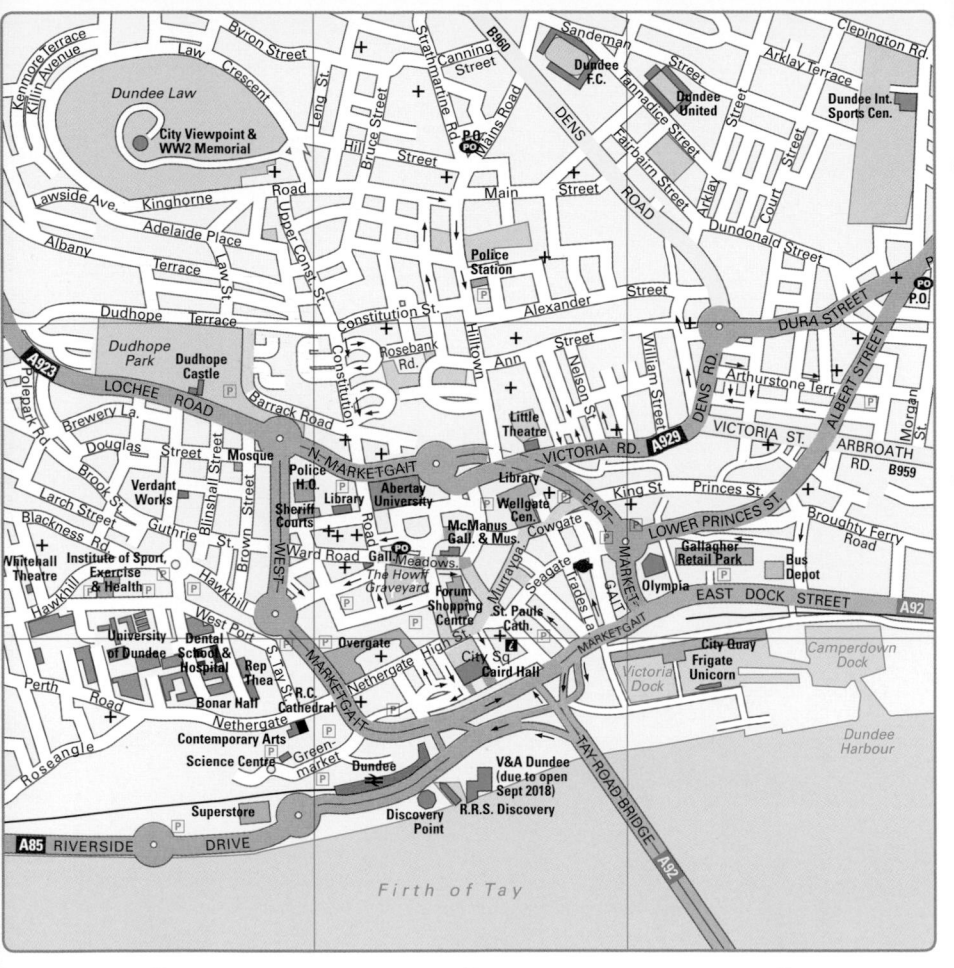

Tourist Information Centre: 16 City Square
Tel: 01382 527527

Adelaide Place	A1	Clepington Road	A3	Kenmore Terrace	A1	Polepark Road	B1
Albany Terrace	A1	Constitution Road	B2	Killin Avenue	A1	Princes Street	B3
Albert Street	B3	Constitution Street	A2	Kinghorne Road	A1	Riverside Drive	C1
Alexander Street	A2	Court Street	A3	King Street	B2	Roseangle	C1
Ann Street	B2	Cowgate Street	B2	Larch Street	B1	Rosebank Road	B2
Arbroath Road	B3	Dens Road	A2	Law Crescent	A1	Seagate	B2
Arklay Street	A3	Douglas Street	B1	Lawside Avenue	A1	South Marketgait	C2
Arklay Terrace	A3	Dudhope Street	A1	Law Street	A1	South Tay Street	C1
Arthurstone Terrace	B3	Dudhope Terrace	A1	Leng Street	A1	Strathmartine Road	A2
Barrack Road	B1	Dundonald Street	A3	Lochee Road	B1	Tannadice Street	A2
Blackness Road	B1	Dura Street	B3	Lower Princes Street	B3	Tay Road Bridge	C2
Blinshall Street	B1	East Dock Street	B3	Mains Road	A2	Trades Lane	B2
Brewery Lane	B1	East Marketgait	B2	Main Street	A2	Upper Constitution Street	A1
Brook Street	B1	Fairbairn Street	A2	Meadowside	B2	Victoria Road	B2
Broughty Ferry Road	B3	Greenmarket	C1	Morgan Street	B3	Victoria Street	B3
Brown Street	B1	Guthrie Street	B1	Murraygate	B2	Ward Road	B1
Bruce Street	A1	Hawkhill	B1	Nelson Street	B2	West Marketgait	B1
Byron Street	A1	High Street	C2	Nethergate	C1	West Port	B1
Canning Street	A2	Hill Street	A2	North Marketgait	B1	William Street	B3
City Square	C2	Hilltown	A2	Perth Road	C1		

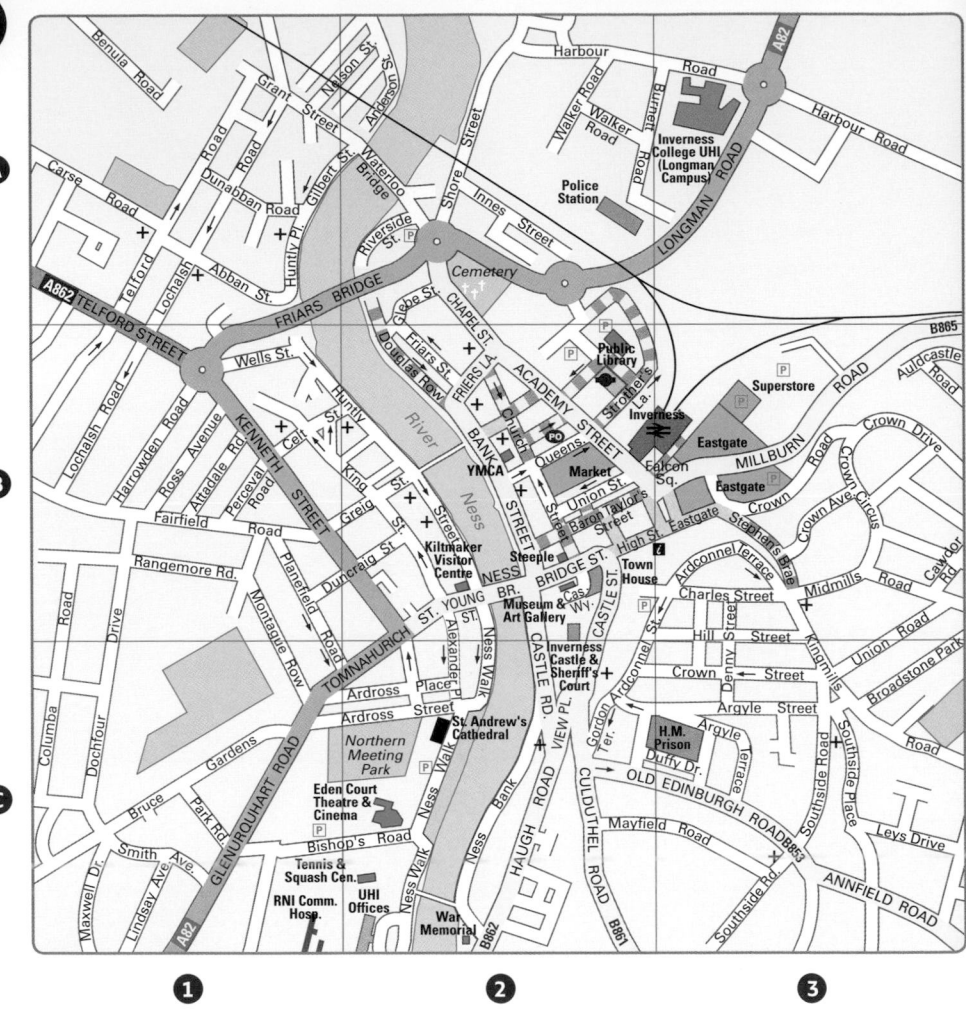

68

INVERNESS

```
0           300 yds
|   |   |
0           300m
```

Tourist Information Centre: 36 High Street
Tel: 01463 252401

Abban Street	A1	Chapel Street	A2	Greig Street	B1	Old Edinburgh Road	C2
Academy Street	B2	Charles Street	B3	Harbour Road	A2	Park Road	C1
Alexander Place	B2	Church Street	B2	Harrowden Road	B1	Perceval Road	B1
Anderson Street	A2	Columba Road	C1	Haugh Road	C2	Planefield Road	B1
Ardconnel Street	C2	Crown Avenue	B3	High Street	B2	Queensgate	B2
Ardconnel Terrace	B3	Crown Circus	B3	Hill Street	B3	Rangemore Road	B1
Ardross Place	C2	Crown Drive	B3	Hontly Place	A1	Riverside Street	A2
Ardross Street	C2	Crown Road	B3	Huntly Street	B1	Ross Avenue	B1
Argyle Street	C3	Crown Street	C3	Innes Street	A2	Shore Street	A2
Argyle Terrace	C3	Culduthel Road	C2	Kenneth Street	B1	Smith Avenue	C1
Attadale Road	B1	Denny Street	C3	Kingsmills Road	B3	Southside Place	C3
Auldcastle Road	B3	Dochfour Drive	C1	King Street	B1	Southside Road	C3
Bank Street	B2	Douglas Row	A2	Leys Drive	C3	Stephens Street	B3
Baron Taylor's Street	B2	Duffy Drive	C2	Lindsay Avenue	C1	Strother's Lane	B2
Benula Road	A1	Duncraig Street	B1	Lochalsh Road	A1	Telford Road	A1
Bishop's Road	C1	Eastgate	B3	Longman Road	A3	Telford Street	A1
Bridge Street	B2	Fairfield Road	B1	Maxwell Drive	C1	Tomnahurich Street	C1
Broadstone Park	C3	Falcon Square	B2	Mayfield Road	C2	Union Road	C3
Bruce Gardens	C1	Friars Bridge	A1	Midmills Road	B3	Union Street	B2
Burnett Road	A3	Friars Lane	B2	Millburn Road	B3	View Place	C2
Carse Road	A1	Friars Street	B2	Montague Row	B1	Walker Road	A2
Castle Road	A1	Gilbert Street	A1	Muirfield Road	C3	Waterloo Bridge	A2
Castle Street	B2	Glebe Street	A2	Nelson Street	A1	Wells Street	B1
Castle Wynd	B2	Glen Urquhart Road	C1	Ness Bank	C2	Young Street	B2
Cawdor Road	B3	Gordon Terrace	C2	Ness Bridge	B2		
Celt Street	B1	Grant Street	A1	Ness Walk	C2		

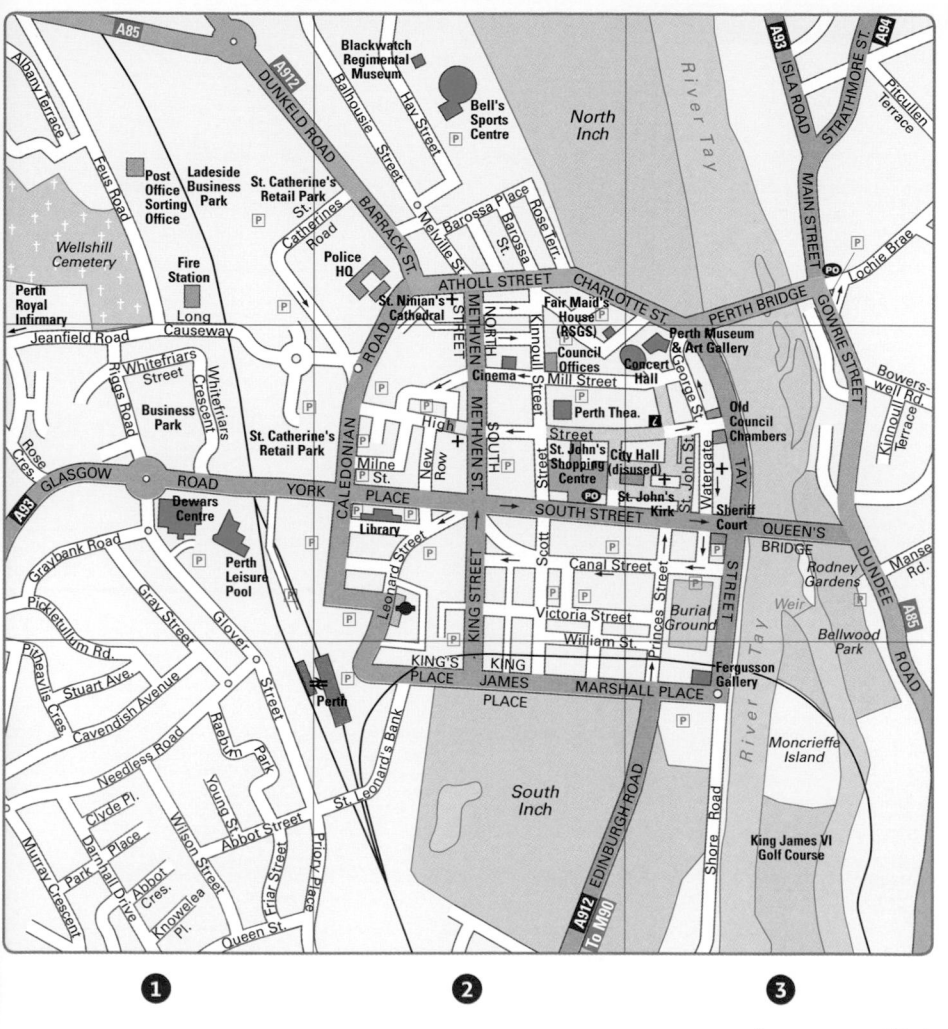

Tourist Information Centre: 45 High Street
Tel: 01738 450600

Abbot Crescent	C1	George Street	B3	Manse Road	B3	Rose Crescent	B1
Abbot Street	C1	Glasgow Road	B1	Marshall Place	C2	Rose Terrace	A2
Albany Terrace	A1	Glover Street	B1	Melville Street	A2	St. Catherines Road	A1
Atholl Street	A2	Gowrie Street	A3	Mill Street	B2	St. John Street	B3
Balhousie Street	A2	Gray Street	B1	Milne Street	B2	St. Leonard's Bank	C2
Barossa Place	A2	Graybank Road	B1	Murray Crescent	C1	Scott Street	B2
Barossa Street	A2	Hay Street	A2	Needless Road	C1	Shore Road	C3
Barrack Street	A2	High Street	B2	New Row	B2	South Methven Street	B2
Bowerswell Road	B3	Isla Road	A3	North Methven Street	A2	South Street	B2
Caledonian Road	B2	Jeanfield Road	B1	Park Place	C1	Strathmore Street	A3
Canal Street	B2	King's Place	C2	Perth Bridge	A3	Stuart Avenue	C1
Cavendish Avenue	C1	King James Place	C2	Pickletullum Road	B1	Tay Street	B3
Charlotte Street	A2	King Street	B2	Pitcullen Terrace	A3	Victoria Street	B2
Clyde Place	C1	Kinnoull Street	A2	Pitheavlis Crescent	C1	Watergate	B3
Darnhall Drive	C1	Kinnoull Terrace	B3	Princes Street	C3	Whitefriars Crescent	B1
Dundee Road	B3	Knowelea Place	C1	Priory Place	C2	Whitefriars Street	B1
Dunkeld Road	A1	Leonard Street	B2	Queen Street	C1	William Street	B2
Edinburgh Road	C2	Lochie Brae	A3	Queens Bridge	B3	Wilson Street	C1
Feus Road	A1	Long Causeway	A1	Raeburn Park	C1	Young Street	C1
Friar Street	C1	Main Street	A3	Riggs Road	B1	York Place	B1

PERTH

Aberdeen to Kirkwall
6 hrs - 7 hrs 15 mins
All Year
North Link Ferries
0845 6000 449
www.northlinkferries.co.uk

Aberdeen to Lerwick
12 hrs 30 mins
All Year
North Link Ferries
0845 6000 449
www.northlinkferries.co.uk

Ardrossan to Brodick
55 mins
All Year
Caledonian MacBrayne
08000 66 5000
www.calmac.co.uk

Ardrossan to Campbeltown
2 hrs 40 mins
Seasonal
Caledonian MacBrayne
08000 66 5000
www.calmac.co.uk

Barra to Eriskay
40 mins
All Year
Caledonian MacBrayne
08000 66 5000
www.calmac.co.uk

Belmont to Gutcher
10 mins
All Year
Shetland Islands Council
01806 244200
www.shetland.gov.uk/ferries/

Belmont to Hamars Ness
30 mins
All Year
Shetland Islands Council
01806 244200
www.shetland.gov.uk/ferries/

Brodick to Campbeltown
2 hrs 20 mins
Seasonal (Saturdays only)
Caledonian MacBrayne
08000 66 5000
www.calmac.co.uk

Cairnryan to Belfast
2 hrs 15 mins
All Year
Stena Line
08447 707070
www.stenaline.co.uk

Cairnryan to Larne
2 hrs
All Year
P&O Irish Sea
0800 130 0030
www.poirishsea.com

Claonaig to Lochranza
30 mins
Seasonal
Caledonian MacBrayne
08000 66 5000
www.calmac.co.uk

Colintraive to Rhubodach
5 mins
All Year
Caledonian MacBrayne
08000 66 5000
www.calmac.co.uk

Coll to Tiree
55 mins - 1 hr
All Year
Caledonian MacBrayne
08000 66 5000
www.calmac.co.uk

Colonsay to Port Askaig
1 hr 20 mins
Seasonal
Caledonian MacBrayne
08000 66 5000
www.calmac.co.uk

Cromarty to Nigg
5 mins
Seasonal
Highland Ferries
07468 417137

Eday to Sanday
20 mins
All Year
Orkney Ferries
01856 872044
www.orkneyferries.co.uk

Eday to Stronsay
35 mins
All Year
Orkney Ferries
01856 872044
www.orkneyferries.co.uk

Egilsay to Rousay
20 mins
All Year
Orkney Ferries
01856 872044
www.orkneyferries.co.uk

Egilsay to Wyre
15 mins
All Year
Orkney Ferries
01856 872044
www.orkneyferries.co.uk

Feolin to Port Askaig
5 mins
All Year
Argyll & Bute Council
01496 840681

Gill's Bay to St. Margaret's Hope
1 hr
All Year
Pentland Ferries
01856 831226
www.pentlandferries.co.uk

Glenelg to Kylerhea
5 mins
Seasonal
Skye Ferry
01599 522273
www.skyeferry.co.uk

Gourock to Dunoon
20 mins
All Year
Western Ferries
01369 704452
www.western-ferries.co.uk

Gutcher to Hamars Ness
25 mins
All Year
Shetland Islands Council
01806 244200
www.shetland.gov.uk/ferries/

Houton to Flotta
35 mins
All Year
Orkney Ferries
01856 872044
www.orkneyferries.co.uk

Houton to Lyness
35 mins
All Year
Orkney Ferries
01856 872044
www.orkneyferries.co.uk

Kennacraig to Port Askaig
2 hrs 5 mins
All Year
Caledonian MacBrayne
08000 66 5000
www.calmac.co.uk

Kennacraig to Port Ellen
2 hrs 20 mins
All Year
Caledonian MacBrayne
08000 66 5000
www.calmac.co.uk

Kirkwall to Eday
1 hr 15 mins
All Year
Orkney Ferries
01856 872044
www.orkneyferries.co.uk

Kirkwall to Lerwick
7 hrs 45 mins
All Year
North Link Ferries
0845 6000 449
www.northlinkferries.co.uk

Kirkwall to North Ronaldsay
2 hrs 40 mins
All Year
Orkney Ferries
01856 872044
www.orkneyferries.co.uk

Kirkwall to Papa Westray
1 hr 50 mins
All Year
Orkney Ferries
01856 872044
www.orkneyferries.co.uk

Kirkwall to Sanday
1 hr 25 mins
All Year
Orkney Ferries
01856 872044
www.orkneyferries.co.uk

Kirkwall to Shapinsay
45 mins
All Year
Orkney Ferries
01856 872044
www.orkneyferries.co.uk

Kirkwall to Stronsay
1 hr 35 mins
All Year
Orkney Ferries
01856 872044
www.orkneyferries.co.uk

Kirkwall to Westray
1 hr 25 mins
All Year
Orkney Ferries
01856 872044
www.orkneyferries.co.uk

Largs to Cumbrae Slip
10 mins
All Year
Caledonian MacBrayne
08000 66 5000
www.calmac.co.uk

Laxo to Symbister
30 mins
All Year
Shetland Islands Council
01806 244200
www.shetland.gov.uk/ferries/

Lerwick to Bressay
5 mins
All Year
Shetland Islands Council
01806 244200
www.shetland.gov.uk/ferries/

Lerwick to Kirkwall
5 hrs 30 mins
All Year
North Link Ferries
0845 6000 449
www.northlinkferries.co.uk

Lerwick to Skerries
2 hrs 30 mins
All Year
Shetland Islands Council
01806 244200
www.shetland.gov.uk/ferries/

Leverburgh to Berneray
1 hr
All Year
Caledonian MacBrayne
08000 66 5000
www.calmac.co.uk

Lochaline to Fishnish
15 mins
All Year
Caledonian MacBrayne
08000 66 5000
www.calmac.co.uk

Longhope to Flotta
30 mins
All Year
Orkney Ferries
01856 872044
www.orkneyferries.co.uk

Longhope to Lyness
30 mins
All Year
Orkney Ferries
01856 872044
www.orkneyferries.co.uk

Luing to Seil
5 mins
All Year
Argyll and Bute Council
01852 300382

Lyness to Flotta
20 mins
All Year
Orkney Ferries
01856 872044
www.orkneyferries.co.uk

Mallaig to Armadale
30 mins
All Year
Caledonian MacBrayne
08000 66 5000
www.calmac.co.uk

Mallaig to Lochboisdale
3 hrs 30 mins
All Year
Caledonian MacBrayne
08000 66 5000
www.calmac.co.uk

Oban to Castlebay
4 hrs 45 mins
All Year
Caledonian MacBrayne
08000 66 5000
www.calmac.co.uk

Oban to Coll
2 hrs 45 mins
All Year
Caledonian MacBrayne
08000 66 5000
www.calmac.co.uk

Oban to Colonsay
2 hrs 20 mins
All Year
Caledonian MacBrayne
08000 66 5000
www.calmac.co.uk

Oban to Craignure
45 mins
All Year
Caledonian MacBrayne
08000 66 5000
www.calmac.co.uk

Oban to Lismore
55 mins
Winter only
Caledonian MacBrayne
08000 66 5000
www.calmac.co.uk

Oban to Lochboisdale
5 hrs 20 mins
Winter only
Caledonian MacBrayne
08000 66 5000
www.calmac.co.uk

Oban to Tiree
3 hrs 30 mins - 4 hrs 15 mins
All Year
Caledonian MacBrayne
08000 66 5000
www.calmac.co.uk

Rousay to Wyre
5 mins
All Year
Orkney Ferries
01856 872044
www.orkneyferries.co.uk

Sconser to Raasay
25 mins
All Year
Caledonian MacBrayne
08000 66 5000
www.calmac.co.uk

Scrabster to Stromness
2 hr 15 mins
All Year
North Link Ferries
0845 6000 449
www.northlinkferries.co.uk

Tarbert to Lochranza
1 hr 25 mins
Winter Only
Caledonian MacBrayne
08000 66 5000
www.calmac.co.uk

Tarbert to Portavadie
25 mins
All Year
Caledonian MacBrayne
08000 66 5000
www.calmac.co.uk

Tayinloan to Gigha
20 mins
All Year
Caledonian MacBrayne
08000 66 5000
www.calmac.co.uk

Tingwall to Rousay
25 mins
All Year
Orkney Ferries
01856 872044
www.orkneyferries.co.uk

Tobermory to Kilchoan
35 mins
All Year
Caledonian MacBrayne
08000 66 5000
www.calmac.co.uk

Toft to Ulsta
20 mins
All Year
Shetland Islands Council
01806 244200
www.shetland.gov.uk/ferries/

Uig to Lochmaddy
1 hr 45 mins
All Year
Caledonian MacBrayne
08000 66 5000
www.calmac.co.uk

Uig to Tarbert
1 hr 40 mins
All Year
Caledonian MacBrayne
08000 66 5000
www.calmac.co.uk

Ullapool to Stornoway
2 hrs 30 mins
All Year
Caledonian MacBrayne
08000 66 5000
www.calmac.co.uk

Vidlin to Skerries
1 hr 30 mins
All Year
Shetland Islands Council
01806 244200
www.shetland.gov.uk/ferries/

Vidlin to Symbister
45 mins
All Year
Shetland Islands Council
01806 244200
www.shetland.gov.uk/ferries/

Wemyss Bay to Rothesay
35 mins
All Year
Caledonian MacBrayne
08000 66 5000
www.calmac.co.uk

Westray to Papa Westray
40 mins - 1 hr 45 mins
All Year
Orkney Ferries
01856 872044
www.orkneyferries.co.uk

Wyre to Tingwall
45 mins
All Year
Orkney Ferries
01856 872044
www.orkneyferries.co.uk

MIX
Paper from
responsible sources

FSC
www.fsc.org

FSC™ C007454

This book is produced from independently certified FSC™ paper
to ensure responsible forest management.

For more information visit: www.harpercollins.co.uk/green

Aberdeen Airport (ABZ)
0844 481 6666
www.aberdeenairport.com

Barra Airport (BRR)
01667 462445
www.hial.co.uk/barra-airport/

Benbecula Airport (BEB)
01870 602051
www.hial.co.uk/benbecula-airport/

Campbeltown Airport (CAL)
01586 553797
www.hial.co.uk/campbeltown-airport/

Dundee Airport (DND)
01382 662200
www.hial.co.uk/dundee-airport/

Edinburgh Airport (EDI)
0844 448 8833
www.edinburghairport.com

Glasgow Airport (GLA)
0844 481 5555
www.glasgowairport.com

Glasgow Prestwick Airport (PIK)
0844 481 5555
www.glasgowprestwick.com

Inverness Airport (INV)
01667 464000
www.hial.co.uk/inverness-airport/

Islay Airport (ILY)
01496 302361
www.hial.co.uk/islay-airport/

Kirkwall Airport (KOI)
01856 872421
www.hial.co.uk/kirkwall-airport/

Stornoway Airport (SYY)
01851 702256
www.hial.co.uk/stornoway-airport/

Sumburgh Airport (LSI)
01950 460905
www.hial.co.uk/sumburgh-airport/

Tiree Airport (TRE)
01879 220456
www.hial.co.uk/tiree-airport/

Wick Airport (WIC)
01955 602215
www.hial.co.uk/wick-airport/

Distance chart

KILOMETRES

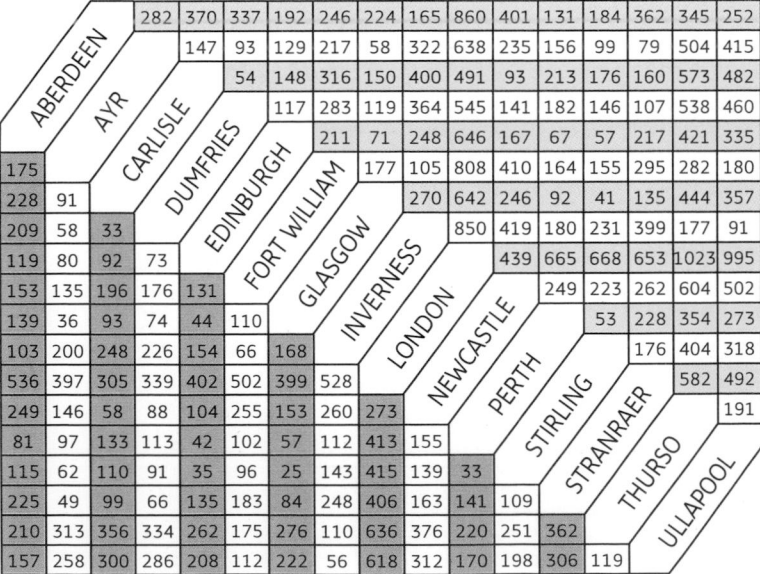

	ABERDEEN	AYR	CARLISLE	DUMFRIES	EDINBURGH	FORT WILLIAM	GLASGOW	INVERNESS	LONDON	NEWCASTLE	PERTH	STIRLING	STRANRAER	THURSO	ULLAPOOL
ABERDEEN		282	370	337	192	246	224	165	860	401	131	184	362	345	252
AYR	175		147	93	129	217	58	322	638	235	156	99	79	504	415
CARLISLE	228	91		54	148	316	150	400	491	93	213	176	160	573	482
DUMFRIES	209	58	33		117	283	119	364	545	141	182	146	107	538	460
EDINBURGH	119	80	92	73		211	71	248	646	167	67	57	217	421	335
FORT WILLIAM	153	135	196	176	131		177	105	808	410	164	155	295	282	180
GLASGOW	139	36	93	74	44	110		270	642	246	92	41	135	444	357
INVERNESS	103	200	248	226	154	66	168		850	419	180	231	399	177	91
LONDON	536	397	305	339	402	502	399	528		439	665	668	653	1023	995
NEWCASTLE	249	146	58	88	104	255	153	260	273		249	223	262	604	502
PERTH	81	97	133	113	42	102	57	112	413	155		53	228	354	273
STIRLING	115	62	110	91	35	96	25	143	415	139	33		176	404	318
STRANRAER	225	49	99	66	135	183	84	248	406	163	141	109		582	492
THURSO	210	313	356	334	262	175	276	110	636	376	220	251	362		191
ULLAPOOL	157	258	300	286	208	112	222	56	618	312	170	198	306	119	

MILES